FOR FREEDOM OR BONDAGE?

For Freedom or Bondage?

A Critique of African Pastoral Practices

Esther E. Acolatse

William B. Eerdmans Publishing Company
Grand Rapids, Michigan / Cambridge, U.K.

Wm. B. Eerdmans Publishing Co.

2140 Oak Industrial Drive N.E., Grand Rapids, Michigan 49505 /
P.O. Box 163, Cambridge CB3 9PU U.K.

www.eerdmans.com

Printed in the United States of America

20 19 18 17 16 15 14   7 6 5 4 3 2 1

Library of Congress Cataloging-in-Publication Data

Acolatse, Esther.

For freedom or bondage?: a critique of African pastoral practices / Esther E. Acolatse.

pages   cm

Includes bibliographical references and index.

ISBN 978-0-8028-6989-0 (pbk.: alk. paper)

1. Pastoral theology — Africa. 2. Theology, Practical — Africa.   I. Title.

BV4011.3.A26   2014

253.096 — dc23

2013038809

Contents

Introduction 1

1. The Church in Ghana: A Window into Contemporary
   African Pastoral Practice 12

2. African Cosmology and African Christian Theology 32

3. Barth's Theological Anthropology: An Overview 72

4. African Theological Anthropology in the Light of Barth's
   Theological Anthropology 99

5. African Theological Anthropology: A Jungian Perspective 134

6. Toward a Model for Pastoral Counseling 173

   Selected Bibliography 209

   Appendix 213

   Index of Names and Subjects 219

   Index of Scripture References 226

128533

Introduction

This book stems out of years of grappling with a new but widespread phenomenon on much of the African Christian scene, including African diaspora groups around the globe, regarding pastoral diagnosis for care and counseling in Independent Evangelical/Charismatic Churches (IECC). Diagnosis is an integral part of any pastoral intervention. But diagnosis is hardly simple or neutral, since worldview plays a large part in both how people perceive and present their difficulties and how pastoral counselors process and interpret presenting problems. If a large source of the problem stems from the worldview through which issues are refracted, then an emphasis on it mitigates rather than helps pastoral counseling. A case in point is the current pastoral practice in Ghana Independent Charismatic churches, in which worldview and diagnosis are inextricably bound to the detriment of the ailing care seeker. In this they are representative of such churches on the continent south of the Sahara as well as in diaspora.

In these churches, current methods of healing are not from the Word of God, as one might assume, but rather from beliefs acquired from African Traditional Religions, with their strong sense of the spirit world and its pervasive influence on natural phenomena. These Ghanaian pastoral counselors interpret almost all problems from a spiritual perspective and treat them with a particular type of theological intervention. But such an approach to diagnosis and counseling is often detrimental to people seeking help, because hidden psychological issues are never adequately addressed. When people are not healed, or receive remediation for their ailments, they often assume that God has failed them, or that they do not have the requisite faith to procure the amelioration of what ails them, which further compounds their problems. This work examines Ghanaian pastoral counseling from a theological and psychological perspective and argues that its basic assumptions about human beings and its methods are inadequate from a Christian perspective.

Drawing from both theological (Barthian) and psychological (Jungian) perspectives, my proposed approach makes a distinction among the causes of presenting problems that allow theological issues to be addressed by theology and emotional difficulties to be addressed by psychology, while recognizing the ultimate need for both disciplines to adequately address the complexity of spirituality. Such a differentiated approach to pastoral counseling offers a more adequate theoretical framework for the daunting task of diagnosis and treatment in African pastoral work on the continent, in African diaspora settings, and in other contexts in which Christian faith meets primal religions and where belief in the spirit world infuses common life.

Personal Assumptions Underlying Research and Concerns

Various approaches could be deployed to explore the current approach to deliverance in many of these African churches. For example one could use a phenomenology of religion approach, allowing the situation to dictate how it is to be studied and expressed, or an ethnographic approach, closely related to the phenomenological, in which the observer is changed by the shared space of observed and observer. In this latter scenario, the interstitial space becomes a springboard for pastoral reflection and care in a congregational setting.[1] But many such approaches hardly escape the tools' tendency toward mere journalistic reporting, offering minimal or no accompanying analysis. There are, however, deep theological questions embedded in the ecclesial practice under investigation that need theological analysis and answers.

As a practical theologian, formed within the Reformed tradition, I confess a leaning toward right doctrine and interpretation of Christian practice, and so I have chosen to explore the situation at hand by means of the most appropriate disciplines available to my field, those of theology and psychology. Moreover, my own faith journey and Christian experience

---

1. Mary Moschella, for instance, argues for the possibilities of ethnography for pastoral engagement and transformation of both the ethnographer and the congregation studied. See her *Ethnography as a Pastoral Practice* (Cleveland: Pilgrim Press, 2011).

cause me to observe that these healing practices need a stronger theological undergirding.

In the fall of 1995 I headed home for Christmas, having just completed my comprehensive exams and brooding over issues of relationality in the African context. I was troubled by what I consider its false relational ethos, framed within the pithy saying, "I am because we are," which, among other things, invariably keeps women sacrificing for the rest of the community.[2] When I got home I saw what could be described as another form of bondage, but this time within ecclesial practice, where the majority of care seekers are women. There I found that a highly educated female friend, a professor, had been coerced into seeking spiritual deliverance treatment for what turned out to be mild clinical depressive episodes. Her ailments, she was told by "word of prophecy," stemmed from her having been conceived after her mother's infertility led her to seek aid from a witch doctor, and since my friend had now become Christian, rather than a devotée of the particular god responsible for her existence, she would find no peace. The remedy suggested was to have her mother confess, renounce, and be delivered from consorting with idols, following which prayers of deliverance would then avail for the ailing friend. I was surprised to find that a person of such status would undergo such an experience, but soon began to notice that it was the norm rather than exception.

This episode, which was by no means an isolated case, opens up endless theological questions and concerns. What does it say about the sovereignty of God? About what it means to be a Christian in a world containing evil spiritual beings? About the efficacy of the cross? About the presence of God in the life of the Christian believer and what that means for security? About the purpose and ends of Christian discipleship?

As I pondered the meaning of this seemingly new phenomenon, I recalled some personal experiences, most of which occurred in Ghana, but also in neighboring West African countries, with a youth evangelistic music team. Though the ministry was focused on evangelism, there was prayer for healing for the sick when it was needed — sometimes with instantaneous results. Many were delivered from demon possession, and we once witnessed a deranged man regain his full mental faculties. I do not believe

---

2. I have since explored this anomaly in "Unraveling the Relational Myth in the Turn toward Autonomy: Pastoral Counseling with African Women," in Stevenson Moessner, J. & T. Thornton, *Women out of Order: Risking Change and Creating Care in a Multicultural World* (Minneapolis: Fortress, 2009).

that the healings came about merely by the psychic suggestion of group influence.[3] Though intense prayer and fasting always accompanied the ministry, we knew that the power was not in us, nor in our prayer, but in the One who called us. There was never undue strenuous effort on our part, nor was such prayer a long, unfruitful, or grueling process. The physical changes in the countenance of the afflicted people after prayer demonstrated the transforming power of Christ.[4]

I have drawn certain conclusions from these experiences, which I believe the Scriptures affirm. Jesus has, and will continue to have, authority over all satanic powers. In his name, as he promised, those who follow him will heal and cast out demons, and the "gates of Hades will not prevail against [them]" (Matt. 16:18). It does not take a particular kind of Christian to cast out demons.[5] The biblical witness attests that demons are afraid of the name of Jesus because of the power and authority given to him by God, who put all things under his dominion.

Nevertheless, I have been perplexed by the recent trend of "deliverance" within African evangelical circles and concerned with the way pastoral counseling functions in the African Christian community. What is a Christian theologian to do to be sensitive to the needs that drive mainly women to these bastions of male domination, while also being careful not to undermine belief in these spiritual powers and being open to the possible work of the Holy Spirit? While I understand that formal pastoral training, which equips the pastoral counselor to effectively integrate theology and other human and social sciences, is too often lacking, the more acute problem in this context may be a cosmology and anthropology deeply embed-

---

3. Autosuggestion is very real, and numerous psychological tests affirm the phenomenon. But there are also ways of testing and sifting reality from fantasy. And there are times when healings and deliverance have occurred within confines that preclude an audience that might be susceptible to autosuggestion. Moreover, in testing the validity of a religious experience, the most common and authentic proof is the end result of the experience. In the Christian context, a changed life lived in and for God through the power of the Holy Spirit is the mark of a true religious experience.

4. A dramatic biblical depiction of a healing that functions as a paradigm is the deliverance of the Gerasene demoniac. "They came to Jesus and saw the demoniac sitting there, clothed and in his right mind, the very man who had had the legion; and they were afraid" (Mark 5:15).

5. Because the term "Christian" encompasses a large group of people with varying beliefs, I need to specify what I call Christian. By Christian, I refer to those who know experientially the saving grace of God through Jesus Christ, who walk in fellowship with God through the indwelling Holy Spirit, and who see bringing others into this fellowship as imperative.

ded in the traditional beliefs and practices of the culture. As Africans ponder humanity's place in the cosmos and how humanity relates to God, they do not seem to actually affirm in practice the rule of God over the cosmos. This is evidenced by their ongoing preoccupation with and fear of spiritual forces that may arbitrarily unleash their power against them. Yet Scripture attests that God has anticipated human fear in the face of this vast cosmos and has addressed our need for structure and assurance.

Thus I wish to argue that African Christianity has yet to truly transcend its cultural moment, and that this failure can explain many of the pastoral problems that beset parishioners. A way forward can be found in a more complete, biblical anthropology that reflects a more Christological approach. A pastoral theology and practice founded on this Christology will enable pastors to interrogate problematic cultural narratives about the relationship between body, soul, and spirit, while offering a more nuanced, constructive, and liberating path towards healing and wholeness.

In order to develop a more viable anthropology and soteriology that will help provide a new theoretical model for Christian therapy in the Ghanaian context, I turn to the Christological theology developed by Karl Barth. I use Barth as one known theological anthropologist whose work converges with African notions properly lived. Barth's theological anthropology gives detailed attention to the relational matrix of the human person. Interpersonal action consists of relationships to God, oneself, and others; humans live within these webs of relationships, and Barth's anthropology sees these webs of relationship as analogous to the inner dynamic relationship within the Godhead. God's being is dynamic because God is Creator, Son, and Holy Spirit. Our relationship to ourselves and to other human beings thus mirrors this inner relationship of God. The subject matter of theological anthropology, therefore, is not merely the human person, but human persons as constituted in their relationships with one another and with God. God's self-revelation undergirds the affirmation that we are made in the image of God and, therefore, our knowledge of who we are as human beings.

Since Barth's theological anthropology gives special attention to the relational matrix of the human being and further places anthropology within the larger context of God's own inner relational being and God's relationship to us, especially as revealed in the incarnation, we can use it both to affirm African anthropology and to critique it. I argue that Barth's theological anthropology affirms aspects of African anthropology, such as its strong sense of (a) the spiritual, including sin and its consequences, and (b) human relationality at both the interpersonal and intrapersonal level. We can see the African emphasis on interpersonal and intrapersonal unity, as well as on the emotional and spiritual interpenetration of discrete persons who are in relationship with each other, as analogous to the Trinitarian affirmation that God is both a single being (unity) and three persons (differentiation). The real strength of African belief is its clear understanding of this unity. On the other hand, Reformed Protestantism emphasizes the clear distinction or differentiation among the three persons. When we draw out the anthropological implications of this Trinitarian affirmation, we come to the analogous understanding that while there is unity within the constituent parts of the human being, there is also differentiation.

The Trinitarian affirmation is that God is one, but God is also three. The Father is neither the Son nor the Holy Spirit. It is this clear differentiation as epitomized within the Godhead that seems to be missing in African anthropology as it reflects on the relationship among body, soul, and spirit. The strong sense of belief in the unity among the physical, psychical, and spiritual is so pervasive that in pastoral situations it is often difficult for the troubled person as well as the healer to see the differentiation that might allow them to make a clearer and more accurate diagnosis.

A closer look at the pastoral care and therapy in these churches displays a close affinity to traditional African religious conceptions of the human constitution, brokenness, and therapy. There are positive elements in African culture, and even in African Traditional Religions, that no doubt aid in the explication and understanding of Scripture to African peoples, and that in turn lend a distinctive character to African Christianity that we need to preserve. At the same time, however, the negative aspects of African cosmology have the capacity to stunt spiritual understanding and snuff out freedom and human vitality. Since our main concern is how these cosmological ideas influence the diagnostic process in pastoral counseling, emphasizing spiritual causes of presenting problems and paying little attention to possible psychological factors, it is my aim to provide a theoretical framework for a more differentiated diagnosis and therapy.

From a practical theology perspective this will entail using an interdisciplinary method that can combine theology and psychology to probe and address pertinent issues in counseling situations. With regard to how theology and psychology should relate to each other and how we can utilize them for pastoral counseling, I need to acknowledge the positive influence of James E. Loder and Deborah van Deusen Hunsinger on my own thinking.[6] With any serious human problem there are many dimensions that need to be addressed, and Hunsinger has developed a method for thinking through both the theological and psychological issues at stake as well as their interrelationship. Her work is valuable to those of us seeking to explicate both the unity and the differentiation between psychological and spiritual dimensions.

In the construction of a psycho-theological model for therapy that draws largely on the worldview and life experiences of Africans, I bring Barthian theological anthropology into dialogue with Jungian analytical psychology as an avenue for exploring the understanding of the life issues that inform African anthropology. We can use Jung's analytical psychology and his understanding of the psyche along with psychotherapy as tools to help with diagnosis and remedy for aspects of African understandings of psychic phenomena. While certain Jungian concepts may prove problematic, especially from the standpoint of Christian theology, Jung holds that human life is rooted in a transpersonal power, and that human experiences (and even the unconscious) have religious dimensions. We can use Jung's understanding of the unconscious, especially the collective unconscious as revealed in the demonic and dreams, to help elucidate aspects of what Ghanaians may term demonic activity. Through concepts like the *persona* and *shadow*, the *anima* and *animus*, we can show how certain phenomena that are now interpreted solely as demonic may be seen in a different light. If we can understand some of these phenomena to have psychological causes and psychological aims, rather than spiritual causes and spiritual aims, then it is possible that we need not reject them as demonic, but rather welcome and transform them to facilitate the wholeness of the person.

Jungian analysis attempts to make unconscious processes accessible to consciousness, so that they can be understood and related to the events

6. Both Loder and Hunsinger have used an interdisciplinary method formally patterned after the Chalcedonian formulation of the relationship between the two natures of Christ. In this formulation, the two natures are seen to be in inseparable unity, in an indissoluble differentiation, and in an asymmetrical order, with the divine nature having logical precedence over the human nature. For fuller understanding, see James E. Loder and W. Jim Neidhardt, *The Knight's Move: The Relational Logic of the Spirit in Theology and Science* (Colorado Springs: Helmers & Howard, 1992). The application of the Chalcedonian pattern of thought to pastoral counseling is Hunsinger's particular contribution. In *Theology and Pastoral Counseling*, she works out the methodological implications of this thesis both theoretically and practically. See Deborah van Deusen Hunsinger, *Theology and Pastoral Counseling: A New Interdisciplinary Approach* (Grand Rapids: Eerdmans, 1995).

of conscious life. Jungian analysis at its best also educates and equips people to continue paying close attention to unconscious material even after formal therapy has ended. In active imagination, for example, analysands explore and play with their fantasies, and through that exploration and play get in touch with material that is ordinarily repressed. They can choose an image from a dream or vision and concentrate on it until it yields its own meaning. For Jung, this process is like a pregnancy; the imagination is pregnant with meaning that will bring forth its own fruit:

> [L]ooking, psychologically, brings about the activation of the object; it is as if something were emanating from one's spiritual eye that evokes or activates the object of one's vision. The English verb "to look at" does not convey this meaning, but the German *betrachten*, which is an equivalent, means also to make pregnant. . . . And if it is pregnant, then something is due to come out of it; it is alive, it produces, it multiplies.[7]

In this regard, a Jungian approach to counseling and psychotherapy could be beneficial for diagnosis as well as therapy in the African context. We can approach aspects of presenting problems, such as dreams, through Jung's method, thus yielding a richer interpretation than pastoral counseling currently accords dreams and visions. Most importantly, individuation (that is, becoming a unified person), which is the goal of Jungian therapy, may prove useful in bringing about the differentiation between psychological and spiritual issues, which will enhance the pastoral theological approach to treatment as well.

The Conceptual Tools: Promises and Challenges

Because of the interdisciplinary as well as the multicultural content of this examination, I need to say a few words about the conceptual tools I used. I have drawn the conceptual tools utilized in this research mainly from Karl Barth and Carl Gustav Jung, but I was not limited to their ideas alone. I bring the ideas of other theologians as well as the religious beliefs of the culture of focus into the theological conversation. The Bible also plays an

---

7. C. G. Jung, *Interpretation of Visions*, privately mimeographed seminar notes of Mary Foote (1930-34, Vol. 6, Lecture 1, May 4, 1932, 3), cited in *Jung on Active Imagination*, ed. Joan Chodorow (Princeton: Princeton University Press, 1997), 7.

important role in this project. It forms the basis of my critique of the anthropological understanding and pastoral diagnoses in the Independent Evangelical churches. My use of the Scriptures in this project draws upon familiar texts that Ghanaian pastors typically refer to in support of their anthropological stance and the pastoral counseling that issues from it. My intention in drawing upon these texts is to suggest possible alternative readings of the texts other than a purely spiritual explication and application. My hope is that a newer, multifaceted reading of these texts will contribute to the kind of differentiated approach to diagnoses that I believe may prove useful for pastors.

David Augsburger has made an important observation about intercultural pastoral counseling:

> The culturally effective counselor has differentiated a self from the culture of origin with sufficient perceiving, thinking, feeling, and *reflecting freedom* to recognize when values, views, assumptions, and preferences rise from an alternative life experience. (Emphasis added)[8]

What stands out in this description, and what is of import to this project, is the capacity of the effective counselor to, as it were, stand outside the culture of origin and to reflect on it, while at the same time recognizing the possibility of other valid life experiences outside the culture of origin. Though Augsburger may have been speaking directly to counselors in the West, where most of the pastoral counseling theories have been formulated, his description can also apply to the counselor from the receiving culture. I am thus stretching this understanding to include the ability to stand just outside the culture of origin, in this case the receiving culture, and to receive from it as well as critique it in order to enrich it. It is this aspect of the stance of the culturally effective counselor that undergirds how I employ theology and psychology in this project.

Before we proceed, I need to say something about what might prove irksome to some readers: the use of ideas garnered from a Western subculture to raise issues with and critique a different socio-cultural space. Perhaps the use of Reformed theology and perhaps even depth psychology *per se* might not raise eyebrows, though it might. But Karl Barth and Carl Jung? Yet I have chosen them precisely *because* they are such cultural out-

---

8. David W. Augsburger, *Pastoral Counseling across Cultures* (Philadelphia: Westminster, 1986), 23.

siders in Africa. That very fact offers them a viewing point that gives pause for reflection. "The one furrowing," according to an African proverb, "is not able to judge whether the path he works is straight, but relies on the perspective of one behind him for direction in order that he might furrow a straight path."[9] Barth's own theological project is grounded in a historical critical edge that remains prophetic because it was spoken in an era of huge political unrest and bondage that required a strong theological voice to speak truth and freedom into the ferment and bring about justice for the oppressed. It is thus an intentional move, and not a case of false consciousness or false identity politics, to utilize Barth's insights. He not only wrestled with similar issues related to damaging outcomes of conservative forces coupled with a strong commitment to culture, but also experienced firsthand what a subtle move to claim divine support for such aims can do to the church. This Barthian approach offers a much-needed release from a false fundamentalism and authoritarianism that currently pervade the theologizing in these ecclesial spaces, and helps bring an imminent critique to the dangers of a burgeoning religion, under the guise of Christianity, to re-subjugate its members, mainly women and the less powerful, to slavery — a slavery to the bondage of the very Word of God that is intended to "set the captives free." Jung is the psychologist I have called upon because even though he operated well outside the African context, his theories make room for the presence of the spiritual within psychic phenomena such as dreams and the demonic.

The first chapter of this book gives a general overview of the problem seen from a particular theological and psychological perspective; the next chapter offers a fuller exploration of African Traditional Religions' understanding of the human being and seeks to demonstrate its strong effect on African Christian anthropology. I give attention to both the strengths and drawbacks of this anthropology from a Christian perspective, and then examine the ensuing problems of bondage, which stem from what I see as an inadequate theological anthropology and Christology, and which in turn hinder the therapeutic process.

The third chapter explores Barth's theological anthropology with its strong Christocentric basis. It pays particular attention to Barth's arguments against claiming a single biblical cosmology, and for understanding the human constitution as body and soul undergirded by spirit, rather than the

---

9. This is an Akan (Ghana) proverb in popular domain, which functions as a teaching tool about listening to others for understanding what one is doing.

tripartite body, soul, spirit, as African Christians traditionally perceive it. Here the emphasis is on the extent of the human being's freedom (especially in the light of the incarnation) on the physical, spiritual, and psychic levels.

Chapter four brings the conclusions gleaned from Barth's theological anthropology into dialogue with African Christian views, supported by biblical and extra-biblical texts. Barth gives us a theological framework from which to challenge certain assumptions in contemporary African theology. In particular, I challenge the assumption that the issues in the present pastoral situation are akin to what prevailed in the biblical times. I argue, contrary to the present African understanding, that there is no kinship between its views and the presumed biblical view, since there is no single worldview as such that the Bible sanctions. In this light, we need to rethink our understanding of the place of cosmology as it affects the life of human beings, as well as our basic understanding of what constitutes the human person.

Through the lenses of Jung's analytical psychology, chapter five deals with the more psychical aspects of some of the causes of bondage. The main concern here is to provide other avenues for interpreting occurrences that have been largely thought of and treated only as demonic within this context. I argue for differentiating truly spiritual phenomena from psychical phenomena and seeing their inner connection.

The concluding chapter braids a three-stranded conversation — African Christian/Barthian/Jungian — to construct a Christian therapeutic model that draws on the worldview and life experiences of Africans and yet transcends these contextual boundaries. I demonstrate how a clearer differentiation can be achieved among the presenting problems in counseling with the help of insights from Barth's theological anthropology and Jung's analytical psychology. The significance for pastoral theology and practice is a more differentiated approach to diagnoses that yields a clearer picture of the individual in therapy, so that counselors can formulate an effective plan of intervention. The ultimate *telos,* of course, is the cultivation of wholeness in persons who are being formed into the image of Jesus Christ.

CHAPTER ONE

The Church in Ghana: A Window into Contemporary African Pastoral Practice

Introduction

In the Ghanaian church today, many people who suffer from a variety of human ills, whether of physical, psychological, relational, or spiritual origin, wander from one pastor to another seeking a spiritual cure. Because of the way cultural beliefs about the spiritual world have interwoven with Christian belief, many Ghanaian Christians live in bondage to their fears of evil spiritual powers. That is to say, traditional beliefs about witchcraft, evil spells, and demonic activity are interwoven with Christian practice in such a way that persons seek Christian pastors to deliver them from spiritual oppression. They see Jesus as a superior power to use against these malevolent spiritual forces.

In the Ghanaian church, pastoral problems are not diagnosed in a differentiated way to indicate a need for medical attention in one situation, psychological insight in another, relational skill in a third, and prayer in yet a fourth (or perhaps all or several of the above in any single situation). Rather, they consider all problems to be of a fundamentally spiritual nature and thus understand them precisely to need a strictly spiritual solution. Consequently, Christians are no different from the rest of Ghanaian society, caught in never-ending battles with spiritual powers.

Yet while the church is not immune to the malevolent spirits in the world, the gospel testifies that in Christ we are free from domination and harm from these forces, which are now under Christ's dominion forever. The Epistle to the Ephesians (6:10-18) gives a clear indication of the scope of the warfare, but also points out that believers are secure because in God they have adequate weapons for waging and winning the war. Moreover, the battle they wage is not restricted to spiritual forces but is also against sin and the flesh, against anything that would inhibit the life they are called to live in the Spirit. These verses address the readers' calling as Christians as they face ordinary daily tasks.

In the Ghanaian churches today, however, these spiritual struggles seem to be at the very center of the Christian life, to the point that spiritual warfare has become both the means and end of Christian existence. The goal of Christian discipleship, however, is more than a struggle against evil spiritual forces, but is rather "to glorify God, and to enjoy him forever," as the Westminster Shorter Catechism states.[1] In their preoccupation with evil spiritual forces, Ghanaians have inadvertently and subtly shifted the focus of the Christian life from gratitude for the salvation God has wrought in Jesus Christ to anxiety about all the necessary steps they need to take each day to ward off evil spiritual powers.

The Church in Ghana: Main Christian Denominational Groups

This shift from gratitude to anxiety appears in varying degrees among the different denominational groupings of the church in Ghana. It is possible to classify Ghanaian churches under three broad categories in order of their appearance on the Christian scene. First are the historic churches, sometimes called the missionary churches, because they were churches planted in the Lower Niger by predominantly European missionary enterprises.

Early missionary efforts were tied in with colonizing activities from the various forts and castles on the coasts. One English clergyman, Thomas Thompson, who served as a chaplain at Cape Coast, took three Fanti boys back with him to England to be educated. Of the three, only Philip Quaque survived and returned to Cape Coast in 1765 after his training and ordination in the Anglican Church. He served as schoolmaster, catechist, and missionary, and "died in 1816 in that position."[2]

However, the Emancipation Act of 1833 became the springboard for the rich missionary work in Africa after centuries of battling bad weather

1. *The Book of Confessions,* "The Shorter Catechisms" (Louisville, Ky.: Presbyterian Church, USA, 1991), 7.001.
2. Lamin Sanneh, *West African Christianity: The Religious Impact* (Maryknoll, N.Y.: Orbis Books, 1983), 112.

and tropical diseases with limited success. This act allowed Africans to work side-by-side with white missionaries, providing them with invaluable knowledge of African cultural values. Moreover, these Africans' immunity to local diseases increased their chances of survival in the region. Their aid had already enabled the successful establishment of Christianity in Sierra Leone, an accomplishment that suggested the possibility of evangelizing all of Africa. A number of missionary societies sprang up throughout Europe to target various regions of Africa for evangelization. In May of 1842 Andreas Riis led a recruiting mission to Jamaica, "and from there the first batch of Christian colonists, twenty-four in all from Jamaica and Antigua, sailed for the Gold Coast" — present-day Ghana.[3] Thus began the first extensive missionary movement to Ghana.

In 1835 Riis arrived at Akropong-Akwapim, beginning the ecumenical Basel Mission in that region. He followed this by opening a station in Aburi a few miles away in 1847. Because traditional modes of missionary work in the coastal regions were overly dependent on European agency among people who had been affected by European contact, the Basel mission sought a new approach by moving inland. After Riis's efforts, church planting began in earnest, spreading all over Ghana, with the Presbyterian mission extending into Togoland. The Methodists and Baptists were to follow shortly after, and the churches planted by these denominations, as well as by the Roman Catholic and Anglican churches, are what are known today as the historic churches.

The historic churches founded by Western missionaries proclaimed a gospel clothed in Western garb with a worship experience that was foreign to the African. Like the Western churches, they laid emphasis on the verbal and cerebral aspects of worship rather than the more celebrative and symbolic approach more likely to resonate in African cultures.[4] In the historic or mission churches people tended to be Christians in name only; in times of crisis, finding it difficult to connect on a deep level with Westernized forms of worship, African Christians fell back on the resources of traditional religions. Subsequently, groups began forming that eventually broke away from the historic churches. These breakaways, beginning as early as the early twentieth century, prepared the way for the emergence of

---

3. Sanneh, *West African Christianity,* 107.

4. The worship atmosphere in these churches has undergone drastic changes since the end of the nineteenth century. Current worship incorporates both Western and African styles, drumming and dancing, and sometimes similar songs, termed "local choruses" because they are born out of the worship experience of the Christian community.

the African Independent Churches (AIC), also known as African Instituted Churches or African Initiated Churches.[5]

While some of these African Independent Churches came into being by separating from existing historic churches (like the Musama Disco Christo Church, which broke away from the Methodist Church of Ghana), others were founded with the emergence of Pentecostalism. Through whatever avenue they came into existence, the African Independent Churches, as J. Pobee observes, are "a place to feel at home," and thus "represent an indigenizing movement in Christianity."[6] From their inception they incorporated a worship and liturgical style familiar to Africans because they borrowed heavily from traditional African rituals. But while adapting Christian liturgy and teaching to an African cosmology made worship more relevant to the African, these tendencies in worship also reinforced "the strong preoccupations of Africans with fears of witchcraft."[7] Throughout Africa this movement to combine the resources of the Christian tradition and those of the African Traditional Religions produced overt and subtle forms of syncretism, in which adherents upheld dual allegiances to both Christianity and African traditional religions.

Several authors have dealt with the issue of nominal Christianity and the tendency towards syncretism among African Christians. These Christians have some affiliation with the church through the rites of baptism and confirmation, but do not incorporate Christian doctrine or Scripture into daily life. For example, Wilson Awasu's research deals with the nominal and syncretistic nature of the church among the Ewes of West Africa, concluding that the historic churches were Christian in name only but not in essence, while the syncretism of the African Independent Churches failed to be an adequate antidote, leaving people's spiritual needs largely unmet. In times of crisis, members of both mission and African Independent Churches visited shrines or other spiritual places for help:

> [They] are unable to know, relate to and enjoy God, as he would have them. By the same token, the impression is created that Christianity cannot satisfy the total Ewe spiritual yearning. That is unfortunate and flawed. Because authentic biblical Christianity, as God's total message

---

5. J. S. Pobee, "African Instituted (Independent) Churches," in *Dictionary of the Ecumenical Movement,* ed. Nicolas Lossky et al. (Grand Rapids: Eerdmans, 1991), 10.

6. Pobee, "African Instituted (Independent) Churches," 11.

7. Pobee, "African Instituted (Independent) Churches," 11.

addressed to the total human situation, is able to satisfy the spiritual hunger of any people anywhere.[8]

What Awasu says of the Ewe could be said of most of sub-Saharan Africa.

The third set of churches in Ghana are the Independent Evangelical/ Charismatic churches, which began to appear on the religious scene during the late 1960s when some fundamentalist groups, discouraged by the lack of biblically based teaching in the historic churches, began to form house-fellowships. Some of these fellowships developed into churches over time, and from the late 1980s to the present have experienced a surge in growth. These groups are mostly charismatic in doctrine and practice, and church services are often filled with displays of the gifts of the Holy Spirit, especially speaking in tongues. In addition to these new churches, there are prayer camps or retreat grounds following a similar worship format, where people go for prayers and where the sick, the demonized, and the barren flock for deliverance. In spite of this plethora of religious and spiritual places, the hunger of the population for a meaningful spiritual life continues. Everywhere one turns there is a new church or house of prayer.[9]

The focus of my research is on this third group, the Independent Evangelical/Charismatic churches, which are mushrooming all over the continent. I am focusing on the Independent Evangelical churches for two reasons. In the first place, though they are new on the Christian scene, they are growing more rapidly than the historic churches. In fact, the historic churches are losing members to these churches at a significant rate. Their message, which is heavily influenced by American televangelism and coupled with contemporary Christian music and vigorous dancing, is especially appealing to young people. Many of the pastors of these churches, however, have little or no theological training, claiming that such training is not only unnecessary but actually blocks the presence of the Holy Spirit in worship. While we may not dispute that the Holy Spirit is present in these churches, many mistakenly equate exuberance and excitement with the Spirit's presence. Furthermore, many parishioners assume that since they are personally experiencing the Holy Spirit in the context of worship, then the words of the pastor or leader

8. Wilson Awasu, "Religion, Christianity, and the Powers in Ewe Society" (Ph.D. diss., Fuller Theological Seminary, School of World Mission, 1988. ProQuest, AAT 8902862), 3.

9. Churches and Christian groups are springing up all over Ghana. There are currently four hundred Christian groups on just one university campus (private conversation with the Traveling Secretary of the Ghana Fellowship of Evangelical Students [GHAFES]).

must be directly from God the Holy Spirit. Because of this belief, the pastor's interpretation of the problems of the people and the solutions he proffers are accepted as the absolute truth.

In light of the fact that their largest audience is the youth of the country, we might say that the future of the church in Ghana lies with these Independent Evangelical churches. Kwame Bediako astutely points out that while African Independent Churches had become a force to be reckoned with on the continent and were the pacesetters for African Christianity, "[a]cademic orthodoxy was still far from recognizing that it was the independent churches which were in fact indicating the trend and direction of African Christianity."[10] If Bediako's claim is correct that these evangelical charismatic churches are poised to become the dominant form of Christianity in Africa, it is important to assess whether the theology and the pastoral ministry practiced in these churches are consonant with the witness of Scripture. These churches claim to adhere closely to the word of God and believe that their approach to pastoral counseling stems from the word of God. I will argue, however, that in certain respects the cosmology of African Traditional Religion has greater influence on the practices of these churches than belief in the saving grace of Jesus Christ.

Method and Procedure

The Context

I have focused this research on a particular culture and intend to speak directly to that culture. It is relevant, therefore, to describe the people for whom I developed this pastoral theological model. This description, though focused on religious beliefs, includes geographical location as well as a brief history of origin of the Anlo and the Akan peoples. While the description focuses entirely on these two because they are the largest people groups in Ghana, what is said of their religious beliefs is not limited to them. Rather, what I say of their religious beliefs is representative of the beliefs of other groups in Ghana, at least in essence. We can make applications from this model, therefore, to pastoral care situations among other groups in Ghana and in sub-Saharan Africa more widely.

---

10. Kwame Bediako, *Christianity in Africa: The Renewal of a Non-Western Religion* (Maryknoll, N.Y.: Orbis Books, 1995), 113.

The Field

I conducted the field research in this project largely through the use of a questionnaire that I developed and filled out through face-to-face interviews with pastors, and also through participant observation at church services and special "deliverance" services. I also recorded several of the interviews for later transcription to allow me the opportunity to reflect on conversations with the pastors. I particularly concentrated on the mode and criteria that pastors used for selection of individuals for various types of counseling or for deliverance sessions.

I interviewed about fifty pastors from various Protestant denominations. Of these, about 15 percent belonged to the mainline or historic churches, 75 percent belonged to the Independent Evangelical churches, including the Apostolic churches and the Assemblies of God, and the remaining 10 percent were from parachurch organizations that provide a form of counseling as well as prayer and deliverance. Interviewing a number of pastors from the historic churches provided a basis for comparison and enabled me to ascertain whether the phenomenon under observation was limited to the focus group. The strictly syncretistic African Independent Churches were not part of the groups researched.

The purpose of each interview was to gather information on how pastors diagnosed presenting problems in counseling situations. The questionnaire was designed to probe the conceptual tools that pastors utilized as they engaged in pastoral counseling, including what theoretical stance, if any, informed their pastoral ministry to the people who sought counsel from them, and how their pastoral interventions were conceived and carried out. Observations from these interviews, as well as participant observation in several churches, led me to conclude that their Christian anthropology is insufficient to accurately discern the complexity of needs that parishioners bring to their pastors. In order to offer more effective pastoral care, ministry practitioners must develop a more robust understanding of the human person that encompasses medical, psychological, and spiritual needs, which in turn means developing more finely-tuned tools for pastoral diagnoses.

Most of the Independent Evangelical churches used questions similar to those in the list in the appendix to determine whether parishioners' presenting issues were of demonic origins or not. These very detailed questions cover all areas of life, from possible physical ailments, through family history, to present spiritual problems. I will explore the significance of some of these questions and their implications for therapy in the churches under focus to clarify the bases and sources of these questions. Such an analysis will also aid in explaining the theological concerns at stake in this examination.

The questions addressed to an individual who comes for counseling fall into seven categories. First are questions dealing with personal particulars. Questions under this category include the person's name and the meaning of the name, gender, age, marital status, hometown, religion or church affiliation, whether or not the person has been "born again," and if so, when. While some of the questions in this category may be for general information, in conversations with several pastors it became clear that some are geared to elicit information about possible spiritual forces at work in the life of the individual.

For instance, the meaning of one's name is often deemed important to determining the significance of the circumstances surrounding the counselee's birth. Since most indigenous names have meaning, and are normally derived from circumstances surrounding one's conception and birth or even from events going on in the family, the meaning of one's name holds clues to vital information about the individual as well as the family of origin. There are several names from all the tribes, for instance, that indicate the birth order of children within particular clans and what those names mean. But there are also peculiar names reserved for infants born after a series of miscarriages, stillbirths, or short-lived babies. The rationale behind these unusual names arises from the belief that those who keep returning to the womb to be reborn will be deterred from coming back to torment their poor mothers if they are given unpleasant names. Some of these names, however, contain subtle messages to the infant to stay and not depart. Often when a family loses several children in infancy, the parents might seek a diviner to intervene in the situation. Pastors believe that the intervention sought from a fetish shrine or diviner makes people vulnerable to attack from evil spiritual beings. The individuals seeking help may thus be suffering because of their past connection with shrines and fetish groves they or their forebears visited, places where rituals were performed following revelations through divination. Since the Christians presuppose that God opposes such practices, and that they are forbidden in Scripture, then visiting shrines and participating in such rituals are sinful, even idolatrous, for which God exacts punishment. Since such shrines and their rituals are of satanic origin (because they could not come from God who forbids it), Satan must therefore have a hold on whoever seeks help from these shrines. When such persons or their descendants become Christians, Satan's hold on them is not immediately or completely relinquished. Ghanaian Christians see the struggles they go through, such as the loss of many children, as signs of a struggle between good and evil powers for control of their lives.

The questions about the counselee's hometown and religious affiliation deal with the presupposition that these could also be avenues for demonic influences. People believe certain towns and villages, for instance, to be strongholds of particular gods, and others to be populated with witches. Hailing from any of these places makes an individual an easy target for witches unless he or she guards constantly against such intrusions. In addition, several pastors reported that individuals who come to them from syncretistic churches, especially those in which worshipers are required to remove their footwear, often presented with symptoms of spiritual attack.

Church affiliation and whether or not the individual is "born again" are considered indicators of the counselee's spiritual state. The knowledge of the individual's spiritual state is vital for effective deliverance as well as preventing spiritual attacks from evil forces. If the individual is "born again" there is less chance of attack from evil forces. Existing idols/gods or ancestral stools[11] in the family provide avenues for harassment from evil spirits, as do parents' affiliation with secret societies such as the Society of Odd Fellows or Freemasons.

After a thorough interview following this extensive questionnaire, the pastors determine whether the individual needs to have further sessions and/or deliverance from demonic assaults. Problems parishioners bring for counseling are of various types stemming from different sources. Consider the following scenarios that took place within hours of each other at one of the churches I visited.

A woman brought her eighteen-month-old son to be prayed for so the spirit of fear might leave him. The infant's aunt, who was a member of the church, had observed that the boy got startled rather easily and interpreted the cause as a spirit of fear. Another woman and her female relatives brought a young police officer who was paralyzed from "unknown causes." He seemed to be in a stupor most of the time. The family wanted prayer for healing for him because they believed he was bewitched. At the close of the service, one of the pastors called my attention to a young woman with an

---

11. Ancestral, or blackened, stools are stools that have attained their black color because sacrificial blood has been smeared on them for years. Among the Anlo, for example, the yearly festivals of clans and tribes provide opportunity for communal worship, and on such occasions the stools are "washed" with blood.

enlarged (probably cancerous) breast who had come for healing for what seemed to be an incurable disease. Two elderly ladies accompanied her. It is striking that all of these persons, with prolonged somatic symptoms, had come to a pastor for help.

The previous day, several people, the majority of whom were women, had gathered together to pray and be prayed for. They gathered to stand together against the forces of evil that threatened to destroy their lives, work, and marriages, and to declare their victory over their adversaries. The day's prayer time ended with a call from the pastor to "hoot at fear" and drive the spirit of fear out of their midst.[12]

In several other Independent Evangelical churches where people waited to be counseled, normally the pastor prayed with the people to find out the root causes of their problems through spiritual discernment. They understood most physical manifestations — some similar to epileptic fits, others as innocuous as fidgeting — to be indications of possible demonic presence and/or activity. Therefore, they saw the individual as either demon-possessed or demon-oppressed, which called for warfare praying and deliverance. Warfare praying — often conducted with trained groups of people — usually involved intense prayer and spiritual battle with demonic forces. Participants would call on the power of God by the authority vested in them as Christians to grant them victory over the evil powers. They used prayer, especially prayers of deliverance, to heal physically, psychically, and spiritually.

The Ghanaian context has some peculiar circumstances that contribute to both the problem and the need to seek out pastors for care and comfort. The current socio-economic situation, combined with the unstable political atmosphere, creates anxiety, and the search for security is at an all-time high.[13] In the face of such insecurity, people turn to the supernatural for hope and reassurance. Many in Africa flock from one revival meeting to another and from one deliverance session to another, all in the hope of

12. Though this project is not specifically about the effect of the prevailing spiritual climate on women, it is striking that most of the people in need of prayer and counseling or who saw the need to bring other people to be prayed for were women. Mercy Oduyoye is right to speak of African women as "religion's chief clients." See Oduyoye, *Daughters of Anowa: African Women and Patriarchy* (Maryknoll, N.Y.: Orbis Books, 1995), 109.

13. The present socio-economic situation in Ghana is like that in most other developing nations. Most people are poor and can barely afford the basic necessities of life. The unstable political systems also make investors shy away from the African market, contributing to a sluggish economy.

alleviating the various pressures on them. In their studies on religious revivalism and cults, Jerome and Julia Frank, admitting that evidence from their research is inconclusive, point out a tendency for "evangelistic sects in affluent societies to flourish more among the economically or socially underprivileged."[14] We would therefore expect that these sects would flourish also in developing countries. They further claim that "the ecstasies of evangelical religions provide outlets for pent-up emotional tensions, offer relief from the impoverishment and monotony of daily life, and gratify important psychological needs."[15] In chapter five, I will explore this assertion in more detail as we examine the psychological implications of some of the presenting problems in pastoral counseling.

Concerns

The focus questions generally used for diagnosing issues brought for counseling had both depth and clarity. The emphasis of the questions weighed toward the spiritual causes of the individuals' problems and paid little or no attention to possible psychological or somatic causes, thus providing little or no differentiation between the spiritual, psychological, and somatic dimensions of the person. Seeing all problems as spiritual, pastors offered only spiritual interventions. Thus, we might say that the underlying theological assumptions of pastoral ministry seem to derive as much from African traditional beliefs as from Christian theology.

We might at first expect that the people involved in searches for spiritual cures would be from the historic churches, whose members are commonly regarded as Christian in name only. However, the churches involved in promoting these "spiritual cures" are not the historic churches, nor are they the African Independent Churches, which are known for their double allegiance to both Christianity and African Traditional Religions. Instead it is members of the newer churches, trying to adhere closely to the word of God, who are most involved in the search for spiritual cures.

Their behavior, however, betrays a failure to understand the nature of true evangelical freedom. The Ephesians passage noted at the beginning of this chapter identifies both a divine initiative and human responsibility

---

14. Jerome D. Frank and Julia B. Frank, *Persuasion and Healing: A Comparative Study of Psychotherapy*, 3rd ed. (Baltimore: Johns Hopkins University Press, 1993), 76.

15. Frank and Frank, *Persuasion and Healing*, 76.

involved in the warfare that the Christian wages. God provides the armor as well as omnipotent presence, and believers are called to live in and trust in this provision as sufficient for their safety. The weapons of God's truth as spelled out in Scripture — of righteousness not based on good works, but on the righteousness of Christ imputed to the believer through faith, and of the peace made with God based on the sacrifice of Jesus — these are the truths believers are to keep in their purview as they live in this world.

As I have already mentioned, many of these churches are led by pastors with no formal theological training or access to ministerial formation. Without adequate theological training, which would include biblical studies as well as some practical theology, pastors fall back on their own understanding of the biblical passages upon which they base their pastoral intervention and theology. They often take these passages literally and without knowledge of the historical and linguistic context of the passages. Theology based on such exegesis risks portraying less than the complete picture of God and of human beings than the Scriptures intended. To give pastoral counsel and care to people based on such an understanding may be unhelpful at best, and dangerous at worst.

Because these churches and their pastors profess a strong desire to be faithful to Scripture, a correct interpretation of the word of God may be our best answer to this problem. If we can develop a new approach on scriptural grounds that would be convincing to these churches — that the theology currently being preached, taught, and practiced in effect causes greater bondage to these very evil forces — then there might be a way to set pastoral ministry on a more secure footing.

The Scriptures are clear that the world is not a chaotic mess. There is order and purpose to every aspect of it. God created the world by bringing order to chaos (Gen 1:1-2) and promised that the structure would be maintained. "As long as the earth endures, seedtime and harvest, cold and heat, summer and winter, day and night, shall not cease" (Gen. 8:22). This is not a passive statement suggesting, as the deists assume, that the world since creation now runs itself. Israel's history, as recorded in the Old Testament, affirms God's involvement in the day-to-day ordering of the universe, an involvement that Christians believe culminates in the incarnation of God in Jesus Christ.

The incarnation is the physical as well as spiritual inbreaking of the rule of God over the world. Jesus began his ministry by declaring that with his presence "the Kingdom of God has come (*ephthasen*) upon you" (Matt. 12:28). To some the Greek word used here points to the proximity of the Kingdom, but others argue, based on usage in other passages, that the verb implies actual physical presence rather than proximity alone.[16] As G. E. Ladd points out, while the Kingdom of God has obvious eschatological implications, there are historical implications as well.[17] Several parables of Jesus illustrate that the Kingdom has both present and futuristic connotations. If we consider God's redemptive work, we find both that the lost are *being* saved and *will be* saved in the final days. If we understand the Kingdom of God as a day of judgment, we find the same present and futuristic connotations: the world was being judged before, during, and after Jesus' life, death, and resurrection. The Epistles also tell of the coming judgment of God.[18] Most importantly, we must bear in mind that, as Ladd says,

> The Kingdom is the outworking of the divine will; it is the act of God himself. It is related to men and can work in and through men; but it never becomes subject to men. It remains *God's* Kingdom. It is significant that although men must receive the Kingdom, this individual human act of reception is not described as a coming of the Kingdom. *The Kingdom does not come as men receive it.* The ground of the demand that men receive the Kingdom rests in the fact that in Jesus, the Kingdom *has come* into history. . . . The divine act requires a human response, even though it remains a divine act.[19]

Ultimately, God is the one who brings about the Kingdom. Its coming does not depend upon our human response.

---

16. New Testament scholarship has broadened our understanding of the concept of the kingdom of God, especially through the study of the parables of the kingdom. See, for instance, J. Jeremias, *New Testament Theology* (New York: Charles Scribner's Sons, 1971); G. E. Ladd, *The Presence of the Future: The Eschatology of Biblical Realism* (Grand Rapids: Eerdmans, 1974); G. R. Beasley-Murray, *Jesus and the Kingdom of God* (Grand Rapids: Eerdmans, 1986).

17. Ladd, *Presence of the Future*, 307. The whole thrust of Ladd's argument is that the Kingdom is not something yet to come. It is already here in a microcosm because of the Christ event.

18. The parable of the Sower appropriately illustrates the Kingdom of God as both a present reality and a future expectation, in respect to redemption and judgment. As a seed harbors within it all that a plant would be, albeit imperceptibly, so also does the Kingdom that has come. It holds in it all that the future will be. As Paul says, "now we see in a mirror, dimly, but then we will see face to face" (1 Cor. 13:12).

19. Ladd, *Presence of the Future*, 193-94. I acknowledge the lack of gender-inclusive language in this text, and ask the reader to consider the date of publication and excuse this failure.

While African Christians know that God is the ultimate ruler of the cosmos, their daily expressions of faith sometimes imply that God's rule extends only to those who voluntarily subject themselves to God. As long as they are preoccupied with what evil forces may do to them through sources beyond their control, and as long as they spend a greater portion of their lives at war with these forces, real or imagined, they infer the presence of independent, powerful beings apart from God's providence. Moreover, they impute to these beings a power beyond that which they are granted by God in their creaturely state. Insofar as they are preoccupied with what evil forces may do, they are robbed of the blessing of the complete freedom that life in Christ brings. Jesus declares, "I came that they may have life, and have it abundantly" (John 10:10). Again, "In the world you face persecution. But take courage; I have conquered the world" (John 16:33).[20]

The tendency to run from one spiritual leader to another and the theology undergirding the pastoral ministry that fosters this behavior reveal two false assumptions. One assumption is that spiritual forces have an independent existence and operate outside the overarching rule of God. The other assumption presumes a power struggle between God and the spiritual forces. The way in which the power struggle is conceived gives the impression that God and other spiritual forces are on the same level of being, but that God will ultimately win the war through superior strength. Not only is such an assumption false, it is also blasphemous because it blurs the distinction between God as creator and all other spiritual powers as creatures. In other words, this primary distinction is a difference between creature and creator rather than merely a difference of degree between omnipotent versus limited power. In the prologue of Job, Satan is clearly depicted as a creature of God, subjected and limited to God's will and purposes (Job 1:6).

I have witnessed the vibrancy of African Christian worship and the response of Christians to the awesome power of God demonstrated in numerous songs, often born spontaneously during worship, and with that in mind I find the current trend in African pastoral ministry perplexing. The faith in God that generates these songs that powerfully invoke the Spirit seems to fade away in time of adversity and stress. It is primarily from this background and the theological insights described above that I address the theological underpinnings of the issues raised by present African pastoral counseling, especially in the Independent Evangelical churches in Ghana.

---

20. The Amplified Version, which carries more nuanced meanings of the Greek text than the other translations, renders this "I have deprived it of power to harm you."

Methodology

Scholars have advanced various approaches to understand the tendency of African Christians to attribute all types of problems to spiritual causes. Usually they see a close affinity between African Traditional Religions and biblical Christianity. Some have argued that African Traditional Religion and biblical Christianity share a common cosmology (especially in regard to the constitution of the human being), as well as a similar approach to health and wholeness.[21] But I believe this basic assumption deserves to be reexamined.

We will explore first whether the Bible presents a single, unified worldview or cosmology, and second, whether there is a natural affinity between this biblical worldview and an African worldview. If there is no single worldview depicted in the Bible, but rather multiple cosmologies that are used in various contexts to make particular theological claims, none of which are the central content of the New Testament witness, then we have a basis for making important distinctions between the Bible and African cosmology. In making these distinctions, however, we must not slide into the error of abstraction, claiming that the Word of God was never truly incarnate, and somehow "floats" above the fray of history, uninvolved and unaffected by the affairs of humankind. On the other hand, we must also avoid the opposite error of claiming a perfect identification between the gospel and a particular culture, as if any people could "own" Jesus or Scripture as its cultural property.

If we are to avoid these twin dangers of abstraction and identification, then, it is particularly important that theologians, pastors, and lay leaders continually attend to the material conditions of Jesus' incarnation. For this reason, when the church proclaims that Jesus is the Christ, she must remember that Jesus is first the Messiah of Israel, and that by taking on Jewish flesh as the Prophet, Priest, and King of Israel, Jesus is also drawing the Gentiles into the sweep of God's promise to Abraham. This is not a claim of national or ethnic chauvinism that seeks to efface or minimize the diversity of human cultures, nor is it a claim that Jesus is the cultural property of a racially construed Israel. Rather, it is a claim about the elective grace of God, who freely created and chose Israel to be the site of God's redemptive action

---

21. In their discussions of the traditional religions, most African theologians start with this basic assumption. See, for instance, Bolaji Idowu, *Olódùmarè: God in Yoruba Belief* (London: Longmans, 1962), 3-4, 202.

in the world — an action brought to its culmination and fulfillment in the incarnation, life, death, and resurrection of Jesus Christ.[22]

We will return to some of these themes in chapter three, and there is much more that we could say about this that would not be relevant to the present argument. For our purposes here, we will simply stress that Christians in Africa stand in the same relationship to Jesus and Scripture as the first Gentile converts in the New Testament: as strangers to the covenant with Israel who have been grafted in by the gracious invitation of Jesus, Israel's Messiah. While inevitably there are many illuminating similarities between African worldviews and the several cosmologies found in scripture, it is dangerous to make the claim to a total identity between the two. Such notable similarities must always be tempered by the memory that African cosmologies are only intelligible as "Christian" insofar as they have been grafted into Israel's covenant with God through Jesus Christ. This grafting is not the imperialistic mode of assimilation, but instead a moment of transcendence by which African Christians find themselves in Christ *as* African, but *more than* African.

In light of these insights, I wish to argue that Christianity in Ghana, and in Africa more broadly, has yet to truly transcend its cultural moment, and that this failure can explain many of the pastoral problems that beset parishioners. A way forward can be found in a more appropriate biblical anthropology that reflects this Christological argument. A pastoral theology and practice founded on this Christology will enable pastors to interrogate problematic cultural narratives about the relationship between body, soul, and spirit, while offering a more nuanced, constructive, and liberating path towards healing and wholeness.

African cosmology has been rightly lauded for its holistic understanding of what it means to be human. The African sees the human person existing in a web of relationships: a web made up of the living, the dead, and the unborn, as well as the rest of creation. At the base of this relational web is the relationship to the supernatural. The supernatural consists of the Supreme Being, to whom is attributed the creation of the world, other spirit beings and lesser gods, charms and amulets, and evil spirits. This interrelatedness operates at all levels of human existence, and whatever crises

---

22. I am indebted to my colleague Dr. Willie Jennings for the Christological insight underpinning this argument. For a more in-depth treatment of this and related themes, see his book, *The Christian Imagination: Theology and the Origins of Race* (New Haven: Yale University Press, 2010), 250-88.

Africans face affect the physical, the psychic, and the spiritual dimensions of life. Thus, occurrences at one level naturally spill over to the other spheres, and often physical and psychical mishaps are attributed to spiritual causes.

These beliefs are strong not only among adherents of African Traditional Religions but also among African Christians. Christians and non-Christians alike are caught up in fear of the supernatural world and its evil effects on them. Like non-Christians, Christians interpret all mishaps from a spiritual perspective. While today Christians do not visit shrines for cures, they do wander from church to church, seeking fulfillment and spiritual protection. While African Christians celebrate through song and dance the victory of Jesus over Satan on their behalf, the habit of wandering from one church to the other seeking protection or assurance from a pastor is an indication that they do not fully understand or appreciate the extent of the victory they profess. African Christology does not take in the full significance of the Christ event, especially the efficacy of Christ's death and resurrection to cast away evil completely and to bring healing and full salvation to all aspects of life.

Very little has been written in the area of pastoral theology or psychotherapy in the Ghanaian context. One exception in pastoral care and counseling is the pioneering work of Emmanuel Y. Lartey.[23] Using Gestalt and family therapy, Lartey attempts to address therapeutic concerns similar to my own. He draws largely on the culture, values, beliefs, and views of the people and works basically within the existing anthropological understanding of the close-knit relationship between body, soul, and spirit. While his model for therapy offers valuable insights for intercultural counseling, it does not address what I think is a basic underlying problem: the lack of adequate differentiation between the three entities in spite of their obvious unity.[24] The African conceives of the person as a relational being: related to God, to itself (as indicative of the close-knit relationship assumed between the body, the soul, and the spirit), and to the rest of the cosmos. Yet an undue emphasis on the interrelatedness among the body, soul, and spirit, coupled with a belief in the influence of the spirit world on human beings, results in giving undue weight to the power of the rest of creation over human beings. Ghanaians lay so much emphasis on the power of the spirit

23. E. Y. Lartey, *Pastoral Counselling in Inter-Cultural Perspective: A Study of Some African (Ghanaian) and Anglo-American Views on Human Existence and Counseling* (Frankfurt am Main: Verlag Peter Lang, 1987).

24. Later in this examination I explore whether human beings are comprised of spirit, soul, and body, or of just two entities, soul and body.

world over the physical creation that the other elements receive inadequate attention. For instance, if one dies suddenly of unknown causes, Ghanaians attribute the death to witches who may have killed the person in the spiritual realm days before the body felt the effect and died.

Ghanaians are so paranoid of spiritual attacks that they constantly live on the lookout for such occurrences. People run from church to church, from one prayer group to another, in search of security. Unfortunately, the help they receive only perpetuates the problem, because the solution operates from the same assumption — that is, that there are powerful, predatory spiritual forces that need to be reckoned with. The interpretative framework for understanding spiritual phenomena itself becomes a form of bondage because it completely ignores the aspects of problems that are purely psychological or physical.[25] When pastors focus diagnosis and remedy almost exclusively on the spiritual, people suffer unnecessarily,[26] bearing persistent psychic and emotional wounds. When suffering persons do not receive the deliverance they seek, they too often come to believe that they have not received it because of a personal inadequacy. They are convinced either that they do not possess the prerequisite faith or that they may have a hidden sin that blocks the flow of God's healing to them. There are reported cases of individuals being beaten in the attempt to drive out evil spirits believed to be harming them.

Most pastors and their helpers have not been formally trained in pastoral counseling, which is understandable since it is a relatively new field of study. But this vacuum of pastoral education and the ongoing lack of any other counseling result in a situation where no one probes other aspects of the problems parishioners bring. They receive a "one-shot prayer and exorcism" with scriptural injunctions to follow. Pastors and sufferers alike expect this exercise to be a permanent cure-all. Such counseling not only fails to touch the deep problems that parishioners bring, but it adds another burden to what they already carry. If counselees already feel that they are failing in their Christian duty by the way they live and then receive a scriptural injunction to exercise more faith or to be patient, they leave feeling worse about their situation than when they came. Their sense of failure is reinforced rather than dissipated.

25. The paradigms through which the African views disease and health are different from those of the West, but I advocate a new paradigm that takes into consideration the possibility and resources of psychological insights as well.

26. Some of these people would have first sought medical help for their physical ailments. The persistence of the problem in spite of medical intervention may bring some to the pastor.

The pattern of counseling described here is not only the direct expression of a particular view that Ghanaian society holds about human beings. It is also a measure of society's understanding of who God is and of the role of the pastor in the counseling situation.[27] For this reason it is important to attend to how the pastor perceives himself, as well as to how parishioners perceive the pastor in his role as spiritual authority. In *Pastoral Diagnosis*, Nancy Ramsay looks at the dynamics of authority in the pastoral relationship as a part of the healing process, indeed as a part of the diagnostic process itself. Ramsay points out that authority, which she defines as "an emotional expression of power," is present in every relationship but takes on certain "distinctive features" in the pastoral relationship.[28] Because the pastor's identity is often tied in with the historic office of the church, which has always been a symbol of authority even in public life, the authority of the church is unconsciously transferred to the pastor. The dynamics present in the pastoral relationship are further circumscribed by geographical and cultural factors. Even the type of congregation affects the dynamics of the pastoral relationship. In Ghana, cultural influences and childrearing practices contribute to the tendency of the individual to show deference to all authority figures, including pastors. In fact, pastors command particular respect among Ghanaians, and this respect, combined with the general deference to authority, shifts the dynamics of power in the pastoral relationship in the favor of pastors. Therefore, pastors need to pay attention to the dynamics of authority in the pastoral relationship and how they affect diagnosis and care.

In order to develop a more viable anthropology and soteriology that will help provide a new theoretical model for Christian therapy in the African context, I will turn to the Christological theology developed by Karl Barth. Barth's theological anthropology gives detailed attention to the relational matrix of the human person. His dynamic view of the person deals not only with motion, but also with interpersonal action. Interpersonal action consists of relationships to God, oneself, and others. The human being lives within these fields of relationships, and Barth's anthropology sees these

27. The word theology is used here to designate both the body of knowledge and the discipline and the concept of God or our understanding of God. There is also a sense in which anthropology presupposes theology and vice versa. Who we perceive God to be affects our understanding of what humanity is, and our understanding of humanity and its place in the cosmos affects our concept of God.

28. Nancy J. Ramsay, *Pastoral Diagnosis: A Resource for Ministry of Care and Counseling* (Minneapolis: Fortress, 1998), 5-6.

fields of relationship as analogous to the inner dynamic relationship within the Godhead. God's being is dynamic because God is Creator, Son, and Holy Spirit. Our relationship to ourselves and to other human beings thus mirrors this inner relationship of God. The subject matter of theological anthropology is therefore not merely the human person, but human persons as constituted in their relationships with one another and with God. God's self-revelation supports the affirmation that we are made in the image of God and, therefore, our knowledge of who we are as human beings.

The main task of this examination is to develop a pastoral theological model that will help African pastors to diagnose presenting problems in a more differentiated way. Since the problems that individuals bring to counseling are multifaceted and stem from all dimensions of life (sociological, psychological, physical, and spiritual), when only one dimension is emphasized and addressed, the whole person is not healed. This analysis will discern not only underlying problems with current diagnostic tools, but also the theological and psychoanalytical resources available for a more holistic response to the problems that beset African Christians.

CHAPTER TWO

African Cosmology and African Christian Theology

Introduction

Worldview or *Weltanschauung*, as the name suggests, is a way of looking at the world and understanding the reality it presents. It comprises the tacit assumptions that a people have regarding the nature of things, assumptions that underlie how they respond to crises. A worldview often becomes clear in response to individual and communal crises.[1]

For the African, religion plays a significant role in culture, and thus in worldview. It permeates all aspects of life and is so integrated with culture that, as Kwesi Dickson points out, "Culture is . . . properly used as an umbrella description which subsumes religion."[2] For this reason, while an individual may not be a practitioner of African Traditional Religion, he or she still participates in it indirectly. In this chapter I examine the worldviews, and in particular, the understanding of personhood of two Ghanaian peoples, to better understand how those beliefs affect their Christian theological beliefs, leading to what we can clearly see as an African Christian theology.

This blending of traditional views with Christianity is not an unusual phenomenon because wherever the gospel has been preached, it has taken on the garb of the culture that it addresses. Though the content remains the same, the expression of it in the various cultures will obviously differ from

---

1. Emmanuel Lartey, *Pastoral Counselling in Inter-Cultural Perspective* (Frankfurt am Main: Peter Lang, 1987), 23.

2. Kwesi Dickson, *Theology in Africa* (Maryknoll, N.Y.: Orbis Books, 1984), 29.

that of the New Testament cultures. And yet, if the mission and vocation of Israel is to be *for* the world, and if Jesus is the embodiment of this mission, then the gospel that Christians proclaim is a gospel that is truly for the entire world. The central message — that God has intervened in history through the people Israel and through the life, death, and resurrection of Jesus, who is the once and for all intermediary between God and human beings — must not be changed or superseded by another dogma. Attempts at contextualization must, therefore, take note of the possibility of syncretism. The problem, then, is how to contextualize the gospel in a way that enables it to come alive for the hearers, without eliding the abiding uniqueness of God's election of Jesus or Israel.

Missiologist Lesslie Newbigin makes an important distinction between true and false contextualization. A true contextualization takes seriously both the message and the mode by which it is delivered, while keeping in mind "the basic fact that there is no such thing as a pure gospel, if by that is meant something which is not embodied in a culture."[3] It is important to take both the content and mode of delivery of the gospel seriously, for:

> If the gospel is to be understood, if it is to be received as something which communicates truth about the real human situation, if it is, as we say, to "make sense," it has to be . . . clothed in symbols which are meaningful to [those to whom it is addressed]. It must, as we say, "come alive." Those to whom it is addressed must be able to say, "Yes. I see. This is true for me, for my situation. But if the gospel is truly to be communicated, the subject in that sentence is as important as the predicate. What comes home to the heart of the hearer must really be the gospel, and not a product shaped by the mind of the hearer.[4]

While contextualization of the gospel is important for effective communication to recipients, it is equally important that the need for contextualization does not override the message delivered. If we lose the message by overly identifying it with a particular culture, there is little gain for the recipients. Instead we should take a balanced approach in our communication of the gospel, such that the content remains constant while the mode of delivery adapts to the message. With this balanced approach, the worldview or the

3. Lesslie Newbigin, *The Gospel in a Pluralist Society* (Grand Rapids: Eerdmans, 1989), 144.

4. Newbigin, *The Gospel in a Pluralist Society,* 141.

culture becomes a channel through which the gospel is delivered. The goal of the gospel message is the total liberation of human beings into a renewed communion with God, neighbor, and creation. In so far as this message disrupts time and space and introduces a tension with a cultural milieu, it calls the hearers to a process of examination, repentance, and transcendence towards a transformed and redeemed worldview. However, this negotiation of adaptation and transcendence is often very difficult due to the deeply rooted, instinctual quality of any worldview.

Anthropologist Michael Kearney has suggested several areas of life with which all known worldviews deal. First, all worldviews classify the reality with which they are presented. Time, event, and space are all organized according to how a people perceive the universe. Above all, a worldview deals with causality, answering fundamental questions regarding origins and power. A culture's understanding of causality therefore tends to be the most entrenched because it deals with the existential questions they live with on a daily basis. While some aspects of culture might change more readily as they interact with other cultures, a people's worldview, especially their understanding of the relationship of the cosmos to themselves, is so ingrained and inheres at such a subconscious level of the psyche that it is difficult to change. At best, it may be modified from time to time, but only by the people themselves:

> As a system, a world view is itself ordered by the dynamic interrelationships among its elements, which are the images and assumptions that form the content of the various world-view universals. . . . [A] world view is to some degree a more-or-less logically consistent and structurally integrated set of assumptions.[5]

Wilson Awasu, following Kearney, suggests that it is the integration and interrelatedness of the various elements of a worldview that make it so resistant to "piecemeal changes."[6] But the gospel, by the very nature of its claims to present what is actually the case about reality, and because of its claim to revealed truth, gives every culture new lenses for apprehending the world. Yet it is often difficult to draw the line between what is merely

5. Michael Kearney, *World View* (Novato, Calif.: Chandler & Sharp, 1984), 123-24.
6. Wilson Awasu, "Religion, Christianity and the Powers in Ewe Society" (Ph.D. diss., Fuller Theological Seminary, School of World Mission, 1988), available from ProQuest AAT 8902862, p. 37.

custom, which can exist side by side with the gospel and be enhanced by it, and what is not.

Ghanaian Cosmology and the Gospel

We can best understand the two Ghanaian peoples' worldviews by looking at their cosmologies. Throughout this examination, I will use the terms *worldview* and *cosmology* interchangeably to mean the deep underlying structure and logic of a people's way of living in the world. A worldview is "the most basic and comprehensive concepts, values, and unstated assumptions about the nature of reality shared by people in a culture. It is the way they characteristically interpret the universe of human experience."[7] As we examine the cosmologies or worldviews of the Anlo and Akan people groups in Ghana, we will see just how entrenched their worldviews are, and how even among Christians the traditional worldviews have not been essentially modified by Christian belief. In order to provide substantive answers to the problems inherent to Ghanaian Christian anthropology, it is essential to understand how people conceive of the deep narratives that undergird their being in the world. I need to underscore the importance of understanding these deep narratives, lest any proposals for change remain merely superficial. Missionary enterprises in Africa have been hobbled by the challenge of syncretism in African Christianity, and the persistence of this phenomenon over the years indicates how deeply a worldview is entrenched in a people. This entrenchment is further underscored by the fact that evangelical Christians, who claim a literal reading of the Scriptures, still exhibit a subtle double allegiance in the daily expressions of faith.

My main concern is how this interpretation of human experience affects pastoral theology and hence pastoral counseling. How does worldview either perceptibly or imperceptibly affect how Christians construe and construct the problems they deal with? How does worldview affect the pastoral response to the construction and presentation of the experiences parishioners bring? How does worldview shape the questions and dialogue that probe the problems of parishioners? What undergirds how parishioners and pastors work together toward an adequate resolution of problems? Above all, are there underlying difficulties and blockages to effective pas-

---

7. P. Hiebert, "Worldview," in *Dictionary of Pastoral Care and Counseling*, ed. R. Hunter (Nashville: Abingdon, 1990), 1338.

toral counseling due to the adherence to particular worldviews? An examination of the cosmologies of the Anlo and Akan in Ghana will provide insights into the present problems in Ghanaian pastoral theology in particular and African pastoral theology in general.[8]

Anlo Cosmology

The Anlo People and Their General Belief System

The Ewe of West Africa today occupy a vast area stretching from the Volta River of Ghana as far as the western borders of modern-day Benin. Though divided and scattered under three different governments, some census accounts put their number around seven million. A common migration experience as a result of tyranny in 1620 under the cruel King Agokoli, the eighty-eighth king of Notsie, gives the Ewe of West Africa a peculiar bond. The Anlo, geographically located in the southeastern part of Ghana, belong to this larger Ewe people. Anlo cosmologies are therefore similar in most respects to beliefs held by the other Ewe groups.

At the center of Anlo cosmology and their view of human existence is a belief in a hierarchy of beings: "a Personal Supreme Creator, personal spirit powers, human ancestral spirits, and an impersonal all-pervasive power," human beings, animals, and plants.[9] The Anlo, like other African peoples, believe in a spirit world that affects the day-to-day affairs of the physical world. In fact, they believe life in the physical sphere to be a replication of life in the spiritual, more "real" world. Thus a person's life here on earth is merely a playback of what the person lived previously on the spiritual plane, leading to an all-pervasive belief in destiny bordering on fatalism that stems from this concept. The result is an attitude of passive resignation that often impedes change on individual and communal levels. When people intone in the face of difficult circumstances, "If God wills it, it will be done," it is hard to escape the impression that they are merely saying that if it is in their destiny, it will happen.

---

8. We can make the larger claim about African pastoral theology because these people groups share common religious beliefs with other African peoples from whom they might have migrated or with whom they share a common migration history.

9. C. R. Gaba, "Anlo Traditional Religion: A Study of the Anlo Traditional Believer's Conception of and Communion with the 'HOLY'" (Ph.D. diss., University of London, 1965), 2.

The Supreme Being

Anlo religion has at its apex belief in a Supreme Being, *Mawu-Lisa,* who is commonly referred to as *Mawu.* The name Anlos give to the Supreme Being is an indication of the fact that they conceive of the creator as both male and female. In Geoffrey Parrinder's research on West African Traditional Religions, he notes that some Ewe at Abomey believe Mawu is female and that Lisa is her male consort. Some (also at Abomey) believe Mawu is male.[10]

They ascribe to the Supreme Being the creation and sustenance of the universe. There have been various speculations as to the origin and meaning of the name *Mawu.* The commonest etymological derivation among Ewe-speaking peoples is *Ema ye wu,* "This is the one who surpasses all." Since Ewe is a tonal rather than an intonational language, meaning changes drastically with stress on various syllables.[11] As a result, others legitimately suggest that *wu* could come from the verb "to kill." In this case *Mawu* would mean "the being that none can kill; the unbeatable." The reverse would also be true: "the being who cannot kill, one who is bountiful, kind and good." In spite of these differing understandings, what is clear is that *Mawu* is a personal being, since he has a proper name. C. R. Gaba suggests that the difficulty in coming to an agreement about what exactly *Mawu* means or derives from "may be the outcome of the same unqualified reverence for the divine name that still makes a riddle of the Tetragrammaton of Judaism."[12] The Anlo conception of God is anthropomorphic and, while it recognizes God as both male and female, in public worship God is addressed as Father. This is no doubt based on the patrilineal organization of Anlo society.[13]

Although there are creation myths among other Ewe peoples, Gaba notes the absence of creation myths in Anlo religious thought. Yet some names Anlos give to their children reveal the belief that the Supreme Be-

---

10. Geoffrey Parrinder, *West African Religion: A Study of the Beliefs and Practices of Akan, Ewe, Yoruba, Ibo, and Kindred Peoples* (London: Epworth, 1961), 17-18.

11. Intonational languages like English effect nuances through changes in inflection on various syllables in a word or words in a single utterance. With tonal languages like most African languages, drastic changes in meaning occur due to stress. So for example, the one Ga word *la* could mean blood, fire, sing, or dreamt depending on how it is said.

12. Gaba, "Anlo Traditional Religion," 48.

13. While there is a tacit acknowledgment in both Judaism and Christianity of feminine characteristics of Yahweh and the Hebrew for the Spirit of God is a feminine form, God is referred to in scriptural testimony exclusively with masculine pronouns. The Ga of Ghana, however, often refer to God as *Atta-Naa Nyogmor* (grandfather-grandmother God).

ing is involved in the day-to-day life of his creation, because most of these names make reference to God and his providence. On the other hand, the names might be a reference to destiny or general providence with no regard to *Mawu* the personal being. The name *Elom*, for instance, is one that most Ewes give to their children. Christians generally assume that it means "God loves me." But the pronoun *E* could refer to either *Mawu* or destiny, and thus the name could mean either "*Mawu* loves me" or "my destiny loves me," with the implication that one has a good or kind destiny. What is not clear is whether the former understanding is a Christian derivation of the latter. There are two possible interpretations. First, Christians wishing to maintain their Anlo heritage, but seeking to move away from the concept of destiny with its fatalistic implications, may have retained the traditional names but given them different connotations from the perspective of their new faith. Second, the prefix *E* may just be the common neuter pronoun that replaces *Se*, the Anlo word for destiny.[14] However that may be, as Gaba points out, "[*Mawu-Lisa*] is not an absentee God who has wound up the world like a clock once and for all, and allowed it to work on its own. He exercises a constant supervision over the universe and he is in an intensely personal relationship with man."[15] In Anlo understanding, however, God's relationship with human beings is not mediated exclusively by Jesus Christ as taught in Christian doctrine but is rather mediated by other spirit beings. It is entirely possible that for the average Anlo the use of God in naming a child or swearing or prayer may have nothing at all to do with God as creator and sustainer of the universe as it is understood in Christian theology.[16]

Spirit Beings

The Anlo believe in the presence of other spirit beings apart from *Mawu*, beings who infiltrate the lives of the community and individuals, and who

14. A single neuter pronoun represents all the nouns in most Ghanaian languages. For Ewe and Ga it is *E*, for Akan it is *O*.

15. Gaba, "Anlo Traditional Religion," 66.

16. This is where the distinction Awasu makes between Ewe supernaturalism and Ewe religious beliefs is most useful. African theologians who are conversant with Judeo-Christian theology and who write apologetically about African Traditional Religions tend to interpret African religious beliefs in Judeo-Christian terms mostly in order to put the two religions on par. When that happens it detracts from accurately portraying what the practitioners of the religion understand the symbols, rituals, etc., to mean to them.

impact their lives for good or ill. Unlike the Supreme Being, the spirit beings are directly involved in the lives of the people both at the individual and communal levels. To these spirit beings, sometimes called children of the Supreme Being, *Mawu* has assigned the work of nurturing and superintending the day-to-day operation of the world. Each lesser god, *Vodu* or *Tro*, has custodians known as priests, literally "the spouse of the god."[17] The gods make contact with the human community through their spouses, *Vodusi* or *Trosi*. These are nature spirits and are most often associated with other natural elements such as mountains, lakes, and lagoons. These nature spirits constitute the direct object of worship and mediate the people's communion with the Supreme Being, because the Anlo believe the Supreme Being is too holy to be approached directly. Shrines are erected for them and human beings communicate with the Supreme Being through the mediums and priests of these shrines.

Another group of gods, the *Legba*, family gods, are guardians of homes, and we normally see images of them at the entrances to compounds all over Anloland. It is customary to give food and drink offerings to these gods daily and on festive occasions. Ancestors feature in this category, and most Ewes in modern times still perform a ritual involving the annual cleansing of ancestral stools, *Togbuizikpui*. At the helm of powers associated with *Togbuizikpui* are the ancestral spirits, followed by the ruling chief, and the traditions and customs all Anlo are to observe. Members of groups or clans derive their self-identity from the *Togbuizikpui*. Awasu suggests that the *Togbuizikpui* constitute what we might consider dynamistic powers, because some people derive power from them. Though there have been endless debates as to whether it is more precise to say that Africans worship their ancestors or that Africans venerate them, it can at least be said that ancestors continue to occupy an important place in the lives of the Anlo and are called upon for blessing and support during all rites of passage and moments of individual and communal crisis. It is also customary for most people in Anloland to place token food and drink on the ground for their ancestors during mealtimes.

Most worship in Anloland is communal and ritualistic. Most of the traditional religious literature underscores the importance of prayer and

---

17. It is interesting to note that this is the description of the church in relation to Christ, e.g., the bride of Christ. Like the *vodusi* or *trosi*, God makes contact with the world through the church, God's bride. The bride of Christ may learn something about ardent devotion from the dedication of these spouses of the gods.

sacrifice in Anlo religion. Indeed, the Anlo do very little without recourse to prayer. Traditionally, prayer takes the form of libation, which involves pouring alcohol, water, or corn dough paste on the ground, while worshippers make petitions and offer thanksgiving specifically to the gods and ancestors. While they address the Supreme Being first in this prayer, they make the requests to the gods and ancestors. In this regard they perceive the Supreme Being as a general overseer who guides the affairs of humans without getting directly involved in them.

In spite of the communal aspect of the religious life of the Anlo, the individual clearly understands his responsibility for communing with the holy. Communal worship addresses significant attention to the individual. Personal religious rites accompany him throughout the life cycle from birth to puberty, through marriage to death. In these rites, "the holy personally confronts the believer; personal moral uprightness, as a prerequisite for worship, becomes part of religion."[18] Uncleanness in any form excludes an individual from participating in communal rituals. As in ancient Israel, an individual's wrongdoing, willful or inadvertent, may bring calamity not only on the household, but also on whole clans or villages. The Anlo make every effort to keep communication open between their house and the spirit world so as to bring blessing, usually equated with fecundity in any enterprise, whether bearing children or running a business. In so far as blessing and fecundity for one's own household is the aim and purpose of Anlo religion, there is little room for love of one's enemies, especially those who go out of their way to harm others. An individual is free to curse and denounce such enemies and drag them before the gods to be punished if they attempt to rob others of life in all its fullness. The Anlo believe curses affect not only the immediately accursed one, but also the entire family for generations to come.

Parallel accounts of such traditional understandings of the spirit world and activity exist among Ghanaian Christians. In many African Independent Churches, ritual baths at the beach at dawn constitute a vital part of individual and communal worship. Many Pentecostals believe that blessings and rewards from God come as a result of good deeds and ritual actions: their cars will be blessed so they will be protected from accidents, or their houses will be blessed so they will be protected from fire and robbers. If the contrary should occur, doubt and confusion set in, and these

---

18. Gaba, "Anlo Traditional Religion," 52. Probably in Gaba, "Sacrifice in Anlo Religion," in *Ghana Bulletin of Theology* 35 (1968): 10-15.

Christians look for other explanations for the cause of the mishap. They usually place blame at the door of a tangible enemy who may be revealed to a pastor or a member of the congregation via "a word of knowledge."[19] While in the church there is no outward cursing of enemies or calling down judgment upon them, there are perceptible signs of leering at them. We observe this often during praise and worship in services when song and dance, which are intended primarily as praise to God, contain words and gestures that send subtle messages to one's enemies. Though the primary targets of such taunts are the devil and other demonic forces, all who wish a person's harm in any form are also invited to see how mightily God works on that person's behalf. An inordinate fear of ancestral curses, which might affect the Christian in one form or other, is also prevalent. Christians are often encouraged to renounce any vicarious involvement they might have in a past ancestral curse. Often pastors who emphasize the need for the special kind of deliverance that they preach claim a kinship between this idea and similar ideas in the Old Testament, examples of which can be drawn from prayers recorded in passages such as Daniel 9:3-19 and Nehemiah 1:4-11.

In most African conception, salvation is tied to material reality in the present and not to something primarily spiritual in the otherworldly life; salvation has to do with the destruction of that which prevents material wealth. In chapter four we will explore this understanding of salvation as it relates to the current pastoral counseling situation. For now, however, it is important to note that, for African Christians, salvation is not complete or effectual if it does not translate into material well-being for oneself, one's kin, and one's property. This is largely due, I believe, to their concept of sin, which Africans associate with evil and conceive of as anything that hinders personal and social wholeness. The import of sin lies in the outcome of the act and not so much in the act itself. It is the death-producing effect of the act that is paramount in the African's conception of sin. Thus salvation is seen as a restoration to material well-being, not necessarily material possessions but to general fruitfulness in all aspects of individual and communal life.

Included in salvation is peace, which is commonly equated with material contentment. The words for peace in the two people groups under investigation all give expression to this understanding of peace as material contentment. The Ewe expression for peace, *nnutifafa*, which translates literally "a cool or calm body," connotes a state of quietude that spills over

---

19. A "word of knowledge" is a gift of the Spirit; through this gift the Holy Spirit communicates with persons, usually by a deep impression and conviction.

into the physical domain, a state in which body, soul, and spirit are at one with each other. The Akan *ahuntor* is similar. But peace and salvation also pertain to the soul, since the African cosmology has no sharp distinction between matter and spirit, and healing is believed to occur first on the spiritual plane. Aspects of this understanding abound in African Christian thought, especially as it shows up in the theology of the new Fundamentalist or charismatic churches springing up all over the continent.

Though the Ghanaian context is the specific focus of this discussion, this insight can be applied to the African situation more generally. While some might argue that there is no such thing as a monolithic African culture, there are places where the cultures of African peoples overlap considerably, and the area of religious belief and practice is one area in which such homogeneity in culture is most evident.[20]

Dynamistic Forces and Magic

The Anlo also believe in an all-pervasive force that issues forth mainly in magic, medicine, sorcery, and witchcraft. So pervasive is this aspect of Anlo belief that it is helpful to distinguish between what Awasu calls "Ewe supernaturalism, a worldview theme, often mislabeled as religion in anthropological literature," and Ewe religion as it truly is.[21] The Anlo, like other Ewes, seek protection from these dynamistic forces by means of amulets, bangles, and other charms, which physically represent the Anlo belief in dynamistic forces and the Anlo's ability to tap into these forces for good or ill.

Dzo, "magic," is the means by which the *dzoto,* "magician," seeks through *dzoka,* "incantation," to command spiritual forces to come to his aid, either for destruction of his enemies or for his protection. The Anlo understanding of spiritual magic is different from a Western understanding of magic as a physical illusion. Westerners normally make a distinction between magic and religion in their function and utilization. Because of the blurred line between Ewe supernaturalism and religion, the Western distinction breaks down, as magic and religion are used in the same way. Anlos are animist and strive through magic to employ the services of spiritual

---

20. For a full discussion of this argument, see especially Ch. 6 of Kwame Anthony Appiah, *In My Father's House: Africa in the Philosophy of Culture* (Cambridge, Mass.: Harvard University Press, 1994).

21. Awasu, "Religion, Christianity and the Powers in Ewe Society," 9.

forces through the magicians, who in a sense make use of spiritual rather than material powers, as in western magic. Awasu points out that the "allies *Dzoka* practitioners have include human and spirit beings. In certain cases, the spirit beings are *Yamenusewo* or archetypal spirits."[22] The *dzotowo* are able to solicit the help of these spirits of the air because by the end of their initiation they acquire the power to transform themselves into whatever spiritual form they choose and travel to their homes. On their homeward journey they establish alliances with these spirit powers, whom they later can call to their aid.[23]

The Anlo strongly believe that magic is contagious, and they operate on the assumption that things once joined must remain forever so and can affect one another. Gaba found a typical use of magic where this is evident: *aza*. The principal ingredient of *aza* is a human skull or ribs. The sorcerer sets *aza* traps by placing bits of different kinds of food near the magic bones. By means of incantations the sorcerer invites the personality soul of the proposed victim to eat the food. If by chance the desired victim takes any food used in the charm for breakfast that day, he will vomit blood and die. Though Gaba does not state clearly that the invitation to eat food placed on the *aza* trap is spiritual, this is implied, since it is only on the spiritual plane that one can invite another person's soul for a meal. To counteract the effect of this kind of magic, the Anlo take preventive steps to ensure that their personal effects, such as organs, body parts, or anything that comes from the body, do not fall easily into the hands of others who might use them against the owner of these things. To this day, in remote villages families store the feces of infants for the first three months to ensure the health and well-being of the baby. Nail trimmings are not just strewn about carelessly; they are carefully disposed of. The same applies to strands from hair trims and cuts. Mothers of new babies demand the umbilical cords and placentas from hospital nurses for proper disposal. In some cases they bury them in the home at dawn so that the child, in addition to being protected from evil spirits, may always find his way home.

Adema magic protects property and home. It buries all the evil intended against the household by stripping evil from the person who intends the harm, while leaving his or her person unharmed. It thus falls into the category of so-called "good magic"; it is purely protective.

Gaba's research shows that every harmful magic has its antidote. An

---

22. Awasu, "Religion, Christianity and the Powers in Ewe Society," 153.
23. Awasu, "Religion, Christianity and the Powers in Ewe Society," 153.

example is *tsi,* which is passed through the blood stream via cuts on parts of the body. When someone suffers harm caused by purely destructive magic as a result of a wrong he has committed, he must confess the wrong done that brought about the mishap, make restitution in kind to the person wronged, and offer sacrifice, which is determined through divination.

Many Ghanaians, including Christians, take part in these practices and therefore take precautions against the possibility of their personal effects falling into the wrong hands. These practices are also in the background of several of the questions pastors ask during counseling sessions as they seek to ascertain the presence or absence of spiritual forces at work in the life of the counselee. Counselees may be asked if they are missing any personal effects, such as clothing or money. They are also asked if they have found money in their possession for which they cannot account. While pure traditionalists employ more dynamistic forces for combating magical effects, Christian fight these magical effects through prayer, in which they invoke the name of Jesus. Yet in many cases these prayers follow a formula that mimics the incantation of witch doctors and fetish priests as they curse enemies. The name of Jesus, then, becomes the charm *par excellence* against all magical charms.

Witchcraft

Witchcraft seems to be the all-pervasive supernatural force affecting all facets of African life today. Whether at home or abroad, Africans are preoccupied with this evil phenomenon and its effect on them. P. J. Johnson describes African witchcraft, which he differentiates from European and American forms, as "the pursuit of harmful ends by supernatural means, usually directed toward family members and neighbors."[24] Testimonies of witches confirm this definition, especially the fact that the target of witchcraft is usually the family. Witches claim that they require a witch within a family before they can inflict harm on a member of that family, as alluded to in the proverb that intones, "something that bites you must come from your cloth" — that which is often the closest to your body.

In my research, I studied the writings of people who claimed to have been delivered from witchcraft. I also had the opportunity to listen to a former witch, who is now a minister of a mainline denomination, share his

24. P. J. Johnson III, "Witchcraft," in *Dictionary of Pastoral Care and Counseling,* 1328.

testimony of conversion from witchcraft to Christ.[25] Whether or not we dismiss witchcraft as a primitive and superstitious residue of a premodern belief system, the fact remains that for many Africans, irrespective of their social or religious standing, witchcraft is a reality they must confront directly or indirectly. Cyril Daryll Forde observes,

> Under primitive conditions of life and in the absence of a coherent body of scientific theory so much more lies beyond the reach of naturalistic explanation, so much more elicits interpretation and action in terms of the mysterious agents called into being in response to hopes and needs. Beliefs of this order are not capable of verification but neither do they require it. In such spheres the peoples of Africa, like those of the West and, indeed, all mankind save the tiny minority which is able to suspend belief, have adopted theories that project on to a plane of supernatural action the desires and aspirations that they know in the realm of human action. Passion and will, virtue and malevolence, compassion and indignation as they are known among men are attributed to unseen powers.[26]

But Africans do not blame things on witchcraft because they are unaware of natural cause-and-effect relationships. Robin Horton points out that while the sick and afflicted may go to diviners to find out the causes of their ailments and to obtain answers involving gods or other spiritual agents, they also require that the diviner tell them "what moved the agency in question to intervene. And this account very commonly involves reference to some event in the world of visible, tangible happenings."[27] The

---

25. This was a visiting pastor at a revival meeting of an Evangelical Presbyterian Church in Ghana. It was not clear whether this pastor was affiliated with that denomination or one of the many evangelical groups with a deliverance ministry, though he was likely of the latter affiliation. This pastor self-published his testimony under the title "From Witchcraft to Christ," a text that was sold at the meeting. A female parishioner commented that she would rather not know about such things, "and if my being in Christ is not enough for me not to worry about what the devil or witches are doing to destroy me, that is God's business." She had purchased one of the pamphlets but thought she ought not to read it. After studying the testimony, I could see how the pamphlet could produce more fear of evil forces than relief in the knowledge that Christ had overcome them.

26. Cyril Daryll Forde, *African Worlds: Studies in the Cosmological Ideas and Social Values of African People* (Oxford: Oxford University Press, 1963), xi.

27. Robin Horton, "African Traditional Thought and Western Science," *Africa* 37 (Jan. 1967): 53.

one who seeks help from a diviner knows that the crops failed because the rain did not come. His issue is with the rain failing for *him* and at just that *precise moment*. Meteorological explanations of the rain cycle alone will not suffice. Again, Africans are perfectly aware that people die of old age, but there must be other explanations for why death occurred on a particular day and at a particular time. Forde suggests that the insistence on explanations other than physical causes for mishaps may be due to the "attendant emotions and the moral ideas of virtue and guilt associated with them."[28] As long as society approves of success and prosperity and sees them as evidence of a virtuous life, it will conceive of misery and catastrophe as the rewards of wrongdoing. The result is anger and anxiety, envy of others, and an incessant attempt to rid oneself of subsequent punishment and the faults that produce these negative consequences. Africans seek avenues to deter these misfortunes or to make atonement for any wrongdoing that may have caused the misfortune.

Another possible explanation, I think, is that witchcraft, already an antisocial behavior, becomes a face-saving device for those unable to climb the culturally acceptable social ladder. It is equally possible that, rather than taking responsibility for misfortunes and figuring out how to respond to them appropriately, those who believe themselves to be victims of witches can simply claim the victim status of those oppressed by the malevolence of others and thus receive sympathy and undue attention. But it is also possible that many self-acclaimed witches or those who allow themselves to be so labeled by society find some satisfaction in being cast in the role of villains who have power over others. In either case, some people simply avoid taking responsibility for responding directly to the misfortune that has befallen them.

There are several ways one can become a witch. The literature on witchcraft attests to at least three primary ways: (1) through inheritance, (2) by inadvertently acquiring the power from an envious witch, or (3) by purchasing it. One can inherit the witchcraft spirit from a member of the family prior to the donor's death. With this mode, food is the main source of transference. There is some apparent ambivalence towards witchcraft. While the Anlo see witchcraft as an antisocial behavior, the personal benefits to the one who has the witchcraft spirit cause it to be passed on to the best-loved girl child. It is entirely possible that unusual behavior of the best-loved child at the loss of her mother is perceived as an indication of

---

28. Forde, *African Worlds*, xii.

possession of witchcraft spirit. If the child herself is also aware of this belief regarding the transmission of the spirit, fear of being rejected during her time of grief might cause her to withdraw from people. Such antisocial behavior in turn yields more accusation from those who already point fingers and suspect her of receiving the witchcraft spirit. Normally the witch passes on the spirit through a prized possession that she leaves for the child. The Westerner might find this confusing, especially if she tries to think it through rationally: how do you give a bad thing to one you love? But perhaps the more appropriate question here is why would you not give a part of yourself to someone you love? At the same time, I doubt that Africans themselves have made sense of it, nor is it meant to be logical and well thought out. Witchcraft seems to be the catchall explanation for things one cannot explain.

The Anlo also believe that midwives who are witches sometimes pass on witchcraft to destroy babies they birth, often out of envy, when they perceive the child to be of good fortune. Anlo thought is not clear, however, as to the process by which such transmission occurs.[29]

Another way of acquiring witchcraft is through inadvertent transference, especially at night. A witch may cast her shadow on unsuspecting passersby, infecting them with the witchcraft spirit. Witchcraft acquired through this process causes the person to have an insatiable appetite for wicked deeds, especially if the "witch spirit agrees with their personality soul."[30] Again, as Gaba points out,

> in dreams, which are real in Anlo thought, some victims of witchcraft practice are decoyed by witches to their night assemblies where they share in a meal and thereby get initiated as practicing witches. It is not unlikely that this belief existing originally on the psychic plane was later gradually and rather imperceptibly transferred to the material plane. When these witches meet at night, their feast presumably consists of human bodies and their drink is human blood. Witches are therefore thought of as spiritual cannibals.[31]

The third primary way to become a witch is by purchasing the spirit, usually at great cost. The one seeking the witchcraft must sacrifice the dear-

---

29. Gaba, "Anlo Traditional Religion," 169.
30. Gaba, "Anlo Traditional Religion," 169.
31. Gaba, "Anlo Traditional Religion," 168.

est human victim. Stories abound as to the procedure involved. The commonest is that the one seeking the witchcraft spirit mentions the name of the best-loved person, whose image then either appears in a mirror or is reflected in a calabash of water.[32] The image is then stabbed with a knife, and this spiritual killing manifests in the physical realm almost instantaneously. Believers attribute sudden wealth following the sudden death of a beloved child, for instance, to a person trading the best-loved person for witchcraft powers. It might seem strange that anyone would go to such lengths to acquire an art that eventually ostracizes her from the society; however, the need for such power emphasizes the distinction made earlier between worldview and religion. While we might see the practice of witchcraft itself as an antisocial behavior, we can only understand the importance of the function of witchcraft to the person who seeks it in the light of the conscious or unconscious hold of worldview on people's actions. Thus a person can practice Christianity, and yet her need to acquire certain powers for protection, or her fear that such powers would harm her, demonstrates the strong hold that the worldview has on her.

The Anlo also believe that witches can recognize each other. Often in the African Independent Churches, former witches who have had the witchcraft spirit exorcized identify other witches to the church leaders. Rank in the coven normally follows that of a typical Anlo society, and witchcraft activity, which takes place at night, is normally held "on the lagoon, the sea and very high trees — coconut palm, baobab and silk cotton for instance."[33] The Anlo believe that the personality soul of the witch attends these meetings. While the soul takes on the form of an animal, the body remains in bed, often immobilized in a semi-conscious state until the soul returns. Oral tradition holds that to be able to attend a night assembly, a witch first smears her body with *adzemi,* "believed to be a mixture of shea butter, palm oil or kernel oil, and some herbs magically prepared."[34] She then lies very still on her back in bed, stark naked. This action transports her to the appointed meeting place. When the witches gather, each takes on the form of a bird, *adzexe* (literally witch bird), and flies away while emitting a very bright light that is reported to look like a ball of fire. The Anlo usually attribute bright lights that they see on the outskirts of villages that do not have electricity as the light coming from these witches. What exactly these witch birds are is not clear in Anlo

---

32. A calabash is a drinking utensil of varying sizes made from a plant/gourd.
33. Gaba, "Anlo Traditional Religion," 172.
34. Gaba, "Anlo Traditional Religion," 173.

thought. Yet when nocturnal birds, such as owls, are heard screeching around suspected meeting places, people conclude that witches are probably feasting on another victim. The owl may seem like a particularly likely witch bird because it has its eyes set like those of humans, and thus has some human facial characteristics.[35] But the snake is the most popular of witch familiars. Regarding snake familiars, Gaba notes:

> Snake dreams are solidly put down to witches in Anlo thought, and the snake familiars are believed to work for witches in dreams when the witch owners happen to be engaged somewhere else. Then in waking life when the witches are not believed to metamorphose, the animal familiars again represent them. Any harm caused to the familiar affects the witch owner, but when the witch suffers the familiar does not. The owners are believed to keep the snake familiars in the secrecy of their bedroom or in their vagina.[36]

This description of witch activity may help explain why only women are thought of as witches. While the description might be offensive, it emphasizes the mysterious nature of that interior space and the quest to understand it.

Gaba suggests that the speed with which the snake moves is the reason it is the most popular witch familiar in Anlo thought. Furthermore, snakes are endowed with the power of protective coloration and may easily disappear from a particular spot. Moreover, the Anlo people credit snakes with fantastic powers, and some species are even the object of worship. The *Voduda* for instance is a snake cult found in Benin. Other animal familiars are frogs, scorpions, cockroaches, and the large common housefly.

35. The Anlo for example call the owl *aye lofl,* "witch bird." I recall an incident during my childhood when I followed a crowd of people in my neighborhood to see an owl perched on a branch. The crowd believed the owl was a witch in her animal familiar because it was unheard of to find an owl in the daytime. They hooted and threw stones at it to no avail. The owl responded only by turning its head away each time the crowed jeered and called it names. Knowing very little about owls in those days, I was struck by the fact that the owl would look our way and then turn its head away, as if in shame. Beyond this behavior, the crowd nearest the tree on which the owl was perched claimed that it was carrying a lady's pocketbook and would occasionally wipe its face. Convinced that this was a witch, they wanted to at the least inflict some bodily injury on it. They thought this would flush out the owner of this animal familiar if someone in the neighborhood showed up later complaining of pain in the exact spot where the owl received bodily injury.

36. Gaba, "Anlo Traditional Religion," 173-74.

In light of this understanding of witchcraft among the Anlo and most African peoples, we can see why many deliverance ministries focus on questions that elicit information about the possible operations of witchcraft in clients' presenting problems. Pastors ask, for instance, if clients ever find themselves visiting with dead relatives, receiving food, or eating in their dreams. The presence of such elements in their dreams indicates the operation of witchcraft.

The list of evil deeds attributed to witches covers a whole spectrum of mishaps. Information about these evil deeds comes primarily through confessions at anti-witchcraft shrines, which are shrines believed to cure people from evils done through witchcraft, as well as to grant freedom from the acquired witchcraft spirit. Confessions come, for example, from wives who have used their powers to cause impotency in their husbands, to those who through spiritual means use the wombs of their rivals as their doormats. Some witch doctors have reported rescuing the wombs of women from their co-wives. There are other women who have become barren from trading their own fertility to purchase witchcraft powers to inflict harm on younger, more attractive co-wives. At the funerals of women who died during childbirth or following miscarriages, it is not uncommon to hear insinuating remarks aimed at a member of the family or the community implying that she is the witch responsible for the death. Illnesses that cannot be easily diagnosed may be attributed to witchcraft spirits:

> all . . . misfortunes which need a reasonably higher amount of education and more scientific knowledge than what the ordinary Anloman possesses, in order to be understood in a better light, cannot in Anlo thought, be anything more than the result of the legally and morally unjustifiable deeds of witches.[37]

However, my research indicates that the attribution of mishaps to witchcraft or to other spiritual factors is not limited to remote villages where the level of education does not easily afford more reasonable or scientific causes for misfortunes. I discovered this tendency to attribute the inexplicable to witchcraft or other spirit beings among some university students and professors of all disciplines.

I found that in pastoral counseling situations, purely psychic or physical causes are rarely considered as possible reasons for the problems that

---

37. Gaba, "Anlo Traditional Religion," 175.

parishioners present. Even when psychic or somatic reasons could be present, they are often overshadowed by larger spiritual considerations. The result is that the counseling that patients receive usually touches only on what might alleviate the spiritual predicament. For example, if there are interpersonal problems between spouses, they are prayed with, and demonic forces threatening to destroy the marriage are cast out or bound in Jesus' name. The couple is counseled to continue in prayer, trust in God, and exercise patience in the face of their trials. Witchcraft is by far the most common diagnosis, which calls for the deliverance of the counselee from satanic powers. There is little or no attention given to considerations that have become a central focus in Western contemporary counseling, such as interpersonal communication or family-of-origin issues from a psychosocial or psychodynamic perspective.

Deliverance rituals as described above are often detrimental to the counselees. Consider the following illustration, narrated to me by a history professor at one of the universities in Ghana with whom I discussed my research concern. The wife of a young man had run away from home because of her husband's maltreatment. Her attempts to talk things out with him had failed. Friends who visited, intending to intervene, reported that the husband immediately attended to prayer as soon as any mention of the problem was raised. He was full of religious talk and allowed no one to interrupt. Not long after the wife ran away from home, reports began reaching their mutual friends of the husband's bizarre behavior in public places. He would wave a Bible at imaginary audiences, preach with enthusiasm on street corners, or fall down on his knees in prayer. Eventually friends and family prevailed, and he was sent by the family to the psychiatric hospital in Accra. There he was diagnosed with a neurological as well as neurotic problem. Subsequently placed on appropriate medication, the young man is now doing well, though his wife is still too terrified to return to him.

In spite of marked improvement in the young man's condition, people still turned to prayer in search of a spiritual cause for his breakdown, and they found it to be his own mother's witchcraft powers. The mother is said to have confessed to causing the apparent neurological problem that caused the marriage to fall apart. Evidence against her was solid because she could recount conversations, and especially arguments the couple had had, though she was never physically present. In some cases she could recount them verbatim. The man's counselors assumed that since witches can turn into animal familiars she could easily have been present in another form to overhear these conversations. Not only did she listen in on their conversations, she also instigated and fanned their conflicts.

Any general failure to make headway in life, especially when one makes strenuous efforts to achieve success, can be attributed to witches. But such a judgment disregards the role of individual differences in the achievement of success — failing to acknowledge, for example, that God made human beings with differing abilities and talents. It also seems to measure success by external criteria alone (affluence in any form) as evidence of God's favor. The new popularity of the "prosperity gospel" and the attendant belief that God's children must be rich and prosper in all things make it easy for Christians to attribute any failure to possible demonic activity.

In this context Ghanaian Christians are left feeling that witches or ancestral curses lie at the root of their problems, or even that they themselves might have been given a witchcraft spirit without their knowledge. The Anlo assume that the conflicts that afflicted individuals experience are at a level above and beyond the common spiritual warfare that all Christians wage. The intensity of their battle is due partly to the fact that they are resisting a witch spirit that is being forced on them. The remedy is for a man of God to do spiritual warfare on their behalf.

Antidotes to Witchcraft

As with magic, there are antidotes to witchcraft that work against a witch's charms as well as expel the witchcraft spirit from people who wish to be rid of it. These antidotes work mainly through herbal medicine. Since in Anlo thought "the physical body is the vehicle of the complex soul, and the two are so inextricably joined in earthly life that what affects one is manifested in the other," herbal medicine applied to the body works toward psychic and spiritual healing.[38] The traditional antidote for witchcraft is much the same as that for sorcery, and is administered by witch doctors. The antidote may be a vaccination with witchcraft black powder or the wearing of charms. Others suggest placing bowls of palm oil in houses so the witches drink that instead of blood. A more effective way to ensure that one is free from the attack of witches is to place a bowl of palm oil near a *Legba* (god) in the community to bribe the witches away. Palm oil is red oil made from the palm fruit, and because of its consistency and color, it can pass for blood. Thus the evil spirits

---

38. Gaba, "Anlo Traditional Religion," 159.

could be fooled into drinking the oil and the household would then be safe from impending attack from witchcraft spirits.

Another antidote is the use of *atadikpu,* "a hot pepper," which is largely employed against money-looting spirits. If, at the end of the business day, a businessperson's account does not balance, or worse, if all goods are accounted for but by the time he arrives home, some of the money is missing, money-looting spirits might be at work. A wise businessperson, therefore, will place short, red-hot peppers in the cash basket, thereby ensuring that the day's earning is safe.

In some Ghanaian churches today, there is a "Christian version" of this same practice. We cannot ignore the connection between this antidote against the money-looting spirits and the recent calls in the charismatic churches by pastors who perform certain acts that ensure God's protection for one's property and business. An illustration of this is the pastoral practice of "anointing" business enterprises as well as anointing individuals for well-being in order to ward away evil spirits. Apostolic tradition teaches the appropriateness of anointing the saints in times of sickness (James 5:14-16), but the use of anointing in contemporary charismatic churches may constitute a misuse of this tradition. Some Christians believe that the act itself, and especially the person who performs it, can bring extraordinary powers to the aid of the person for whom prayer is offered.

Anti-witchcraft shrines also promise protection through initiation into the shrine. Practitioners claim that this initiation produces a protective mystical union with whichever deity is invoked. Gaba notes that the syncretistic churches also put forth their own method of protection. The Apostles Revelation Society (ARS) and the Musama Disco Christo Church are examples of churches that enjoin fasting and other rituals to ward off witchcraft spirits. These groups promise protection through prayer and fasting and the wearing of copper rings and crucifixes. Fasting and prayer must be carried on regularly for full, effective protection, because the symbols are inadequate in themselves. Prayer and fasting are accompanied by anointing in severe cases.[39] Gaba notes again that some "orthodox Christians and traditional believers are of the opinion that African magic is employed behind the scenes

---

39. What exactly this anointing is and how it is done is not clear. According to Gaba, the "'ointment' seems to be olive oil, slightly perfumed with 'florida water'. Olive oil and florida water are generally considered by many, especially the formally educated with an inclination for magic, to be endowed with some mythical powers of cure. It is not, therefore, surprising that these syncretistic churches with a bent for indigenous beliefs, may be tempted to hold olive oil and florida water in a mysterious esteem" ("Anlo Traditional Religion," 180).

by these syncretistic churches."[40] Those who hold this view cite as evidence the presence of former witch doctors and wizards in the ARS in Anloland.

If a witch desires to be cured of witchcraft, she must first publicly denounce the practice. This denunciation is the prerequisite in both the shrines that purport to produce cures by the traditional method and the syncretistic churches, which effect cures by means of prayer and anointing. Normally the witch reports harmful things she has done to others and discloses the location of witchcraft paraphernalia, including her animal familiar. However, since the sources of the content of the confessions are those who claim to bring the cure and not the witches themselves, we might well be skeptical of them. Moreover, there is the possibility that in their confession, witches may "confuse their dreams with realities."[41] Yet among a people for whom "dreams are regarded as realities constituting the activities of man's psychic nature, all other phenomena connected with dreams must naturally be [thought of as real]."[42] While the literature on the Anlo suggests that they do not practice witch hunting, and so these confessions may not stem from compulsion, we must note that coercion can be indirect. Gaba, for instance, notes that sometimes these confessions follow long periods of illness after which the witches visit places for a cure from their acquired witchcraft powers where confessions may be demanded. Interestingly,

> many of those who supervise these confessions and cure victims report that some of their patients, because of too much harm they have done with the witch spirit, are punished by the Supreme Being with madness and that they have been removed to the mental hospital in Accra. These confessions could equally be in the early stages of the mental unbalance of the witch patients — a time when it may not be easy to draw a sure line between sanity and insanity. At other times these confessions are made on the death bed of victims and are regarded as the Supreme Being sitting in judgment over the victims.[43]

Confession as an avenue to healing and wholeness is a tradition of the church. While the Catholic church still practices formal confession on a regular basis, the Protestant churches are not known to make confession to

40. Gaba, "Anlo Traditional Religion," 180.
41. Gaba, "Anlo Traditional Religion," 181.
42. Gaba, "Anlo Traditional Religion," 181.
43. Gaba, "Anlo Traditional Religion," 181.

a pastor a requirement of the Christian faith and practice. But some Protestant churches, such as the Evangelical Presbyterian Church, Ghana, provide the opportunity during the week prior to communion Sunday for people desiring confession and absolution.

It is possible that if pastors encouraged regular confessions from parishioners, incidences of forced confessions at anti-witchcraft shrines might diminish. Making confession a regular part of church practice might also be a great help to those needing to utilize this resource of the church for healing and wholeness. It would also curtail the tendency to bottle things up until they fester, which causes people to be in such distress when they finally do seek help that they are coerced into confessing things they have not done and are then stigmatized for them.

Removing the *adzedede,* "witch spirit," is the principal cure for witchcraft, but sometimes the "human owner is 'destroyed' along with the witch spirit."[44] This normally happens to obstinate witches whose arrogance causes them to partake of the special meal reserved for the ancestors and deities; the offended ancestors and deities inflict the punishment of death. Inflicting bodily harm on the witch along with the witchcraft spirit also occurs in churches where, in the act of casting out demons, the demonized have been physically beaten. Death occurs in some cases, especially with prolonged exorcism of this nature. Rituals for *adzedede* include handing over any tools of the trade, usually witchcraft paraphernalia. Here we find similarities with what happens during mass deliverance sessions. These sessions normally end with newly-converted witches handing over the tools of their trade to be publicly burned by the evangelistic leaders.

The Anlo, like other African tribes, seek through witchcraft to establish communion with the Holy, either for destruction or protection. All of the beliefs and practices that the Anlo people classify as witchcraft are consonant with Anlo cosmology, which undergirds their knowledge and understanding of the meaning of life and of how that life ought to be lived to the fullest.

Divination and Sacrifice

We cannot really deal with Anlo cosmology without reference to divination, especially regarding the harnessing of dynamistic forces for one's per-

---

44. Gaba, "Anlo Traditional Religion," 182.

sonal benefit. Divination plays an important role in Anlo life and thought. Through divination, the Anlo obtain information regarding the future, especially information that will help forestall misfortune. The typical Anlo does not question misfortune; in fact, misfortune is seen as an integral part of life. However, the Anlo hopes to have some frequent respite from "the dreadful clutches of this inevitable and inescapable anxiety."[45] As with other African peoples, the Anloman seeks out a diviner before a betrothal or a marriage, before making an important life decision, or after any kind of loss. He seek out diviners in times of crisis to ascertain which god he has offended and what appropriate sacrifice he must make to propitiate the avenging god. In times of sickness, or if an infertile woman desires children, or when anyone is disturbed by strange dreams, the Anlo seek out the diviner. The outcome of many divinations is a prescription of sacrifice to the gods or to the ancestors, as the case may require. Generally, the Anlo sacrifice for the same reasons that they seek the help of diviners. Sacrifice occurs at both the individual and corporate levels, especially during times of communal crisis, as when a famine or plague threatens the whole community. But a cult adherent may also offer sacrifices at any time to show gratitude to a deity. Gaba notes that there are two types of sacrifices, *dza* and *nuxe*. The former comprises gifts to the Holy, where the Holy is conceived in this context as what Rudolf Otto calls the *mysterium tremendum et fascinans*.[46] Sacrifice may be a votive, a thank offering, or a meal offering. "Votive sacrifice, 'dzadodo,' is anything that a worshipper offers the Holy to beg for certain favors, in return for which he makes a vow to offer something later when his wishes are met."[47] The two forms of sacrifice made when the people need to drive away a dangerous manifestation of the Holy from among them are *nuxe* (derived from *nu*, "thing," and *xe*, which could be either "pay" or "prevent," thus "a thing paid" or "that which is used to prevent something," *nuxexe*) and *vosa* (from *vo*, "sin," and *sa*, meaning "bind" or "pass by," *vosasa*, implying that which nullifies sin by either binding it or passing it by or ignoring it). *Nuxe* and *vosa* describe sacrifice that is propitiatory, substitutionary, preventive, or purifying in function but which aims at the expulsion of the dangerous manifestation of the Holy from the affairs

45. Gaba, "Anlo Traditional Religion," 184.

46. Rudolf Otto, *The Idea of the Holy: An Inquiry into the Non-Rational Factor in the Idea of the Divine and Its Relation to the Rational* (London: Oxford University Press, 1970), esp. 12, 35.

47. C. R. Gaba, "Sacrifice in Anlo Religion," *Ghana Bulletin of Theology* 3.5 (Dec 1968): 13.

of human beings. However, *nuxe* is the term used for this type of sacrifice among the Anlo.

In *nuxe,* unlike *dza,* the person on whose behalf the sacrifice is being made must be present if the rites involve the curing of a disease. But where the defilement is largely ritual and has not resulted in sickness, a priest can present the sacrifice on behalf of another. *Nuxe* is usually offered at night because it is believed that evil spirits operate mainly at night. According to Gaba, every *nuxe* sacrifice must make contact with the body of the sacrificer in order to be efficacious. This is usually done by rubbing the sacrificial animal on the person while the priest pronounces a wiping away of death, sickness, poverty, trouble, and general failure in life from the person:

> [A] sacrifice completely takes the place of the sacrificer. It also takes away with itself any evil that may be suffered as a result of a dangerous manifestation of the holy in human affairs. The plain truth is that in Anlo thought the sacrificer has used the sacrifice to exchange his life which the holy will have claimed. . . . Once the head (life) of a sacrificial animal is offered . . . the head . . . of the sacrificer can no more be claimed (by the holy).[48]

The Anlo do not regard a god's demand for blood sacrifice as a vindictive act; the god is being strict and thus intolerant of wrongdoing. As in ancient Israel, the economic status of the sacrificer is considered, and the sacrifice demanded is on a sliding scale. Normally the Anlo offer direct sacrifice to lesser gods and the ancestors, but they may also give sacrifice when the impersonal spirit power is "personalized," as in magic and witchcraft, and then given moral quality. They offer sacrifice to the Supreme Being through the ancestors and the lesser gods. But as Gaba points out, the Supreme Being himself *never* requests any sacrifice from human beings.[49] Also, a ritual specialist must offer every formal sacrifice. Such a sacrifice involves more than throwing bits of food or drink on the ground. Sometimes it entails calling in *Afa* diviners. These diviners are specially trained in divination and knowledge of the appropriate sacrifice for propitiation. Awasu writes:

> *Afa* diviners undergo a rigid twelve-year training under experienced experts in the *Afa* "seminaries." . . . *Afa* enjoys a universal reputation of

48. Gaba, "Sacrifice in Anlo Religion," 15.
49. Gaba, "Sacrifice in Anlo Religion," 16.

being able to unravel and resolve situations that have proved unmanageable with other means through its divination-healing machinery.[50]

Human Beings–Personhood

Gaba notes that there is no literature of help to the theologian on the Anlo people with regard to their concept of personhood. What is available is mainly anthropological or social data compiled from the perspective of a cultural anthropologist. But the oral literature, of which the Anlo have a rich store, provides valuable information on the Anlo concept of personhood and human existence. In Anlo thought the human being is made up of the body, the soul, and the spirit. The body, *nutila*, is literally the covering or flesh of the "thing," in this case, the self. It is the outer covering of the real person. While the body and spirit are single entities, the Anlo see the soul as multi-layered, and they differentiate between types of souls.

The Anlo conception of the soul reveals that the real animating principle, termed the "complex soul," is *gbogbo* (divine or life soul), the divine bit of *Mawu* in every person. *Gbogbo* can also be translated as "spirit" and has the same connotation as *ya*, or wind. In day-to-day usage, however, the Anlo know from the context whether *gbogbo* means wind or the life-giving spirit. Anlo believe that at birth a number of psychic elements come together to form the complex soul, which is regarded as the animating principle of the material body. In Anlo thought, the complex soul has no name in its own right but is often referred to periphrastically as *amea nnuto*, "the real person,"[51]

There are other soul elements in the complex soul. One element is part of the father's personality soul that a man passes on to each of his children. There is also the maternal counterpart of the paternal soul. And the Anlo believe that resemblance between children and their parents results from the possession of these two soul elements. Divination may also reveal a different source of resemblance of the child to another member of the family. The child's complex soul could be part of the soul of an ancestor or any other dead relative. But there are only two major soul elements: life soul and personality soul.

The Anlo concept of creation holds that the material world has a spir-

---

50. Awasu, "Religion, Christianity and the Powers in Ewe Society," 164-65.
51. Gaba, "Anlo Traditional Religion," 258.

itual counterpart on which it is modeled. Everything in creation, including human beings, has a spiritual counterpart. The human being's state on earth simply reflects a pre-earthly spiritual existence. The personality soul, or death soul, had a previous existence in *amedzofe*, "the origin of human beings," which they believe is patterned after the earthly one. At the end of earthly existence, the personality soul goes to *tsinyefe*, "land of the dead." The Anlo believe that the personality soul has the capacity to leave the body and travel at night while the life soul is asleep. In this state, any mishap that touches the personality soul manifests in the body. It is this aspect of the soul that acts and is acted upon in dream states. The life soul, *gbogbo*, comes from God and is the same in all human beings. The personality soul, however, differs from person to person.

The complexity of Anlo thought regarding the soul is further revealed in the equivocal way they refer to differing aspects of the soul. The personality soul, for instance, is *luwo*, the name for the complex soul, which is the personality soul and the divine, or life, soul. The personality soul translates into English simply as soul. In dreams, which are the soul's activity, the life soul, which acts as guardian genius, can prevent the personality soul from leaving and engaging in activities during the dream states that may be detrimental to it. Unexplained scratches on a person's face and arms would be evidence of the struggle between these two soul elements.

A strong personality soul equates with a strong life soul. The activities of witches can hardly affect a strong personality soul. This is rather confusing considering that the life soul comes from God. The only explanation is that the Supreme Being gives different qualities of life souls to different people. This then would fit well with the concept of *dzogbe se*, "destiny." The same life soul can be found in different people at different times. It "can be joined to many other personality souls in successive earthly existences."[52] *Vovoli*, "shadow," can mean the personality soul and the complex soul because in the shadow one's physique is defined. The life soul does not cast a shadow, probably because of its origin from God, who is never thought of in corporeal terms. Through the shadow, spiritual forces can attack the body. Thus, they attribute sores in the mouth, nostrils, and private parts to the psychic harm the *adoglo asikevee*, "two-tailed lizard," inflicts on the shadow — and not, for example, to vitamin deficiency.[53]

In general, the Anlo believe that every individual is composed of two

52. Gaba, "Anlo Traditional Religion," 266.
53. Gaba, "Anlo Traditional Religion," 267.

principal soul elements: the *gbogbo*, "immortal life or divine soul," which is the real animating principle, and *lowo*, "the personality or death soul," which has lived in the pre-earthly world. In reality, however, they use the term *lowo* as the Hebrew use *nephesh*, as a metonym to refer to the living being, the person.

Akan Cosmology

The Akan are a very large group consisting of various ethnic groupings located mainly in Ghana, with a few in the Ivory Coast. Oral tradition locates their earliest home along the Niger bend in the region lying between Djenne and Timbuktu (present-day Mali) until they were ousted by Muslims. Though today there are about fifteen subgroupings of the Akan, they share a common ancestry. Eva Meyerowitz points out,

> It would appear that the founders of Akan states were the descendants of Dia or Za (Diaga or Zaga); Libyan Berbers; and the Gara of the Tibesti region, who emigrated when the Arabs conquered North Africa and pushed the Lemta Tuaregs from the Fezzan into their territory. Settling along the Niger bend they incorporated many of the inhabitants into their clans, as was the custom among matrilineally organized peoples. These people were originally of much the same stock as themselves but in the course of time had intermarried with negro aboriginals.[54]

In light of the conquests and intermarriages of this and other Dia, Libyan Berber, and Gara refugees, it is likely that the belief among the Akan that their ancestors were of a white race and came from beyond the Sahara is true. It is interesting to note the similarities in belief among certain North African and Middle Eastern civilizations and the Akan.

The Akan believe in a universe full of spirits. They believe in the existence of a Supreme Being, the creator of all things, "who manifests his power through a pantheon of gods."[55] Below the gods are other numerous spirits who animate trees, rocks, and charms. Then there are the "ever-present spirits," *nsamanfo*, "the ancestors." They are the ones who mediate

---

54. Eva Meyerowitz, *The Akan of Ghana: Their Ancient Beliefs* (London: Farber, 1958), 18-19.

55. K. A. Busia, "The Ashanti," in Cyril Daryll Forde, *African Worlds*, 191.

between the world of the spirits and the life of humans on earth. Not everyone can be an ancestor, however. This is the exclusive privilege of those who have lived exemplary lives, contributed to the community, and lived to a ripe old age. These are the ones who have proven themselves worthy to become ancestors, guardians of the state. The Akan revere the ancestors second only to *Onyame*, the Supreme Being. The Akan crave their blessing and pour libations to stay in favor with them.

The Akan believe that the Supreme Being is too far removed from mortal men to be reached directly and can only be reached through intermediaries, *abosom*, "the pantheon of gods," who derive their power from the Supreme Being. Some call them *Nyankopong mba*, "the sons of the Supreme Being." According to K. A. Busia, the most powerful of these gods are the spirits of the rivers. But even the most powerful of the gods require shrines and priests through whom they speak.[56]

In addition to the group of gods they refer to as sons of the Supreme Being are *asuman*, "minor deities." These derive their power from the souls of plants or trees. The Akan believe that though animals and trees have souls, most are not powerful enough to cause harm to human beings. But those that do have such power must be propitiated. An Ashanti craftsman, for instance, would not cut down the *odum* tree without first addressing the spirit of the tree and asking that no harm befall him.[57] The *asuman*, sometimes represented in the form of beads or other charms worn on the body,

> could be regarded as impersonal forces acting in obedience to secret formulae and operations; the Ashanti themselves, however, believe that ultimately all *asuman* derive their power from some other supernatural beings. A *suman* [singular of *asuman*] protects the wearer and guards him against harm, or assists him to gain his personal ends, and functions effectively or not, according to the care given to it.[58]

Thus the effectiveness of the *suman*, "charm," depends on the wearer's ability to care for it. The Akan also believe in witchcraft and black magic, and that even the forests are inhabited by dwarfs who taught the hunters their art of healing. But they make a distinction between *beyie pa*, "good witchcraft," and *beyie bone*, "evil-causing witchcraft."

56. Busia, "The Ashanti," 193.
57. Busia, "The Ashanti," 194.
58. Busia, "The Ashanti," 195.

Human Beings

There are four important components of the *nipa*, "human entity," which Akans believe they receive from father, mother, and *Onyame*. These are the *mogya* (blood), *nnipadua* (body), *kra* (soul), and *sunsum* (spirit).

According to Meyerowitz, the stories of the origin of the *Okra* vary. One story has it that when the "deity of the cosmos Nyame Amowia, visible as the moon, gave birth to the Sun god, she gave him her *kra*, her eternal soul or life-giving power; hence his name, the Only Great Nyame,"[59] or *Nyankopon*. The *kra*, like the deity *Amowia*, is considered both male and female. The female component is seen in the moon, in substance or body, while its male component is seen in the form of fire or the spirit, which is perceived as truly divine. The Akan believe that *Nyankopon* gives *kra* to all human beings, hence all people are Nyankopon's children: *Nnipa nyinaa ye Onyame mma, obi nye asaase ba*, "none is earth's child." When a child is about to be formed in the womb, *Nyame* gives it life in the form of the *kra* through the help of *Nyankopon*. *Nyankopon* "shoots a particle of the sun's fire into the blood-stream of the child, thus bringing its blood to life"; hence the Akan saying, "*Kra ne mogya*, the *kra* is live blood."[60]

Akan philosopher J. B. Danquah brings from his Western philosophical background another element. According to Danquah, a person's life has a physical basis, which he calls *E-su*.[61] "*E-su* has some form of consciousness but is without conscious self-direction, the attribute of reason. The latter quality, the attribute of reason, is acquired in the act of 'leave taking' whereby a soul, *okara*, or personality, in the full sense, comes to inhere in man's being."[62] The human being in this state comes to *Nyankopon* and receives a soul, "the distinctive capacities of a truly human being with a corresponding responsibility to realize those capacities."[63]

The *kra* is present in man as long as he lives, though its strength varies with life's occurrences. Misfortunes affect it by diminishing its life force. A person who has experienced shock or grief would normally say, "*me kra*

---

59. Eva L. R. Meyerowitz, "Concepts of the Soul among the Akan of the Gold Coast," *Africa* 21 (1951): 24.

60. Meyerowitz, "Concepts of the Soul," 24.

61. It is important to point out that this word is very akin to the word that translates as character. One could either have *suban pa* or *suban boni*, good or evil character respectively.

62. J. B. Danquah, *The Akan Doctrine of God: A Fragment of Gold Coast Ethics and Religion* (London: Lutterworth, 1944), 111.

63. Danquah, *The Akan Doctrine of God*, 111.

adwane afiri me ho,' or *'me kra atu ayera,'* that is, 'my *kra* has gone [or flown] away.' . . . [W]hen a person, dogged by his conscience, is getting thinner and more lifeless daily, people say of him *'ne kra ayera neho,'* 'he is losing his *kra.'* "[64] In this way the *kra* is seen as the real essence of man, his vital force, "the source of his energy, his great reservoir of strength and sustenance."[65] It is also a divine spirit and the carrier of inspirations, dreams, and fantasies. It is the repository of man's instinct, which acts as protector and guardian, and thus also man's guardian spirit. But it is never merely the source of good luck, because an individual's fate depends for the most part on the extent to which he is able to harness his uncontrollable impulses. "The *kra* is visualized as man's twin or double; it is said *'ne kra nedii n'akyi ntira anka owni,'* 'but for his *kra* that followed him, he would have died.' "[66]

Another version of the story involves ancestors. As already mentioned, ancestors are very important to the Akan, who believe that the soul of a matrilineal ancestor representing *Nyame,* the deity of the cosmos, embraces a child during a good-bye ceremony in heaven and thereby gives the child its own *kra.* The child then receives a command to be a good human being and to do good deeds during his life. This kind of leave-taking is more crucial if the child's ancestor had failed to live a good life and his soul is unable to unite with that of *Nyame,* for to be united with *Nyame,* the soul has to become a *saman pa,* "good spiritual being." Sometimes the *akragya,* one of the seven patron deities of the seven days of the week, acts for *Nyame* and gives the child his *kra.* In this regard, the deity of the day on which the child is born imparts the *kra* to the child. These *akragya* are the deities of the planets *Awusi* (Sun), *Adwo* (Moon), *Abena* (Mars), *Aku* (Mercury), *Awo* or *Abrao* (Jupiter), *Afi* (Venus), and *Amen* (Saturn). Any child born on a day sacred to one of these deities lives under his protection. In this version, the child receives the *kra* after he is formed from the blood of his clan and endowed in the *samandow* with the *sunsum* ("personal soul"), and with the *ntoro* ("spirit of his patrilineal ancestors"), and is then taken by an *akragya* to *Nyame.* "A golden bath is brought, and the *akragya* bathes the child by pouring water over it. Nyame then rises and, having uttered *nkrabea,* the message of destiny," drops water from a leaf into the child's mouth.[67] "This is the water of life, *nkwansuo,* 'the pure water that boils yet does not burn.'

---

64. Meyerowitz, "Concepts of the Soul," 24.
65. Meyerowitz, "Concepts of the Soul," 24.
66. Meyerowitz, "Concepts of the Soul," 24.
67. Meyerowitz, "Concepts of the Soul," 25.

It is said to have at its center a breathing image of Nyame 'like the figure of a person in a mirror.' The water then penetrates the whole body of the child until, when filled with the *honhom* (breath of life), it wakes up to live. The *kra* in this version is envisaged as the water of life in the veins of the child."[68]

Whatever the version of the story may be, it is quite clear that the soul is a gift from God and is a vital part of the human being as well as the human being's relationship with the creator and giver of the *kra*. What happens to the body also affects the *kra*, though sometimes the *kra* acts as if it were external to the body when it is conceived of as the twin of the person. It can be reincarnated until it becomes good enough to be rejoined to its source, *Nyame*.

The Sunsum

Meyerowitz describes the difference between the *kra* and the *sunsum*. "Whereas the *kra* is seen as the divine, impersonal soul, the *sunsum* [spirit] is regarded as the personal soul. . . . The *sunsum* is not divine; it is only a shadow, which lives as long as a person can throw a shadow, and can therefore not be reincarnated."[69] As in the earlier version of how the child acquires a soul, the Akan believe that the patrilineal ancestor, prior to the bestowing of the *kra* by *Nyame*, and with the help of a matrilineal ancestor, imparts the *sunsum*. "The unborn child receives the *sunsum* after it has indicated the manner in which it wishes to express itself, and the plans it desires to put into action."[70] This is the *nkrabea*, "destiny or the manner of taking leave." With the former version in which the *nhebea*, "command," comes from *Nyame*, the Akan believe that "*Onyane nkrabea nni kwatibea* — what *Nyame* has destined cannot be evaded."[71] To the Akan, free choice or actions are determined not so much by rational decision as by the *kra*, "the impulse, the irrational driving factor." The *kra* and the *sunsum* together form a whole.[72]

Each person is expected to fill to the brim with goodness *honhom*, "the spirit-breath," that dwells in his *kra*. Inability to do so disqualifies him from entrance into *samandow*, "the land of ghosts or place of the dead,"

68. Meyerowitz, "Concepts of the Soul," 25.
69. Meyerowitz, "Concepts of the Soul," 26.
70. Meyerowitz, "Concepts of the Soul," 26.
71. Meyerowitz, "Concepts of the Soul," 27.
72. Meyerowitz, "Concepts of the Soul," 27.

where those who have committed little sin live on after they have become *saman*, "ghosts." But those who are very wicked are not wanted there and "are condemned after judgment in heaven to live to eternity in the *abronsamgyam*, the place of wickedness or hell."[73] But the concept of reincarnation includes a provision to help those who are willing to gain entrance into the land of ghosts: the imperfect *kra* is believed to return to earth through reincarnation. "But *okrabiri*, people with a thoroughly bad *kra*, who have omitted to fill it with goodness, are refused permission to stay in the Upper Kingdom and become evil spirits on earth. If they repent, however, they are pardoned; and their *kra* is reincarnated in a child born blind, lame, or otherwise infirm."[74] The spirit on the other hand flies back to *Nyame* upon death, "but when it is filled to the brim with goodness it becomes one with the Sun-god."[75]

The *Nnipa*, "human being," thus comprises the *hunam*, "body," which includes the *mogya*, "blood," and *kra* and *sunsum*, "the various soul components," into which *Nyame* has breathed his *honhom*, "spirit." The Akan place great emphasis on the *kra* and *sunsum* and very little on the *hunam*.

Normally the Akan blame the evils that attack the soul or spirit and manifest in the body on various forces. The Supreme Being for instance, though he does no evil, may send down disease as a punishment for a crime. But usually these diseases are of communal or tribal proportions. Some good spirits can cause sickness as a result of violation of an interdiction. The evil spirits, like *sasabonsam*, however, cause disease senselessly because they delight in doing evil. Ancestors, like the good spirits, would afflict an individual for failing to pay them due reverence, especially with regard to the offering of sacrifices. Sometimes the Akan explain continual misfortunes as one's destiny, which could be either self-chosen in the pre-earthly existence or laid down by the Supreme Being. But they attribute some diseases to natural causes, which is normally when a disease attacks a very old person who is considered a witch. The assumption is that such people have received their just rewards.

Despite the differences in the description of their religious beliefs, there are certain evident commonalities between Anlo and Akan cosmologies. They

73. Meyerowitz, "Concepts of the Soul," 27. It is difficult to know if this latter thought is original to Akan cosmology, or whether it is the influence of Christian thinking on the afterlife introduced by Christian missionaries, or whether it reflects Meyerowitz's desire to help readers understand the term.

74. Meyerowitz, *Akan of Ghana*, 97.

75. Meyerowitz, *Akan of Ghana*, 97.

share a belief in the Supreme Being, the creator and sustainer of the universe, and in the presence of other spirit beings who govern the universe and who, with the help of their priests and priestesses, enforce rules that maintain order in society. Additionally, they have a common belief in ancestors, though the Akan have by far the more highly developed belief system regarding ancestors and their veneration. They share a common understanding that human beings are composed of body, soul, and spirit, and that occurrences at the physical level have already taken place on the higher spiritual plane. In this regard, the influence of the spiritual world upon individuals, especially through witchcraft, receives a great deal of attention. Antidotes, in the form of charms and amulets against witchcraft and other malevolent forces, are available from anti-witchcraft sources. For preventive purposes, diviners can foretell the future and provide intervention for possible mishaps.

The evangelical community as a whole may not believe that destiny or lack of veneration of ancestors or other spirit beings causes them spiritual harm, but many believe that witchcraft spirits, ancestral curses, their own sins, and curses cast by other human beings can have an impact on them. They attempt then to ward off all possible attacks from the spirit world. Some of these attempts, it has been noted, are detrimental to the individual and families involved.

Summary of Ghanaian Theological Anthropology

We can sum up Ghanaian Christian anthropology as it is affected by Ghanaian cosmology among the Anlo and Akan as follows:

1. Human beings are persons in relationship with God, self, and others, both the living and the dead, and in particular a person's own direct ancestors.

2. A human being consists of three basic entities — body, soul, and spirit — of which the spiritual component supersedes the other two components, since it is an aspect of the creator and is immortal.

3. The spirit world impinges on the natural world and affects the human person through his or her spirit.

4. In order to guard against destruction, people must live in such a way as to invite the protection and blessing of the gods and ancestors.

5. Christians enjoy protection from spiritual forces through Jesus, on the condition that they do the right things, especially renouncing any part they may have in ancestral and familial curses.

6. Only the prayers of particular spiritual Christian leaders gifted to do so can effect deliverance from bondage to particular spiritual forces.

While the background provided here is focused on the Anlo and Akan, observations we make about their cosmology is applicable in varying degrees to all the people groups in Ghana. With this cosmological background in mind, we will examine the theological basis for the content and direction of pastoral counseling in the Ghanaian context. This is of primary importance because a certain theological stance informs the work of pastors. Pastors, as well as parishioners, ask basic theological questions that need theological answers. There must be a reason why a person suffering from an ailment of unknown causes, whether physical or psychological, seeks out a pastor for help rather than any other professional. The cosmological assumptions I presented influence the content and direction of present pastoral practice in Ghana. Ghanaian Christian theology intertwines subtly with African religious ideas that sometimes appear to take the foreground, especially in the pastoral counseling practices currently going on in the Independent Evangelical churches.

Since Ghanaians believe that human beings are in relationship with God as well as seen and unseen others, particularly their direct ancestors, they have no concept of the kind of individual autonomy assumed in the West. They make major life decisions in conjunction with the family, both living and dead. And yet the fear of ancestral curses (and their effect on future generations) remains a major concern, and libations, sacrifices, and divination function to make communion, appease, and stay in favor with these ancestors. Ghanaians satisfy their need to know and be rightly directed in important life-changing decisions through divination. While libation is not a specialized task and the average person can pour libation, divination and some forms of sacrifice require training and a calling.

The effect of these beliefs in pastoral practice is that Ghanaians lay emphasis on renouncing ancestral curses and sins that they perceive are the causes of the problems they face. In place of libation to appease these ancestors, prayer, especially the prayer of deliverance, becomes the means of access to higher, more supernatural powers that counteract the effect of these curses.

One cannot state too emphatically the importance of the place of ancestral and other spirit forces on the life of individuals and families. Ghanaians believe strongly that ancestral curses are passed on from generation to generation, and they are constantly called to renounce complicity in curses pronounced over the family. As far as back as the first century, there have been rites of passage, typically called "out-dooring," for babies on the eighth day of life. Traditionally, this is the first time that the child is welcomed into the land of the living. The rite involves invitations to the gods and other ancestral spirits to protect and guide the new member of the community. Apart from this event, at yearly festivals mainly associated with the harvest, it is customary to appease the gods and to place all in the household as well as the extended families into their hands. Rather than protecting the people placed under their care, this act, some Christians believe, allows the spirit of these gods to adversely affect the lives of people placed in their charge, regardless of the people's allegiance to God. These occasions create avenues for demons or other spirit forces to affect the lives of believers, especially if their faith is not strong.

Confessing with the mouth and believing that Jesus Christ is both Lord and God does not automatically rid them of these demonic possessions or oppressions. What occurs is rather an ongoing battle between the conflicting powers that takes place in dreams and visions, and which is made manifest in attendant physical symptoms. This belief is exemplified in the approach to pastoral diagnosis and counseling that pertains in contemporary Ghana. This belief that the living and the dead are interrelated and that curses persist even after one has become a Christian drives the need to ascertain from the parishioner whether there are any ancestral gods or known ancestral curses in his family. A case in point was an incident in one of these churches where the individual who had come for counseling was told that the cause of his ailment lay in the fact that his mother had visited a shrine prior to his birth. For deliverance to be effected, he was required to bring his mother to confess her wrongdoing.

In light of the need and tendency to seek out diviners to predict the future, with the hope that one might at least prepare for it, the recent surge of "prophetic all-night prayer meetings" among the Independent Evangelical churches is not surprising. As part of my research, I attended some of these meetings and had occasion to interview some of the leaders. These meetings were not limited to any particular ethnic group; in fact, one of the churches, Faith Foundation International, led by a Ga minister, has a branch in Canada. At these meetings, where his future is foretold by the leaders of the church or by prophets brought in especially for the occasion, the African is in familiar territory once occupied by diviners. What goes on in these prayer meetings, therefore, is a direct response to the Ghanaian worldview and the need to know and manipulate the cosmos to one's favor.

What is interesting is that some of the leaders of these new ventures in the church in Ghana receive their teaching from Western church leaders, particularly from North America. Most of these leaders are televangelists, whose teachings emphasize the need for "wealth and health" in the life of the believer as outward signs of God's favor, and who attribute the lack of these things to lack of faith or sin. The basic assumption for such groups is that Christians should not have emotional or financial problems because God is their father. Dwight L. Carlson expounds and critiques this belief, stating that it hinders Christians from receiving the help that they need.[76] According to Carlson, Christians are not availing themselves of psychological and other resources for their emotional well-being because they have bought into an "emotional-health gospel."

The emotional-health gospel assumes that if you have repented of your sins, prayed correctly, and spent adequate time in God's Word, you will have a sound mind and be free of emotional problems. Usually the theology behind the emotional-health gospel does not go so far as to locate emotional healing in the Atonement (though some do) but rather redefines mental illnesses as "spiritual" or as character problems, which the church or the process of sanctification can handle on its own. But this is a false gospel, one that needlessly adds to the suffering of those already in turmoil.[77] While this "gospel" is not limited to the Ghanaian context, the Ghanaian cosmologies that we have examined thus far create fertile ground for such prosperity preaching. In the same way that one can avoid attacks and receive blessings by living to please the ancestors, a Christian enjoys protection from spiritual forces through Jesus on the condition that he does the right things, especially renouncing any part he may have in ancestral and familial curses. While it is true that right living and right doing are part of what it means to be a child of God, the emphasis here seems more on preventing mishaps than on experiencing fellowship with God as Father and friend.

We can also note a similarity between the practice of calling upon trained diviners and diviner-healers and the practice of calling upon particular kinds of Christians gifted in "deliverance" to rid the demonized of the spirits that ail them. As mentioned earlier, Anlo diviners undergo a rigid,

---

76. Dwight L. Carlson, "Exposing the Myth That Christians Should Not Have Emotional Problems," *Christianity Today* 42:2 (Feb. 9, 1998) [journal on-line], accessed 13 Dec. 2000, available from http://www.christianitytoday.com/ct/8t2/8t2028.html.

77. Carlson, "Exposing the Myth."

twelve-year training under experienced teachers and enjoy great prestige for their ability to unravel and resolve difficult situations. The assumption is that these deliverance-gifted Christians have attained a certain level of spirituality or Christian maturity that affords them the power to bring deliverance to the demonized.

Exorcism is not a new phenomenon; the church has practiced exorcism since its inception. But today, the church seems to ask, who can pray for deliverance? In Ghana, especially among the Independent Evangelical churches, the answer seems to be that an exclusive group of Christians particularly called and anointed by God are the only ones to do any and all types of deliverance. However, the testimony of the Scriptures as well as church tradition give a much more complex picture of who is qualified to perform exorcism.

Prior to the formation of the church, Jesus commissioned the disciples to go out and cast out demons (Luke 10:1-20). Apart from this mission of the disciples, one of the five signs that attend believers is the ability to drive out demons in his name (Mark 16:17). All who believe in Jesus are thus given the authority to drive out demons or to pray for deliverance for those who need it. This practice continued in the early days of the church. It is said of Philip, a deacon appointed to oversee the distribution of food in the church and who evangelized Samaria, that his mission included exorcism. Evil spirits, "crying with loud shrieks, came out of many" to whom he ministered (Acts 8:7).

In *Deliverance from Evil Spirits*, Francis MacNutt draws on the traditions of the early church in an attempt to answer the question of who is qualified to pray for deliverance. Citing several church fathers, he notes that one did not need a special calling to perform exorcisms. There was no "special class of Christians to whom the ministry of deliverance was restricted,"[78] and following the death of the Apostles all believers performed exorcisms. MacNutt therefore asserts that all believers have a role in casting out demons. He notes that Origen, for instance, mentioned that several Christians cast out demons "merely by prayer and simple adjurations which the plainest person can use. Because, for the most part, it is unlettered persons who perform this work."[79] Tertullian said that the noblest aspect of the Christian life is "to exorcize evil spirits — to perform cures . . . to live

---

78. Francis MacNutt, *Deliverance from Evil Spirits: A Practical Manual* (Grand Rapids: Chosen/Baker Books, 1995), 131.

79. Origen, *Against Celsus*, vii, 4, cited in MacNutt, *Deliverance*, 131.

to God."[80] It is clear from these sources that the Apostles and early church fathers believed that all Christians could exorcize.

Looking to scripture, many have seen the special ability to cast out demons as one of the gifts described in passages like 1 Corinthians 12, though Paul himself does not list this gift among the charismata. Such a reading is inferred from their understanding of the "gift of miracles." Some of the early church fathers affirm this reading, and MacNutt agrees that it makes sense to include the ability to exorcize under the gift of miracles.

Ghanaian pastors are therefore right in so far as they contend that spiritual gifts differ within the church and that some people are equipped with the gift to cast out demons. But when they limit this gifting only to certain individuals, they erect a spiritual hierarchy that forms the church and people to become unduly dependent on these "men of God."

Conclusion

Currently, Ghanaian pastoral theology seems to be unhelpfully conditioned by African cosmological ideas. This situation renders diagnosis and pastoral intervention unhelpful to Christians seeking counseling for their problems. In fact, the very thing for which they seek help — fear of harm from evil spiritual forces — becomes the focus of counseling in a negative way that often induces more fear rather than alleviating it. The counselee goes away knowing more about what evil spiritual forces have done or could be doing to him or her rather than discovering the freedom that Jesus Christ offers through his death and resurrection.

---

80. Tertullian, *De Spectaculis*, para. 29, cited in MacNutt, *Deliverance*, 131.

CHAPTER THREE

Barth's Theological Anthropology: An Overview

Introduction

Ghanaian pastoral counseling today is based on a set of beliefs and practices that it inherited from African Traditional Religion and blended with certain cosmological ideas from the Old and New Testaments that seem to give weight and authority to this traditional way of looking at the world. The dominant worldview that underpins Ghanaian pastoral theology assumes that spiritual (and not physical) reality is ultimate, and that the universe is filled with malevolent spirits. Following from these assumptions, the purpose of religion becomes spiritual warfare, a struggle to fight off these dangerous spirits. Jesus figures into this religious landscape as a supremely powerful god who helps ward off these dangers. On the anthropological level, Ghanaians traditionally imagine human beings as body, soul, and spirit, with the spirit being the point of vulnerability in spiritual warfare. Those who are not "born again" (implying that they do not belong to God) must act with even more vigilance in order to protect their well-being from spiritual attack. How might Ghanaian theological anthropology be set free from a cosmology that reinforces fear in order to proclaim a gospel message of hope?

The theology of Karl Barth has been helpful as I have pondered the magnitude of the theological and practical challenges facing the African church today. As I searched for substantive theological guidance on these complex issues, I turned to Barth for several reasons. First, African Christians (myself included) seek to understand themselves in the light of Scripture. They have a high view of the authority of Scripture and are convinced by preaching and teaching that is scripturally based. Karl Barth undertook his entire theological enterprise for the sake of faithfully preaching and teaching the scriptural witness.

Second, Barth has developed a way of ordering the relationship between theology and culture in ways that would be helpful to African Christians who are sorting through various strands of belief and practice. Which beliefs and practices are consonant with the New Testament witness and which ones stand in tension? Is it possible to distinguish between a theological affirmation and how it is conveyed through cultural symbolic forms? Barth is helpful as we seek to make crucial distinctions between the gospel and the cosmologies that developed over time through the biblical era.

Third, Barth is a practical theologian par excellence. His theology is not speculative or esoteric, but is closely allied with the practices of the church. His discussion of the true nature of human beings, of human beings in the cosmos, and of the relation of the soul to the body all have important implications for the practice of pastoral counseling in the African context.

The Basis and Scope of Barth's Theological Anthropology

According to Barth, a theological perspective is the proper starting point of anthropology. While the various anthropological approaches, such as cultural anthropology or social anthropology, have their value and contribute in important and diverse ways to our understanding of the human being, they are limited in one crucial respect: they do not offer us a picture of what Barth calls *wirkliche mensch,* "real man." By "real man," Barth means Jesus Christ as God's self-revelation, and by inference human beings as God sees them on account of this "real man." Barth's theological anthropology affirms the place of other bodies of knowledge in our understanding of human beings in so far as these disciplines own the contingency of such knowledge. He opposes them when they claim the ability to show us the "real man":

> At this point we find ourselves in basic opposition to philosophy, but we are all the closer methodologically to the inductive sciences based on observation and inference. The latter are differentiated from theological science by the fact that their object and source of knowledge are neither identical with each other nor with the Word of God. The source

of their knowledge lies in the process of observation and inference and therefore not in faith in the Word of God.[1]

For Barth, the hypothetical exact sciences and the speculative philosophies are based on facts and assumptions that arise from within the limited horizons of human subjectivity, rather than from faith in the word of God. When these forms of knowledge take their rightful place in subordination to God's revelation in Jesus Christ, then they can contribute to theological knowledge. If, however, these bodies of knowledge set themselves over and against revelation, they stand in opposition to the Christian confession.

The speculative philosophies, which belong to the realm of worldview or cosmological theories, are often a combination of myth and philosophy. They sometimes take their point of departure from the exact sciences or from "pure self-intuition purporting to be axiomatic."[2] The sources of the exact sciences' knowledge are mainly observation and inference; thus they are preoccupied with the appearance of things, i.e., the external person and not the "real man." The danger with the speculative philosophies is that they leave the moorings of hypothetical sciences and begin to propose their observations and inferences as worldviews. Rather than see what they offer as hypothetical, they go beyond their proper boundaries and offer intuition as fact.

Like worldviews, these speculative philosophies thrive where the word of God has not taken root. Barth says that a speculative philosophy

> ... arises in the arid place — unspiritual in the biblical sense of "spirit" — where man has not yet heard the Word of God or hears it no longer. In this place man supposes that he can begin absolutely with himself, i.e., his own judgment, and then legitimately and necessarily push forward until he finally reaches an absolute synthesis, a system of truth exhaustive of reality as a whole. On this assumption he also and primarily thinks that he can know and analyze himself. . . . Anthropology on this basis is the doctrine of man in which man is confident that he can be both the teacher and the pupil of truth.[3]

---

1. Karl Barth, *Church Dogmatics*, III/2 (Edinburgh: T&T Clark, 1960), 12.
2. Barth, *Church Dogmatics*, III/2, 22.
3. Barth, *Church Dogmatics*, III/2, 22.

The reason that we cannot be both "teacher and pupil" is that we are fallen creatures. Sin distorts our understanding of ourselves. By starting with ourselves we can know only our possibilities and not our actual situation. The human being can only be known from revelation, as given in the biblical witness to Jesus Christ.

The human being should and can only be known from a theological perspective because the relationship between God and human beings is the central theme of the Scriptures, the word of God. We can obtain no true knowledge of the human being without reference to this relationship between God and humanity.

> Anthropology confines its enquiry to the human creatureliness presupposed in this relationship and made known by it, i.e., by its revelation and biblical attestation. It asks what kind of a being it is which stands in this relationship with God. Its attention is wholly concentrated on the relationship. Thus it does not try to look beyond it or behind it. It knows that its insights would at once be lost, and the ground cut from beneath it, if it were to turn its attention elsewhere, abstracting from this relationship. Solely in the latter as illuminated by the Word of God is light shed on the creatureliness of man. Thus theological anthropology cleaves to the Word of God and its biblical attestation.[4]

According to Barth, the real human being can only be known within the relationship of the Creator to the creature as explicated by the word of God. The unique example of real humanity is found in Jesus Christ. We can see how God sees and relates to real humanity in God's perception and relationship to this man, Jesus. "As the man Jesus is Himself the revealing Word of God, He is the source of our knowledge of the nature of man as created by God."[5] Jesus Christ is the source of our knowledge about human nature as it has been created by God. The true *nature* of human beings behind our *fallen* nature is seen only in Jesus Christ. In Jesus Christ alone do we see humanity without sin, and in Jesus Christ alone do we see God's attitude and relationship to unfallen humanity.

When we understand human beings on the basis of Christology, we see that

---

4. Barth, *Church Dogmatics*, III/2, 19.
5. Barth, *Church Dogmatics*, III/2, 41.

1. All persons are to be understood in relationship to God.
2. All persons are conditioned by the fact that Christ's deliverance is for them.
3. Persons are not ends in themselves, but exist for the glory of God.
4. All persons stand under the lordship of God.
5. Every person participates in what God does as deliverer and has the *freedom* to decide in favor of God.
6. Every person is to render God service.

It is a dangerous enterprise for a person to assume the role of "both teacher and pupil" on a subject of which he knows only a partial truth by virtue of being a creature.[6] The danger is accentuated when we base our lives on such a partial truth. According to Barth, it is even unacceptable for persons to consider God as one factor among many as they pursue this self-knowledge, because their process still arises from sources other than God's self-revelation. It remains but a human word about themselves with reference to God, and thus is limited and only partially true, leading them into an endless and fruitless search for what they hope will be the final truth about themselves.

Barth's conclusion about speculative philosophy is that such a subjective, self-referential starting point for knowledge about human beings is opposed to God and to Christian theology, and that the church should oppose it. The Christian church should not behave as though it too lived in the sterile, unspiritual corner where the word of God has not yet been heard. Barth warns that if the church were to embrace speculative philosophies, which morph into worldviews without recourse to the word of God, it would cease to be the church God called into being. Rather than embracing the speculative philosophies, which belong to the realm of worldview theories, the church should be on its guard, making sure that its own anthropology stems from the word of God. In short, speculative philosophies should have nothing to do with theological anthropology. The church should not emulate the kind of self-knowledge and "unlimited self-confidence" that speculative philosophy exudes.[7]

The other kind of non-theological anthropology arises from the study of what Barth calls "the exact science of man."[8] These include physiology

---

6. Barth, *Church Dogmatics*, III/2, 22.
7. Barth, *Church Dogmatics*, III/2, 23.
8. Barth, *Church Dogmatics*, III/2, 23.

and biology, as well as psychology and sociology. The major difference between these and the speculative philosophies is that they do not claim to give us a picture of the "real man." Properly engaged in, the exact sciences have no worldview *per se*. They are satisfied to maintain their proper place and see themselves as giving information about the appearance of the human being and not the being of the human. They describe the human as a phenomenon, not human beings as they are in themselves. The exact sciences do not usually offer their findings as dogmas to live by; rather,

> [a] sense of relativity will always be maintained. To the extent that science is exact, it will refrain from consolidating its formulae and hypotheses as axioms and therefore treating them as revealed dogmas. It will always be conscious that its concern is not with the being of man but the appearance; not with the inner but the outer; not with the totality but with the sum of specific and partial phenomena. It will realize that its temporarily valid picture or system can be only a momentary view for to-day which it may have to replace by another to-morrow, for the flux of phenomena is reflected also in the conclusions of science.[9]

According to Barth, then, misunderstandings may occur when the exact sciences do not recognize the boundaries set by their own discipline. When they follow the guidelines of their field by recognizing the limits of the knowledge they offer, however, we can use their findings in tandem with those of theological anthropology for the well-being of persons.

The findings of the exact sciences change as their knowledge of human beings changes. As such, they cannot make any kind of definitive assessment of what Barth calls the "real man." It would be false for science to suppose that its findings for any period constitute the complete finding and thus a definitive theory of human beings. If the scientific anthropologies maintain their allotted realm of enquiry and see themselves as describing and explaining aspects of human phenomena, that is, something about human possibility and aptitude, but not the essential nature of human beings, then they can contribute to theological anthropology. Their contribution is valuable because their findings and their anthropology give us precise and relevant information that can be of service to our understanding of the functioning of human beings. Furthermore, their findings neither hinder nor promote the hearing or receiving of the word of God, and in this sense

9. Barth, *Church Dogmatics*, III/2, 23-24.

they are a-spiritual. They do not interfere with the claims of theological anthropology. Thus theological anthropology only differentiates itself from scientific anthropology, but does not necessarily oppose it on account of the difference between them. Barth does not dispute the fact that scientific enterprises are informed by the theories of their field or that theories would be generated from their findings. But he believes that the results of their findings should be confined to the understanding of aspects of human phenomena. If the focus of scientific inquiry shifts from fact-finding and data-generating into the sphere of dogma by proposing definitive theories about human nature, then it must be opposed in the same way as the speculative philosophies. At that point, it ceases to be pure knowledge. According to Barth, pure knowledge "confines itself to the study of phenomena but does not lose itself in the construction of world systems."[10]

Barth stresses the point that true knowledge of humanity (i.e., "real man") comes only from the word of God, which is the only source of complete truth regarding human beings. The true relationship between God and humanity exists only through, in, and from Jesus Christ, the word of God. In Christ, this relationship is not concerned merely with "man as a phenomenon but with man himself," both his possibilities and his reality.[11] Our knowledge of the relationship between creature and creator, and of the boundaries of human existence, is conditioned by what God says about humanity.[12] It is for this reason that it is a false starting point to begin anthropology from a foundation of human autonomy and self-determination. Such anthropologies deny the created purpose of the human person as a covenant partner with God, and therefore miss humanity's true reality and essence. The only place to find and understand human beings as they really are is in the Scriptures, which bear witness to God's self-revelation in Jesus Christ. In other words, Jesus Christ reveals to us not only the truth about God, but also the truth about human beings, because Jesus Christ is the only human being whom we know who is without sin.

Yet the human being that confronts us in Scripture is not "real man" but rather a humanity marred by the effects of the fall. How do we move from the humanity in its fallen state to the "real man," i.e., to his true humanity? We need to understand that God still regards human beings in their sinfulness as beloved creatures and as such, human beings are still real before God. The

10. Barth, *Church Dogmatics*, III/2, 13.
11. Barth, *Church Dogmatics*, III/2, 25.
12. Barth, *Church Dogmatics*, III/2, 4.

imago Dei is not destroyed by the fall. As Barth asserts, "[I]n the radical depravity of man, there is also hidden his true nature; in his total degeneracy is his original form."[13] This insight can become clear to us only by the piercing light of God. Our sinfulness makes it impossible for us to see ourselves as we truly are, both as sinners and as those redeemed by grace. Sin robs us of the capacity to see ourselves as we really are and distorts our self-awareness, hiding itself from our view so that we underestimate the power of its impact. We need revelation to show us how much our self-perception is distorted. Yet since the *imago Dei* is intact in human beings, the covenant relationship between God and human beings is not destroyed.

We can therefore understand and know the *wirkliche mensch,* "real man," when we hold together these two opposing truths: on the one hand, human beings are fallen, and on the other, our original form is still embedded within us even in our fallenness. This is the work of grace alone. So, Barth concludes, the "real man" is not only the object of divine grace but also participates in divine grace. If human beings are the object of divine grace, our self-contradiction may be radical and total, but it is not the last word about us. Our present state is not the final and total picture of humanity, at least not as God sees us. Because of the covenant relationship that God has with us, our future transcends the present boundaries set for us by sin, and our future transcends the subsequent judgment that should rightly befall us as those who have broken this covenant relationship. Our fate is determined in a totally different way from what it would have been because of the faithfulness and mercy of God.[14] God's omnipotence and the splendor of God's grace would be thwarted if any assessment other than God's determined human identity:

> If he is the object of God's favour, his self-contradiction may be radical and total, but it cannot even be the first word about him. The fact that he became a sinner cannot mean that he has spoken an originally valid word about himself, even in respect of his own origin and beginning.[15]

Any other understanding presupposes that the devil, or sin, or we ourselves have creative power and can therefore refashion ourselves in a form other than that which God has created, and which in Christ God has

---

13. Barth, *Church Dogmatics,* III/2, 29.
14. Barth, *Church Dogmatics,* III/2, 31-34.
15. Barth, *Church Dogmatics,* III/2, 31.

redeemed. We must therefore be careful in our anthropology not to imply that the effects of sin have produced a new kind of humanity, a *malum substantiale*, a humanity substantively different from that which God has created. To base anthropology on any footing other than on what God says about human beings is to impute creative power beyond that of God to Satan, who is the cause of humanity's fall. The sin through which human beings fell and the resultant corruption of humanity through that sin are not the same thing.[16] The sinful human being is not the "*real* man." Sin indeed has no creative power and therefore it cannot constitute a new human being. For this reason we belong to God and not to Satan or even to ourselves, even though we sin and make our condition hopeless in itself.

Barth's understanding of the "real man" is a stance that is evident in the creation saga. Here we encounter a God who in his mercy first clothes human beings and then ushers them out of the Garden of Eden to prevent them from eating fruit from the tree of life. While the expulsion from Eden has traditionally been interpreted as a punishment resulting from disobedience, Barth sees the grace that was implicit in that action. If Adam and Eve had stayed in the garden they would have had access to the tree of life after they had fallen into sin, resulting in an eternal life lived in a fallen state.[17] If sin could not totally destroy human beings, nor re-create a new person other than the one that God created, then sin seems to be in the final analysis less powerful than we have traditionally made it out to be. But because of God's merciful act of expulsion, the destructive power of sin did not have its full effect on humanity. Barth contends for the final sovereignty of God's grace when he asserts that "sin itself is not a possibility but an ontological impossibility for man."[18] Yet this does not imply that sin is of no consequence. It was and is evil and consequential, and it therefore calls for divine judgment — a judgment, however, that does not conflict with divine mercy. Sin is so terrible because it takes place within the covenant with a gracious God.

Human sin does not change the fact that we are created by and for God. In spite of sin, we are still creatures of God. In addition, in the new covenant God identifies with humanity in Jesus alone: God is always the Lord, and humanity the partner of the covenant. God does not let humanity go, hence humanity cannot be released from its status as a creature in relationship with

---

16. Barth, *Church Dogmatics*, III/2, 28.

17. Barth, *Church Dogmatics*, III/2, 635.

18. Barth, *Church Dogmatics*, III/2, 136. See also Barth, *Church Dogmatics*, IV/1, 408-10, for a fuller discussion of this point.

its creator.[19] He can flee, but he cannot escape either God or himself. God knows the truth about human beings beyond their sin. God alone knows what we, in our guilty blindness, can never know through our own initiative.

I need to emphasize that Barth is by no means making light of sin, nor of its consequences, for this would be contrary to the scriptural witness on sin. The cross, a sign of God's love, is also the clearest evidence that God takes sin very seriously. Barth therefore says,

> When man is truly and seriously viewed in the light of the Word of God, he can be understood only as the sinner who has covered his own creaturely being with shame, and who cannot therefore stand before God even though he is the creature of God. . . . If we try to deny this or to tone it down, we have not yet understood the full import of the truth that for the reconciliation of man with God nothing more nor less was needed than the death of the son of God. . . .[20]

The Scriptures indeed give us both pictures of human nature. On the one hand is the fallen human being and the resultant enmity with God, with herself, with others, and with the rest of creation. But in Christ the human being is judged and proclaimed righteous and restored to a new covenant relationship with God. Both noetically and ontically, anthropology rests on Christology. It is only on the basis of who Christ is for humanity that human beings know themselves in both their neediness and their redemption. The logical structure of Barth's thought is to move from Christology to anthropology, from this *particular* man, Jesus, to human beings in general. Formally, therefore, Barth's thought follows that of Paul when he proclaims that there is no condemnation for those who are in Christ Jesus (Rom 8:1-4). No condemnation awaits them, either in the present or in eternity, for the judge has justified them, and no other judgment counts.[21]

---

19. Barth, *Church Dogmatics*, III/2, 32.

20. Barth, *Church Dogmatics*, III/2, 27.

21. Barth's soteriology raises the question of whether humans have any agency in being counted righteous in Christ. Is justification dependent on human belief, or is it dependent on the finished work of Christ? Or is it the case that it is equally dependent on both the finished work of Christ and human belief in Christ as Savior and Lord? How we answer these questions depends on how we understand the efficacy of Christ's death. I believe that its efficacy does not depend on the magnitude or strength of human belief. Regardless of human belief, God still sees us through Christ and the finished work of the cross. Otherwise, faith itself becomes the "work that saves."

Human Beings and the Cosmos

This human being who together with God is the object and subject of the Scriptures is always a part of God's creation. While humanity is not a prototype of the cosmos but is merely a minute part, the lens of Scripture is nevertheless focused on this particular creature. When Barth considers humanity in the cosmos, he begins with humanity as a creation of God, emphasizing that humanity is *a* creation and not *the* creation of God. Humanity is always humanity *in* the cosmos: "Man is a creature in the midst of others which were directly created by God and exist independently of man."[22] It is, therefore, wrong to detach humanity from creation, biblically as well as ecclesiastically. Always humanity is humanity in the cosmos, part of creation. Human beings are dependent on other aspects of creation that are superior to them.[23] In this regard, Barth is wary of those who blur the distinction between human beings and God, as well as those who separate human beings from the rest of the created world. To blur the distinction between the creature and the Creator is to lose sight of the fact that God has created human beings for communion with God. There can be no real communion unless there is differentiation, unless there are a self and other. "That real man is determined by God for life with God has its inviolable correspondence in the fact that his creaturely being is a being in encounter — between I and Thou. . . ."[24]

Though humanity is always humanity in the cosmos, Barth does not give the cosmos or cosmology undue attention. He argues that the Bible itself does not regard cosmology as a distinct and independent concern worthy of separate attention. Scripture itself has no single cosmology, for while it employs several, it adopts none.[25] There is, thus,

> no world outlook which can be described as biblical, or even as Old Testament, or New Testament, or as prophetic or Pauline. There can be a welter of cosmological elements in the Bible deriving from the most diverse sources, and none of them is given in its totality, none is expounded as a doctrine, and none is made obligatory for faith.[26]

22. Barth, *Church Dogmatics*, III/2, 4.
23. Barth, *Church Dogmatics*, III/2, 14.
24. Barth, *Church Dogmatics*, III/2, 203.
25. Barth, *Church Dogmatics*, III/2, 6.
26. Barth, *Church Dogmatics*, III/2, 9.

No particular cosmology is central to the Scriptures. Barth makes several pertinent points to uphold his argument. In the first place, the theme of Scripture is always humanity in the cosmos, and never the cosmos itself. Scripture, therefore, is free to employ any cosmology it sees fit for a particular illustration, but it is also free to set aside any or all cosmology. It is not wedded to any particular cosmology to make its point. The creation saga that depicts the unfolding of humanity's relationship with God, as well as with the rest of creation, is filled with various implicit worldviews. In fact, it warns us against being captured by any *particular* worldview, because it can become our focus rather than Christ.[27] This being the case, the Bible can even be disloyal to any cosmology without detracting from its own central message. It can and does oscillate between and within worldviews while keeping its central theme in focus.

In arguing for a recognition of the variety of cosmologies found in the Bible, Barth is not, however, denying the import of the cosmos. He goes so far as to own that humanity as part of the cosmos "must remain loyal to the earth."[28] However, of greater importance is the knowledge that humanity stands between heaven and earth and thus is equally bound and committed to both. Now, if heaven is the dwelling of God, then what heaven says of human beings holds greater sway than what earth speaks regarding them. Barth asserts that "we shall never truly understand him . . . if we forget that heaven is above him."[29] Again, it is true that

> the New Testament has a "cosmic" character to the extent that its message of salvation relates to the man who is rooted in the cosmos, who is lost and ruined with the cosmos, and who is found and renewed by his Creator at the heart of the cosmos. In the present exposition we must not and will not be guilty of any failure to appreciate the significance of the cosmos, of any insulating of man from the realm of the non-human creation.[30]

27. Colossians 2:8, 20 tells believers, "See to it that no one takes you captive through philosophy and empty deceit, according to human tradition, according to the elemental spirits of the universe, and not according to Christ. . . . If with Christ you died to the elemental spirits of the universe, why do you live as if you still belonged to the world? Why do you submit to regulations . . . ?"

28. Barth, *Church Dogmatics*, III/2, 4.

29. Barth, *Church Dogmatics*, III/2, 4.

30. Barth, *Church Dogmatics*, III/2, 4.

We can thus affirm and embrace the place of the cosmos in the life of human beings as long as the cosmos is placed in the right perspective with regard to human beings as those who live in a covenant relationship with God. Barth's concern is to understand the cosmos in a proper perspective, that is, not making it into something other than what it was intended to be or according it undue attention. He argues against making a commitment to a particular view of the cosmos *per se* and interpreting all reality through that lens.

When we make a commitment to any particular cosmology, we have slipped off the foundation of Christian faith by allowing it to become captive to a human worldview. However careful and intentional we may be about adhering closely to the faith we profess, intercourse with any cosmology brings the attendant temptation to identify it with Christian faith, thus taking the faith captive to human ideology and shifting its focus away from its proper subject. It is for this reason that Barth talks of faith always being in "some contradiction with the cosmologies with which it associates."[31] He argues that the proper attitude to adopt about worldviews is to discern the Bible's own attitude, which is to hold loosely to all worldviews and pay homage to none. Barth says of the Christian faith,

> In so far as its confession is pure, it will always be able to make an eclectic and non-committal use of current world-views. If it allows itself to be bound by them, its confession has ceased to be true confession. It is then limited, conditioned, determined and challenged by the autonomy of the alien body to which it has wantonly fettered itself. . . . That at least a partial obligation towards dominant world-views is axiomatic, was no less an opinion of the ancient than of the modern Church. But a faith embroiled in this self-contradiction and a partial commitment to a specific world-view cannot be the norm which we must accept in this matter.[32]

How do people of faith become so embroiled in the issues of cosmology as to assume that the word of God, which speaks of God and also of human beings, contains either directly or indirectly some disclosure about the nature and being of the cosmos in and of itself? Barth's answer is that

31. G. W. Bromiley, *Introduction to the Theology of Karl Barth* (Grand Rapids: Eerdmans, 1979), 122.

32. Barth, *Church Dogmatics*, III/2, 10.

fascination with the worldviews occurs when we no longer hear and obey God as revealed in the Scriptures. For cosmology

> can arise only in the sterile corner where the Word of God with its special revelation has not yet found, or has lost again, hearing and obedience on the part of man. Only then can the cosmos be a third force between God and man and thus become the object of independent attention and consideration.[33]

Rather than give ourselves fully to the God of the Bible and the relationship we have with this God, we attach ourselves to an alien worldview, one devoid of the covenant we know as revealed in Scripture.

Although we do not want to be unduly embroiled with worldview themes, we do need to understand the place of the created world in the covenant between God and humanity. Barth claims that creation names a cosmological boundary between that which is divine and uncreated, and that which is temporal and created. The division within the cosmos between heaven and earth is a boundary that points and corresponds to this more fundamental difference between creature and Creator. Heaven is the invisible creation inaccessible to humanity, while the earth is the visible creation that lies under human control and activity. For Barth, "heaven corresponds to the being and action of God," and earth "corresponds to the being and action of man," while the "conjunction of heaven and earth corresponds to the covenant in which the divine and human being and action meet."[34] This point or junction is forever concretized in Christ, an event that is evident in all aspects of human action. The history that God began among human beings by calling Abraham has reached its perfect distillation in Jesus Christ. In Christ God has fulfilled the promise to Abraham and pitched a tent among human beings forever. Thus, the cosmos is in some harmony with the history that is now enacted in it. It is in this state that the word of God addresses humanity, that is, human beings in their existence under heaven and on earth, human beings in the in-between state, not what they could become and yet not what they used to be. Thus the word of God is not interested in cosmology as such, but with the specific history of humanity in which God through Israel and Jesus Christ has become incarnate and acted in and through human

33. Barth, *Church Dogmatics*, III/2, 11.
34. Barth, *Church Dogmatics*, III/2, 12.

beings.[35] We speak thus of the very human being that God has become, Jesus Christ, who is God for humanity and humanity for God. If in Christ God and humanity are conjoined, and Christ in that conjunction stands in the place of human beings before God and in the place of God before human beings, then God has indeed come to humanity as Servant and Deliverer.[36] While nothing is the same on earth again because of Christ, neither will anything be the same in heaven. Forever a mediator stands between God and human beings. If we believe this affirmation in faith, as Barth does, then "there arises irresistibly the demand that anthropology should be based on Christology."[37] In all respects, Jesus is the "real man," the man for all human beings. His person is therefore the place from which we start if we are to understand human constitution. It is from Jesus that we know humanity because he is the sinless man, the human being whose nature has not been distorted by sin and its consequences. So we do not first know humanity and then understand Jesus Christ relative to this general knowledge; rather we first know the human Jesus and then understand all human beings relative to this particular knowledge.

Jesus, the "Real Man"

This man Jesus, who is the human being for all humanity, is both God and human. For this reason Christological anthropology is the only possible approach to understanding human nature in general.[38] Barth's decisive thesis is that "[a]s the man Jesus is Himself the revealing Word of God, He is the source of our knowledge of the nature of man as created by God."[39] Our starting point must be "Jesus, man for God"[40] and the "man for other men."[41] We are not dealing with a neutral, abstract, and unhistorical view of Jesus. Instead, we are dealing with the historical Jesus of Nazareth, whose human nature was manifested within a specific history which takes place between God and humanity.[42] According to Barth, this is the only place to

35. Barth, *Church Dogmatics*, III/2, 159-60.
36. Barth, *Church Dogmatics*, III/2, 159-60.
37. Barth, *Church Dogmatics*, III/2, 46.
38. Barth, *Church Dogmatics*, III/2, ix.
39. Barth, *Church Dogmatics*, III/2, 3.
40. Barth, *Church Dogmatics*, III/2, 55.
41. Barth, *Church Dogmatics*, III/2, 203.
42. Barth, *Church Dogmatics*, III/2, 55-71, 203-22.

start if we are to avoid anthropological abstractions.[43] Other anthropologies start from human observation of the self and others, which is by definition a limited approach distorted by fallen human perception. This man of the people of Israel did not become a generic human being but a particular person in whom a decision was made concerning the nature of all persons. In Christ humanity finds a "Neighbor," a "Brother." What we say of Jesus includes "all other men, those who were before him and those after him, those who knew him and those who did not know him or did so indirectly, those who accepted him and those who rejected him." Because of this man, "everyman in his place in time is changed."[44] According to Barth, this is the good news: human beings are different from what they would have been if God had not assumed human flesh, and because God took on flesh in the man Jesus Christ, human beings will never be the same again. If we take the incarnation seriously, then in Christ we are to regard humanity at once as assumed, judged, redeemed, and handed to us.

Barth notes that we can run into problems when we ground anthropology in Christology. The dual nature of Christ, the divine and the human, held together in differentiated unity within him, threatens to make any analogy between Christ and other human beings break down at some level. Nevertheless, this is a characteristic of all analogies, especially when the comparison is between God or God/Man and human beings,[45] for humanity is a mere copy of what is actualized in Jesus as the original. If Jesus Christ is sinless, it is because he had a unique relationship to God. Fallenness is, therefore, not a necessary result of human nature. It was acquired, what might be called a *nonessential accretion*. In Christ, human nature becomes knowable and recognizable precisely because in him it is neither distorted nor ruined by sin. What we were meant to be is laid bare for all to see. We participate in the same human nature with Jesus. The status of Christ's humanity is different from ours, but the constitution of his human nature is not. He was just as human as we are; the difference lies in his relationship with God.

In Jesus Christ, there is forever a concrete relationship between God and human beings. For this reason, all of a person's relationships with the self, with others, and the cosmos must rest on this concrete relationship. If

43. Barth, *Church Dogmatics*, III/2, 132.

44. Barth, *Church Dogmatics*, III/2, 133.

45. See, for example, Thomas Aquinas's exposition on the use of analogical language and Holy Scripture in his *Summa theologica* I, 1, 9, 10 (New York: McGraw Hill, 1964).

Jesus is the "real man," then to understand the constitution of human beings, we must look to this "real man."

> We find our bearings and our instruction as we look to the constitution of the humanity of Jesus. With the clarity and certainty that we gain here, we can then set out the propositions in which the Christian understanding of the constitution of all men generally may be expressed and comprehended.[46]

Jesus, the one on whom our humanity is patterned, is soul and body. He is one complete whole, not a union of two complete substances. He is an "embodied soul and besouled body."[47] It is in this constitution that he was born, lived and died, rose again, and now sits in heaven at the right hand of God. In the same constitution he will come again. It is in this same constitution that he has fellowship with the community of believers today. Of all the ways to describe the constitution of Jesus and thus that of all humanity, Barth chooses to use soul and body because "they keep us closest to the language of the Bible."[48] Nevertheless, we might say that the language used in the Scriptures to describe human beings, and even the man for all human beings, includes spirit and mind as well as soul and body. According to Barth, however, these other descriptions are peripheral, subsumed under the main constitution of human beings as soul and body. In the creation story, God forms the human body and breathes God's spirit into it so that "man became a living soul" (Gen. 2:7, KJV).[49] The human being is, therefore, soul and body undergirded by the Spirit of God, which gives and sustains all life. He receives the Spirit and is able to do things by the power of the Spirit. "From the general anthropological standpoint, however, possession of the Spirit is not a human state according to the Bible. In those events, the Spirit is imparted only 'by measure' (John 3:34)."[50] Perhaps, a better way to describe the relationship between the Spirit and human beings is to say

---

46. Barth, *Church Dogmatics*, III/2, 327.

47. Barth, *Church Dogmatics*, III/2, 327.

48. Barth, *Church Dogmatics*, III/2, 326.

49. Barth further clarifies this point in his exegesis of the annunciation of the birth of Jesus by calling attention to the distinction between what is messianic about him and what is anthropological. The presence and movement of the Spirit in Christ from conception through his ministry days speaks of a special relationship between this man and the Holy Spirit who is God. See *Church Dogmatics*, III/2, 333-66.

50. Barth, *Church Dogmatics*, III/2, 334.

that the Spirit has humans, rather than that humans have the Spirit, even a human spirit. An important distinction is being made between the Spirit of God and what has become known as the human spirit. It is not that the Spirit is not fully available to human beings; it is rather that human beings are only able to appropriate a certain measure of the Spirit. This is the case because, as Barth writes, human "life is only transitory and partial: transitory, since it comes only to go; partial, since death and corruption are always near it."[51] Herein lies the marked difference between this Jesus of Nazareth and all other human beings: His life is not transitory or partial.

There is another marked difference between the human being and Jesus, a difference found in the way the constitution of body and soul is ordered. The constitution of the human being is ordered with lower and higher elements. Yet Jesus' life is lived so wholly and truly that he is both the higher and the lower, the dominating and the dominated, the leader and the follower. Barth writes:

> He is whole man, a meaningfully ordered unity of soul and body. That His human existence unfolds in these two moments — not in one only, but also in the other — is as visible in Him as it can possibly be. But there is lacking in Him all cleavage between the moments, and to that extent the problem of their relationship is resolved. . . . The two moments are indestructibly different even on this higher level, for it is a matter of divinity and humanity. But abstractions and separations are impossible. In the place of man stands the One who is God Himself in man; and in the place of God stands the same One who is man in Jesus. And in this wholeness and oneness the relationship of God and man, of man and God, in Jesus is itself a meaningfully ordered relation. Here already there manifestly operate superior and inferior, lordship and service, command and obedience, leadership and following — and this is in a constant and irreversible relation.[52]

51. Barth, *Church Dogmatics*, III/2, 334.

52. Barth, *Church Dogmatics*, III/2, 340-41. Barth's use of the terms *superior* and *inferior* to describe how the soul and body of Jesus relate might seem problematic until we understand how the terms function within an asymmetrical relationship. In the terms of a hierarchical relationship, when one has more, it automatically implies less for the other. Leadership of one suggests subjugation of the other. In an asymmetrical relationship, however, this is not the case. Asymmetrical relationships pertain to realities that share no common frame of reference. In this regard, more for one does not mean less for the other. In short, there is no comparison implied in the relationship to warrant a hierarchical interpretation. Barth

Jesus lived as one whole person. Any other way of living would destroy the oneness of his being. While soul and body completely intertwine in him, they are nevertheless differentiated and ordered such that the soul has ultimate precedence over the body. It is not that one is superior and the other necessarily inferior in the way we understand it, but that one takes priority over the other, in the same way that in ordinal numbers, for example, the number 1 precedes the number 2. The number 1 has no intrinsic characteristic that sets it apart from the number 2. They are both numbers.

The soul and the body exist in a differentiated unity by an inner ordering. Barth refers to the constitution of this creaturely being as "soul and body in their interconnection, in their particularity, and in their material relationship."[53] Barth's understanding of the constitution of the human being gives each entity a certain autonomy within an interdependent relationship.

Soul and Body in Their Interconnection

By soul and body in their interconnection, Barth refers to the unity of soul and body: the human being is one whole, soul and body. The soul has no existence apart from the body, and the body has no life apart from the soul. To have one is to have the other. The soul can only be what it is and can be known and experienced only through the medium of the body. In this regard, whatever is done to the body affects the soul and vice versa. This understanding is of primary relevance in the Ghanaian context, where the obverse is dominant: things affecting the body (diseases, death, etc.) are believed to have first occurred in the soul and secondarily manifested in the body due to the internal unity between the two entities. By contrast, Barth argues that

> The soul is not a being for itself, and it cannot exist for itself. Soul can awake and be only as soul of a body. Soul presupposes a body whose soul it is, i.e., a material body which, belonging to soul, becomes an organic body.[54]

---

employs the terminology of superior and inferior because of the necessary delimitations of language, especially in any theological enterprise. If we read Barth in the context of his theology, however, the confusion due to the choice of languages diminishes. For further insight, see George Hunsinger, *How to Read Karl Barth: The Shape of His Theology* (New York: Oxford University Press, 1991), 185-224.

53. Barth, *Church Dogmatics*, III/2, 366.
54. Barth, *Church Dogmatics*, III/2, 373.

There is a mutual interdependence between the soul and the body such that one cannot exist without the other. The same thought cannot be expressed, however, of the relationship between soul and spirit. While the soul needs a body for existence, "[t]he Spirit cannot be said to need a body" in the same way.[55] The spirit exists independently of creation and the creature and is the basis of soul and body and, therefore, of life. But we can only speak of life if there is *something* alive, quickened, in motion, acting. For this reason, we cannot speak of the soul of inanimate objects. We also cannot speak of a cosmic soul, since not all of nature lives in an independent manner, although all creatures are alive and act.[56]

The Old Testament affirms the understanding of a besouled body, and the same Hebrew word can denote both "soul" and "life." The word *nephesh* can mean bodily life in general as well as an individual corporeal being. Here a distinction is made between the material and organic being. In a note in Barth's discussion of the interconnection of the body and soul, he explains that the Old Testament *nephesh* (נֶפֶשׁ) is the life of the body in much the same way as the New Testament *psyche* (ψυχή).[57] What we see from the standpoint of Scripture is that human beings do not have the capacity to destroy the soul. However, the Creator has the power to destroy both the body and the soul in the nether world.[58] The promise of the New Testament, and to some extent the Old Testament, regarding the soul or life of the body, is not immortality, but rather the future deliverance of the body in the resurrection.[59] Thus, immortality is not an inherent property of the human soul: God is able to destroy both the body and the soul.

Exactly how we are to understand the destruction referred to here is debatable. The Scriptures present us with an interpretive challenge because there are passages in the New Testament that stand in tension with each other. In John's Gospel, for instance, Jesus says to the sisters of Lazarus that those who believe in him shall not see death (John 11:25). In Paul's expositions of

55. Barth, *Church Dogmatics*, III/2, 373.

56. Barth, *Church Dogmatics*, III/2, 377.

57. Barth, *Church Dogmatics*, III/2, 379. Barth explains the inability of both English and Greek to delineate the different understandings of the word. The Greek and English use *sōma* and *body* respectively, for corporeal and organic being, and thus the distinction, which the German maintains, is lost. In the German, *Körper* is corporeal being, and *Leib* is life.

58. In Matthew's Gospel, Jesus says that we should not fear those who are able to destroy only the body, but should fear instead the One who is able to destroy both the body and the soul (Matt. 10:28). For Barth, the "One" is the Creator. Barth, *Church Dogmatics*, III/2, 379.

59. Barth, *Church Dogmatics*, III/2, 379.

the end times in Thessalonians, he says that those who die in the Lord are not dead, but merely sleeping (1 Thess. 4:13–5:11). Concerning his own life or death, Paul speaks of absence in the body as being present with the Lord. From just these few references and many like them, we could arrive at the conclusion that the soul is immortal and that it separates from the body at death. What exactly are we to understand by the term "immortal," especially in the light of the biblical witness? As with all arguments pertaining to the Scriptures, in order to draw any conclusions we must allow Scripture to be its own interpreter. By this I mean that all interpretive methods and meanings derived from biblical passages should align themselves to the totality of the message of the Scriptures, rather than relying on isolated verses.

Given the conclusion of our discussion of the union between soul and body, to impute immortality to the soul and mortality to the body would negate that unity at a very basic level. If soul and body part from each other at death, if one is spiritual and otherworldly and the other is mortal, corporeal, and this-worldly, can we still say that one is the life of the other? Can we still argue for such a basic interconnection? Could there still be an indestructible unity between them? If what is said of one can also be said of the other, and if what is done to one is automatically done to the other, how then can we impute immortality to one and corruptibility to the other? This kind of belief arises from a failure to understand the Scriptural witness to the unity between body and soul.

The Scriptures are the source of neither current Christian beliefs about the immortality of the soul nor of negative portrayals of the body. Rather, the source of such notions can be found in Greek and Latin antiquity, which bequeathed to the church a dualistic conception of human nature that posed a separation of body and soul. Furthermore, this dualism hierarchically ordered the soul as superior to the body.[60] I believe, however, that this anthropology has no place in Christian theology because the Bible gives a clear indication not only of the unity of the body and soul, but also of the inestimable value of the body as the temple of the Holy Spirit (1 Cor 6:19). Various passages of the Old Testament implicitly affirm the body when they refer to God anthropomorphically, attributing to God human feelings, thoughts, and actions.[61] In the New Testament, this same God

---

60. Barth, *Church Dogmatics*, III/2, 390-94.

61. Notable examples include references to God walking (Gen. 3:8), grieving (Gen. 6:6), to God's right hand (Exod. 15:6) and nostrils (Exod. 15:8), and to the palm of God's hand (Isa. 40:12).

takes on human flesh as Jesus of Nazareth. Through his death, resurrection, and glorification, Jesus Christ banishes forever the notion that the body is inferior. If we accept this affirmation, we cannot subordinate the body to the soul.[62] While the soul antedates the body because it is grounded in the Eternal Spirit, there is no scriptural basis for imputing a dominant/subordinate hierarchy to the relationship between the soul and the body. However, an inner ordering exists between the two, which I shall discuss in the next section.

There is a final point I wish to make regarding the interconnection between soul and body. Theories and practices abound that stress one entity over the other: certain theologies and strands of spirituality stress the importance of the soul over the body, while materialistic currents of thought effectively negate the soul by claiming that what we cannot experience with the five senses must not exist. The claims of the former make humans objectless, while the stance of the latter makes them subjectless.[63] The truth lies midway between these two extremes. It is possible to maintain a balance between them only if we understand the importance of "soul and body in their particularity."[64]

Soul and Body in Their Particularity

A distinctive hallmark of contemporary spirituality is a growing emphasis on holistic approaches to the human person and to therapeutic practice. It has become common to speak of the interconnection between the somatic and the psychic and the spiritual. Practitioners go to great lengths to emphasize this interconnection and chide those who maintain a dualistic approach. For this reason it may seem as if calling attention to soul and body in their particularity, and insisting on the distinction between these two entities, is to contradict the broad consensus of the therapeutic community. Yet, it is precisely because of our concern for the total human being and the desire for healing to reach every aspect of the human personality that we must attend to each component of the human person.

62. There are various Scriptures that allude to abasing the body so that the soul might be saved. However, all of these Scriptures are treating the theological metaphor of "the flesh," which is the human tendency and propensity toward sin (e.g., Mark 9:42-49, Gal. 5:24), rather than the body in itself.

63. Barth, *Church Dogmatics*, III/2, 392.

64. Barth, *Church Dogmatics*, III/2, 394.

Barth calls our attention to soul and body in their particularity in a unique way. Barth's understanding of soul and body in their *particularity* holds each entity accountable for its being and action. Both soul and body as individual components stand before God in their temporal as well as eternal existence. The distinction that Barth makes is not always apparent, however, because his emphasis on the unity between body and soul usually takes the foreground. This is because he makes the distinction while simultaneously upholding the unity of the body and soul. Barth calls this kind of distinction a differentiation within unity.[65] A human being is "soul and body totally and simultaneously, in indissoluble differentiation, inseparable unity and indestructible order."[66] Imperceptible though it might be, an important distinction exists between soul and body, and exploring this distinction may yield new possibilities for therapy in the Ghanaian context.

Barth begins his discourse by stressing the inherent unity of the human being who stands before God. The human being's creaturely nature is always as a besouled body called into fellowship with God. While the human being is a "besouled body" and an "embodied soul" and the two are inseparable, nevertheless,

> the two moments of this human creaturely nature are differentiated. The centre is not as such the periphery. The person is not as such the representation. The inner is not as such the outer. The soul is not as such the body. That it could not be without it is of course true. But it is not for this reason directly identical with it.[67]

The body is distinct from the soul, and while one needs the other, they are not identical. We could say that it is characteristic of soul to have body and vice versa.

This distinction between body and soul is vital to understanding how the human being apprehends an other as other, as distinct from the self. It is within this distinction that a human being stands before God and other persons and makes decisions and acts upon them. It is as a "besouled body" and as an "embodied soul" that a human knows the self. It is in the body that humanity lives the life it is disposed to live. Living is a shared

65. Barth, *Church Dogmatics*, III/2, 399.
66. Barth, *Church Dogmatics*, III/2, 437. We recognize in this terminology the same formal pattern as the Chalcedonian definition of the relationship between the divinity and humanity of Christ.
67. Barth, *Church Dogmatics*, III/2, 397.

task between the body and the soul. As soul of the body, the person gives guidance and direction to his or her life. As body of the soul, the person acts on the decisions made. The soul cannot displace the body or do for it what only the body can do. This might sound as if one being is actually two beings, or two substances within the same being, one the leader and the other the follower. In other words, it may seem as though the soul is the leader and the body merely the follower. Barth maintains that this is not the case. Rather, what we have is what Barth terms "two moments" of the same human being as creature.[68] To be and to act as a creature is to have these two moments. Barth stresses the fact that we are not talking about two substances within the human being, but rather a distinguishing between two moments of the human being as creature: "For within man, the animating factor and the animated, the soul and the body diverge, and are distinct from one another."[69] We can see the distinction between the two moments to which Barth alludes in how a human being relates to God, to other people, and to the self.

Barth uses an analogy to explain the distinction between the body and the soul: the distinction between awareness and thought during the act of perceiving. During perception, awareness is received through the senses via the bodily organs, what we normally term the natural senses. Thought belongs to the soul, making soul the rational aspect of human life. Perception is a single act of the human being, but the body and the soul together cooperate to bring about human perception. While this sounds simple enough, there is more going on. It is not merely a shared task with each component doing its part. Barth writes:

> The situation is rather that man as soul of his *body* is empowered for awareness, and as *soul* of his body for thought. Understood thus, the two are different and cannot be interchanged.[70]

It is in the body and through awareness that human beings encounter each other as well as the spiritual, and thus God. In this regard, the outer, or peripheral, has great importance in our apprehension of the other as other. It is not just the soul that initially apprehends the other, while the body merely receives the aftershocks. The body of the soul receives and posits

---

68. Barth, *Church Dogmatics*, III/2, 399.
69. Barth, *Church Dogmatics*, III/2, 399.
70. Barth, *Church Dogmatics*, III/2, 400.

the other as other. The body is thus *sine qua non* to our being human, i.e., beings in relation. In the next chapter, we will elaborate this further as we call attention to the importance of understanding the components of the human being in their particularity. While the bodily awareness of another makes relationship possible, in the soul and through thought the human being can take another into the self. The human being is thus able to make another his or her own. Perception is not subdivided into two parts, one pertaining to the body and the other to the soul. But "it can be affirmed that a special relation to the body is proper to the one, and a special relation to the soul to the other."[71] In desiring and willing, we find the same cooperation between the soul and the body at work. Desire pertains to the body, while willingness, the decisive factor, pertains to the soul. The soul thus insures that the desire is either acted upon or resisted.

There are implications of these affirmations in assessing African Traditional Religion and its appropriation by African Christians, the focus of chapter four. When we can recognize the place of the body in the grand scheme at work in our human creatureliness, we can give the body the attention it requires for proper function. Proper functioning of the body is necessary for the overall effectiveness of the human being. Proper functioning means more than simply functioning as an organism. In positing a "differentiation within the unity" between body and soul, we circumvent dualism and in its place we arrive at a balanced view of the human being.

The Scriptures affirm what we have been saying about the soul and the body in their particularity. We find in the Christian Scriptures that God is interested in both awareness and thought, in both desire and willingness. This means that God is interested in what we do in our bodies as well as what we do in our souls. In the Decalogue, for example, we receive warnings against actions as well as desires. This same point is emphasized in the Sermon on the Mount, where Jesus calls attention not only to acts, but also to desires that lack the attending actions, claiming that both are equally sinful (Matt. 5:21ff.). God will judge both the body and the soul for their involvement in acts of sinful behavior. More importantly, God meets us in our bodies as well as our souls, and we, in turn, meet others in our bodies as well as our souls. Both body and soul are important in our humanness and in living fully the covenant relationship into which we are called. We are indeed besouled bodies, souls of our bodies and embodied souls.

71. Barth, *Church Dogmatics*, III/2, 401.

Soul and Body in Their Ordering

I do not support dualistic approaches, nor do I affirm monistic understandings of what constitutes the human person. At the same time, I understand and agree with Barth that the two components or moments of the one human being are ordered in their relation to each other. In Barth's understanding, this ordering is based on the anthropology of Jesus, "the man for God" and the "man for all men." This one on whom all human life and living is forever patterned is again the starting point of our understanding of how the two moments of the one human being are ordered.

In his discussion of soul and body in their order, which he bases on the anthropology of Jesus, Barth focuses on the human as a rational being created as such by God, who stands apart from all creatures. The rationality that is characteristic of humanity is not self-imposed or acquired over time. It is seen as the imperative that God imposes on humanity.[72] If this is true, then human beings can either live fully within the rationality given them before God, to live within this truth, or they can cling to the falsehood that leads them to negate their calling and thus themselves. They can conduct themselves seriously as rational beings or fall into complete error in relation both to God and to themselves. If they elect to defy the revelation and will of God, they end up choosing their own nothingness.

Yet human beings in general are aware that they are rational beings and at least try to live as such, fulfilling the calling imposed on them by the Creator. According to Barth, if human beings understand themselves thus, then there are some specific things to be said about them and how they are to live. In the first place, we meet with a human being who rules herself and, as such, "is called and claimed by God."[73] As a person thinks and wills, she fulfills the human act of living. As a "besouled body," and as the soul of the body, the person precedes the body in controlling and using it and having dominion over it. When a person is able to do this, she is a "spiritual soul."[74] The person is undergirded by God and lives as such before God. In death, in which such activity ceases, freedom is lost, as the dominion or precedence that the soul exercised over the body is broken. Without deliverance from death, the human being's life, as it ought to be, ends. Since in Christ there is a negation of death, however, then this ordering, which makes the human

72. Barth, *Church Dogmatics*, III/2, 423.
73. Barth, *Church Dogmatics*, III/2, 423.
74. Barth, *Church Dogmatics*, III/2, 424.

being who she is, remains intact. The ordering does not end with death as we would assume; rather it supersedes death and remains the final word about humanity. The human is and will continue to be a "besouled body," always preceded by the soul.

Summary

Our argument thus far can be summarized this way: first, theological anthropology needs to be based on Christology. Because of human sin, human beings do not have access to knowledge of their true human nature. But through the revelation of Scripture, we are shown how we were created to be as we look to Jesus Christ who is fully human, yet without sin. By looking at Jesus, we know "real humanity" as created by God. He is the source of true knowledge of human beings.

Second, we can use non-theological anthropologies (both the exact sciences, such as psychology, and the speculative philosophies, such as various worldviews) eclectically and noncommittally as sources of knowledge. They can give us valuable information about human phenomena, but when these disciplines set themselves up as axiomatic or dogmatic, they are to be opposed unless they function within a context set by theological anthropology. When they become foundational (rather than peripheral) to our theological anthropology we are to oppose them because they usurp the place that needs to be accorded to God's self-revelation in Jesus Christ, as witnessed by Scripture.

Third, human beings are constituted as soul and body undergirded by God's Spirit. Our souls and bodies are patterned after Jesus Christ as "embodied souls" and "besouled bodies," existing in a differentiated and ordered unity. While there is no dualistic separation between body and soul, neither is there a confused enmeshment between them. We must give each its due in the ordered relationship.

In the next chapter, we will see how Barth's rejection of speculative philosophy can have a striking impact on the African apprehension of Christian theology, which in turn has profound implications for pastoral practice. We will also see how his understanding of the relationship between body and soul affects how we can differentiate, unify, and order pastoral theology in Ghanaian practice.

CHAPTER FOUR

African Theological Anthropology in the Light of Barth's Theological Anthropology

Introduction

This chapter examines African theological anthropology and its cosmological underpinnings through the lens of Barth's theological anthropology. Present pastoral counseling is based on the understanding that human beings are body, soul, and spirit existing in almost undifferentiated unity. Things affecting the individual are first experienced at the level of spirit and only then felt in the body and/or soul. That is, evil spiritual powers have access to the individuals through their spirit and can then gain power over the body and soul. Evil spiritual agents, such as demons and witches, are responsible for inflicting harm on human beings through their spirit; this then enables them to gain power over a person's body and soul. Witchcraft spirits can also be transferred to unsuspecting individuals through articles of clothing, trinkets, and other personal items, as well as through food and drink. Christians are not immune from these attacks and may even be susceptible to witchcraft spirits, thus becoming witches without knowing it.

Many Ghanaian Christians, for example, assume that their beliefs about the spirit world and its effects on human beings are also those of the Scriptures. All of the Independent Evangelical church pastors that I interviewed for this study referred to this connection between their practices and their interpretation of Scripture. They pointed to examples of healing and exorcism from the Gospels, for instance, to support this view. These pastors would contend that if in the Gospels Jesus healed all manner of diseases through prayer and exorcism, then Jesus understood diseases as spiritual problems needing spiritual intervention. Based on these and other passages that address evil spiritual powers, the pastors claim a natural affinity between a biblical worldview and the African worldview, especially as it relates to current pastoral practice. For this reason, they first seek to identify the cause of disease and other forms of human brokenness through prayers of discernment and then, depending on whether they identify demonic causes as the root of the problem, they may offer exorcism to bring healing to the troubled individual. If it is the case that human ailment, as Ghanaian pastors understand it, primarily stems from spiritual causes to be healed through prayer and exorcism, then we would assume that prayers of exorcism alone would effect the desired change and restore the individual to wholeness.

In my research as well as in my personal experience of these phenomena, however, I found that not all problems go away with exorcism. The problems perdure, leading the individual to continue seeking out one "man of God" or another in search of healing. Many of the questions pastors ask parishioners in an effort to understand their problems, as well as the assumptions behind the questions, are derived from African cosmological ideas and not strictly from biblical narratives. For instance, the meaning of their name, the type of church they attend, whether or not they have ancestral gods in their family, whether they have frequent dreams in which they eat with someone or are involved in sexual relations, are all concerns and questions that have little direct or explicit link with Scripture. They do, however, have a direct link with African religious ideas. For example, many Africans believe that frequent dreams involving eating with others or receiving food are an indication that a witchcraft spirit is being given to an unsuspecting victim.

Many Africans also believe that their understanding of human beings as made up of body, soul, and spirit, and of the spirit as the means by which disease affects the individual, are both beliefs similar to what the Bible teaches. They believe that diseases depicted in the Bible stem from demons and sometimes from Satan himself, even when this is not the case. Since malevolent spirits cause diseases and other human ailments, human beings must protect themselves from these spirits through spiritual means. The individual must watch the places he visits, the kinds of churches he attends, what he eats, and whom he receives those food items from. Christians are not immune from acquiring and being oppressed by these spirits unless they are in a special supernatural relationship with God. Only strong or mature Christians, those who are in constant fellowship with God through intense prayer and fasting, are able to withstand demonic onslaughts. Questions posed during pastoral diagnoses, as I have already pointed out, work to elicit such information.

Are these really ideas that come from the Bible and the teaching of the church or are they more in line with African cosmological ideas? Is it true, for instance, that a certain level of maturity in the Christian life or walk with God offers protection from evil spiritual powers that the less mature do not have? If that is the case, what happens to the new convert to the Christian faith?

When African Christians claim biblical support for their African Christian cosmology, not only are such claims overstated, they also keep these Christians from recognizing the bondage that ensues from such assumptions. However, because African Christians also understand the Bible to be the final authority on all issues pertaining to life, we can hope that if they recognize the fact that the Bible has no single cosmology, they will come to see the liberating potential of its message for pastoral practice. If Scripture has no single cosmology, then we can see how cosmological concerns are peripheral rather than central to the biblical witness, and we need not adhere to any one worldview at the expense of the Bible's central message. We might then encourage African pastors to hold lightly rather than tightly to the cosmological assumptions from which pastoral practice is performed, with the hope that pastoral intervention will be more beneficial to the counselee. For this reason, it is helpful to examine those biblical texts that seem to offer a rationale for African cosmological assertions and for the theological anthropologies that ensue from them.

African Cosmology: The Case for Biblical Continuity

I must underscore the importance of Scripture in the lives of Africans. While Scripture by its very name is written, the average African Christian receives and expresses the assertions of the word of God mainly as oral tradition. In the hands of pastors, many of whom are great orators, Scripture comes alive in very tangible ways for those who hear it. For these Christians, the word of God is infallible, timeless, and often taken literally. It is their source of hope, encouragement, and strength, and the means by which all things are possible. That most Africans readily find meaning in the Bible and are drawn to it lends some credence to the idea of a kinship between the experiences of the people depicted in scripture and African peoples today. The late Ghanaian theologian Kwame Bediako has said the following about the relationship between Christianity and primal religion and African Traditional Religion in particular:

> Not only have we learnt to understand these primal religious traditions as the background of the Christian profession of the vast majority of all Christians of all generations and all nations in the twenty centuries of Christian history, and therefore as the most fertile ground for Christian conversions, but also this peculiar historical connection between the primal religions of the world and Christianity may have implications for understanding possible affinities between them.[1]

For Bediako, African traditional religious ideas are seen as fertile soil for the gospel. There are, no doubt, aspects of African Traditional Religion that bear a close resemblance to ideas and practices in the Old as well as New Testaments. Some of these common beliefs include the interdependence and kinship between human beings and creation, and a concept of sin, especially as an abomination for which whole families and clans can be destroyed. Other commonalities include beliefs about the need for sacrifice as expiation for sin, and the need for a scapegoat who can absorb punishment on behalf of an individual or community. All these ideas are familiar themes in the Old Testament. Because Africans already believe and practice rituals of sacrifice to appease the gods, the idea of the death of Jesus Christ as a supreme sacrifice is usually not incomprehensible.

Bediako stresses the importance of understanding the affinities between the gospel and primal religions for current theological enterprises in Africa. Work is already underway in this area, and his own work with a group of lay church members at the Center for Mission Research and Applied Theology in Akropong, Ghana, provides the basis for some of his pertinent observations about how the gospel, especially the uniqueness of Jesus Christ for all peoples, can be made tangible for Africans. His treatment of the subject of Christology within the context of African Traditional Religions focuses on three areas of religious meaning in African traditional life in Ghanaian society: the practice of sacrifice, priestly mediation, and ancestral function.

Based on a study of the Epistle to the Hebrews in the Twi language, which adds concreteness to the text, he suggests the possibility of seeing

---

1. Kwame Bediako, *Christianity in Africa: The Renewal of a Non-Western Religion* (Maryknoll, N.Y.: Orbis Books, 1995), 83.

"Jesus as 'Ancestor' and sole mediator."[2] This is because Akan religious thought holds the ancestor, as the examination in chapter two points out, as second only to the Supreme Being. The ancestral cult is the ground of being and pervades all spheres of Akan life and action. In his invitation to view Jesus as Supreme Ancestor, Bediako bases his argument in the fact that Jesus Christ in his person and action is the ancestor *par excellence,* something the Akan can easily recognize through reading the Scriptures. The nuances of the text of Hebrews 1:3 in the Twi language then hone the argument.

> When he had made purification for sins he sat down at the right hand of the Majesty on high. . . . (NRSV)

> After achieving forgiveness for the sins of mankind he sat down in heaven at the right hand side of God, the Supreme Power. . . . (TEV)

The Twi version of the same text reads:

> Ode n'ankaso ne ho dwiraa yen bone no, okotraa anuonyam kese no nifa so osorosoro (Apam Foforo).

The word "odwiraa," which derives from "dwiraa," would easily strike any Akan speaker who reads these words because it is a yearly festival in which the Akan-Akwapem perform traditional purification rituals. In Jesus, however, the purification rites have already been performed.

> If Akan speakers read their Bibles only in the English versions, . . . it is conceivable that they would dutifully attend and participate in every annual *Odwiraa* Festival without ever coming to the realization that the traditional purificatory rituals of *Odwira,* repeated year after year, have in fact been fulfilled and transcended by the one, perfect *Odwira;* that Jesus Christ has performed once and for all, and for *all* people everywhere, a perfect *Odwira* which has secured an eternal redemption for all who cease from their own works of purification and instead trust in him and his perfect *Odwira.* . . .[3]

2. Kwame Bediako, *Jesus in African Culture: A Ghanaian Perspective* (Accra, Ghana: Asempa, 1990), 16.

3. Bediako, *Jesus in African Culture,* 45. This more nuanced understanding is based in the vernacular text, but in many ways, as Bediako has pointed out, the vernacular is the appropriate vehicle for the transmission of the gospel. In this way it gives expression to the

Here in this brief passage and exposition we gain insight into both the affinity between the two worldviews as well as how that affinity is utilized to construct a theology that is at once biblical and culturally centered. Yet such an achievement is not always possible, and Bediako himself acknowledges that "the challenge is that of relevance without syncretism."[4]

While affirming these similarities and agreeing with Bediako's assertion that primal religions contain within them an avenue for understanding and appropriating the gospel message, I believe it is important not to overlook the differences between them, because problems emerge when the affinities are overemphasized.

Many maintain that Traditional African Religions do not understand God as a Personal Being, a being who is involved in the day-to-day affairs of the whole cosmos. Such an assertion is difficult to support, however, because African Traditional Religions have a strong anthropomorphic element in their descriptions of the Supreme Being in everyday affairs. The daily expressions for the Supreme Being are very personal. For instance, the Supreme Being is called Obaatan, "the good mother" (Akan). Other expressions are theophoric names, proverbs, or wise sayings that give the impression that God is near and very present. It is often unclear whether these are expressions of trust in a good and powerful God or simply resignation in the face of malevolent or even benevolent fate.

In contrast to the God of Creation, who is unseen even though believed in, there are the lesser gods, typified in nature, that Africans can see and feel and therefore more readily approach. It is very likely that the geocentricity of the African cultures, which makes it easier for Africans to live within the concrete realm rather than the abstract, contributes to this phenomenon. There is, for instance, the pervasive belief that the presence of "spirit" activity at every level and at every turn dominates the individual's life. To mitigate this domination, one has constantly to manage the world of these spiritual powers in a way that produces benefits and increases fecundity. The total well-being of the individual, the family, and the community at large depends on how one manages these "spirit powers." At the same time practitioners of African Traditional Religions believe that basic necessities — food, clothing, shelter, abundance of children, and so on — depend on the gods and spirit ancestors, who may choose either to grant or

---

scriptural witness in the way it was first heard at the inception of the church, where all who were gathered at the feast of Pentecost heard the Scriptures in their own language.

4. Bediako, *Christianity in Africa*, 85.

withhold blessings. However, this fecundity can be threatened by demonic activity and the work of witchcraft spirits.

The idea that we are engaged in cosmological warfare is not peculiar to African thought. We can see some validity to this claim in St. Paul's Letter to the Ephesians. There he warns that the Christian wrestles against principalities and powers and dark forces in the heavenly places (Eph. 6:12). While Paul was speaking directly to the Christians at Ephesus, he was speaking indirectly to all Christians everywhere. The difference between what happens in the African scene and the rest of the world (according to these pastors) is that in the African world the beliefs that have been handed down open Africans up to the cosmos in a way that allows cosmic powers to infiltrate their lives. African Christians are, therefore, not immune to these powers. Christian or not, they are brought forth into a family that for generations has worshiped other gods, and there are still members of the extended family who worship these gods. Because of the sins of their forebears as well as contemporaries who might be committing idolatry, they are vulnerable to spiritual attacks from demonic sources. There is biblical precedent for this concept. The people of Israel went through a period in their religious journey when they blamed their ancestors for the misfortunes they faced. The prophets, however, proclaimed in no uncertain terms that while that may be true, God's justice also requires that those who eat wild grapes would have their own teeth set on edge (Jer. 31:29-30). People will pay for their own sins.[5]

African Cosmology: The Case against Biblical Continuity

While there is evidence of a cultural continuity between certain biblical cosmologies and the African worldview, a claim that there is a monolithic biblical cosmology that stands in continuity with African cosmology can-

---

5. James Hyatt proposes that the saying "the one who eats wild grapes would have one's own teeth set on edge" expresses the ancient Hebrew belief in collective responsibility and may have been widely used as an explanation for the Babylonian conquest and subsequent exile. What is being prophesied here by the mature Jeremiah is the idea that each man must be responsible for his own freedom. Many commentators suggest that this passage presupposes the longer discussion found in Ezekiel 18:1-4, and Hyatt argues that, since Jeremiah held to a doctrine of corporate responsibility, he would not have said this. Furthermore it seems to conflict with the hope expressed in verse 34. James P. Hyatt, "Jeremiah," in *New Interpreter's Bible*, vol. 5 [Nashville: Abingdon, 1956], 1036.

not be sustained. Since this erroneous claim centers around the spirit world and its influence on human beings through demons and demon possession, I will first examine the biblical understanding of demonology.

The passages normally deployed to support the claim that African cosmology and pastoral theology are consonant with the biblical world-view are often taken from the apocalyptic literature of the Old and New Testaments. Other passages are taken from the miracle accounts found in the Gospels, especially those in which Jesus is depicted casting out demons or healing people of various diseases. The question that concerns us here is whether the African reading of these accounts overstates the claim that there is a single biblical worldview and that there is an affinity between that and the African worldview.

For the African Christian, miracles often seem to be an end in them-selves: a church is a wonderful church if it supports a "powerful man of God" performing miracles, and people flock from one prayer meeting or house of worship to the next just for the sake of witnessing works of power. Tied in with this emphasis on miracles is a focus on spiritual warfare between Jesus and demons that fails to appreciate the full significance of the victorious in-breaking of God's kingdom in the incarnation of Jesus. It is as if Jesus and the demons are locked in a never-ending battle between two equal but opposite forces. Pastors base this understanding partly on the readings of apocalyptic literature that speak of wars in the heavenly places in which each Christian is a participant. And as long as the Christian is constantly at war with these spir-itual powers, then Jesus is at war with them too. The biblical picture, however, is not quite that simple; we find a tension between Christ's completed work on one hand and human responsibility on the other.

John Driscoll tells us that in the Gospel accounts the aim of Jesus' miracles

> is the glory of God in the manifestation of Christ's glory and in the salvation of men. . . . A saving and redeeming mission was the purpose of the miracles, as it was of the doctrine and life of the eternal Son of God. . . . Their motive was mercy. Most of Christ's miracles were works of mercy. They were performed not with a view to awe men by the feel-ing of omnipotence, but to show compassion for sinful and suffering humanity.[6]

6. John T. Driscoll, "Miracles," in *The Catholic Encyclopedia*, vol. 10 (New York: Robert Appleton, 1911), 346.

Jesus' miracles always focused on the glory of the Father and the breaking in of the kingdom. The miracles were never an end in themselves. Though the immediate end was the healing or rescuing of the needy person, the theological meaning of the miracle was a sign of the salvation that had been inaugurated in Christ. Jesus spoke many times about the Kingdom of God and the onslaught against the Kingdom of Satan. He viewed his age as the age in which Satan was permitted by divine sovereignty of God to exercise authority over men. Satan is referred to as a strong man who guards his house and who will not allow anyone to enter it and take his property without force (Mark 3:27). He also aims at frustrating the Kingdom of God on earth, and only the age to come will bring an end to his power. G. E. Ladd points out that we cannot ignore the dualistic terminology that Jesus himself employs in his teaching about the kingdom of God.[7] But in the advent of Christ, the kingdom of God has come and the defeat of Satan has begun because human beings are already freed through the good news of the kingdom. When we shift the focus from the deliverance or healing that occurs to the warfare between Jesus and the demons, we miss the import of Jesus' message. In the same way we also miss the point of the means of deliverance.

Another oft-cited source for Africans' focus on spiritual warfare is the apocalyptic literature found throughout the Bible. The book of Daniel, for example, includes several references to "wars in the spiritual realm." The ninth chapter recounts such a war. Daniel prayed, and at the inception of his prayer God dispatched a messenger to give him the answer he needed. It took twenty-one days for the messenger to arrive because the "prince of the kingdom of Persia" held the messenger captive (Dan. 10:13). African Christians usually interpret the account in this passage literally. It might well be that a heavenly being appeared to Daniel in a vision and told him how he was delayed until a backup appeared to aid his deliverance. The warfare and its implications are often highlighted as the reason why we should persist in prayer and why we should believe that there are actual spiritual, territorial forces assigned to various regions.

However, we can also benefit greatly from additional interpretations of this passage found in biblical scholarship on apocalyptic literature. Paul Hanson's *The Dawn of Apocalyptic* offers us valuable insight into these

---

7. G. E. Ladd, *The Presence of the Future: The Eschatology of Biblical Realism* (Grand Rapids: Eerdmans, 1974), 115.

sometimes difficult-to-understand books of the Scriptures.[8] He reminds us that this literature reflects the stories of those who suffered such severe affliction "that they began to lose their moorings in reality."[9] Therefore, we can attribute the surreal feel of the stories to the fact that they arose out of the nether regions of the psyche. In Hanson's view, dreams and visions represent sociological, as well as possible psychological, breakdown, making apocalyptic literature a "literature of desperation."[10] He claims that dreams can be avenues offering release from oppression. These are "images of what could be, what may be, and, most dramatically, what will be."[11] We could say that these dreams and visions are defense or survival mechanisms. But they are more than that. They have not only psychic significance but also spiritual and social significance.

Perhaps the most significant spiritual impact of these dreams, visions, and words from God is that they seek to draw Daniel, as well as the whole Israelite community, to God. Both before and during these visions, Daniel is in prayer, confessing his sins and the sins of the whole community. Often it is in the condition of admitting one's sins and brokenness, as well as that of all humanity, that God comes to people with healing and deliverance. Several references in the Bible show confession as a prerequisite for healing and deliverance. A vivid example is the injunction in the Epistle of James for the Christian community to make confession not merely to God but to one another so they may be healed (James 5:16). It is as if until such healing comes, people are held in the arms of mercy through these dreams and visions. Dreams and visions, even those that are bizarre and difficult to interpret, may be the means by which healing comes to the mind and then to the body.[12] But healing also comes through the compassionate care of the community as Christians share their common stories.

In addition to passages from the Gospels and explicitly apocalyptic literature, passages like Ephesians 1:20, 2:1, and 3:10, as well as Colossians 2:15 all speak about spiritual warfare. In about forty of the fifty churches

8. Paul Hanson, *The Dawn of Apocalyptic: The Historical and Sociological Roots of Jewish Apocalyptic Eschatology* (Philadelphia: Fortress, 1979).

9. Hanson, *The Dawn of Apocalyptic*, 30, cited in Daniel L. Smith-Christopher, "Daniel," in *New Interpreter's Bible*, vol. 7 (Nashville: Abingdon, 1995), 106.

10. Hanson, *The Dawn of Apocalyptic*, 30.

11. Hanson, *The Dawn of Apocalyptic*, 30.

12. Jungian analytical psychology, for instance, gives insights into the psyche's way of attaining wholeness through dreams. We will explore this concept in greater detail in the fifth chapter.

and parachurch organizations I visited, pastors quoted Ephesians 6:12 and similar passages directly during the interview or used it as an exhortation to the congregation during deliverance sessions. Constant reference was made to the Christian's struggle "against principalities and powers and spiritual forces of wickedness in the heavenly realms." The Ghanaian pastors I interviewed interpreted this passage to mean that Christians are in a battle with evil spirit beings, particularly demons. These spirit beings are pervasive, and thus Christians must be exhorted to vigilance even though they know that in Christ they are "more than conquerors." Thus pastors explain "principalities and powers" strictly as evil spiritual beings. Biblical scholars, however, propose other possible explanations of this terminology and how to understand it in terms of the context in which it was first employed.

In discussing the meaning of the terminology used to describe these powers, Hendrik Berkhof raises a series of questions aimed at deciphering Paul's intended meaning. He asks whether it is possible that Paul's "powers" "indicate various sorts of Powers, or various functions, or various names for more or less inclusive classifications."[13] His conclusion, based on several passages in Paul's epistles, is that "Paul means to suggest broadly, by the variety of expressions, the number and diversity of the Powers."[14] He further suggests that Paul's employment of this terminology was not his own invention, nor can it be conclusively said to be borrowed from Jewish apocalyptic literature, but "at least it is definite that these terms were not new to the religious vocabulary of Paul's readers."[15] Whether Paul's language refers to figurative or real beings is not very clear; what is clear is that "Paul sees them as structures of earthly existence."[16] These are real entities seeking to dominate human affairs. They are not ethereal spiritual beings, as Africans sometimes assume. At the least we can admit the possibility of seeing these "principalities and powers" who work in the "heavenly places" as being part of earthly physical structures, such as rulers and those in authority.

This does not mean that demons are not real or personal. Personalization of evil in Paul's day and in the African worldview today might be problematic to modern minds. Modern understandings of evil tend to depersonalize and split evil into psychological complexes or sociological

13. Hendrik Berkhof, *Christ and the Powers*, trans. J. H. Yoder (Scottdale, Pa.: Herald, 1977), 14-15.

14. Berkhof, *Christ and the Powers*, 15.

15. Berkhof, *Christ and the Powers*, 17.

16. Berkhof, *Christ and the Powers*, 23.

determinations.[17] It is not uncommon, however, to encounter situations or persons whose actions constitute something that we can only name as evil. Documented evidence of exorcisms in the modern church indicates that we cannot discount reports of personal evil.[18] Barth himself views the demonic as both real and metaphorical.

We should also bear in mind that if God is able to empower the church by the Spirit to do acts of healing and reconciliation, it is certainly possible for the Evil One to empower people for destructive acts as well. What we need to stress is neither the personalization nor the depersonalization of evil. Rather we should take account of both forms of evil, that is, both personal and impersonal evil, in such a way that human beings might come to acknowledge and confess their part in the evil that pervades their life.

Again it is clear that there is no single biblical understanding of the term "principalities and powers," and we cannot assume from the language of "spiritual hosts and wickedness in heavenly places" that only heavenly spiritual beings or demons are implied, as African pastors teach. A balance between the two positions, between personalization and depersonalization of evil, is necessary to address all aspects of presenting problems in the pastoral context. Such a balanced approach would prevent pastors from assuming *a priori* the presence of evil spiritual beings as the root of every pastoral problem. The pastor would be aware that there could be other impersonal powers at work, such as strict familial rules, that could be at the root of the problem. But above all, pastors should stress that *deliverance* comes because One who is like us has conquered and destroyed evil once and for all.

Demons and Other Spirit Powers

African Christians see continuity between their worldview and Scripture insofar as both acknowledge the domain and the extent of the spirit world. Not only do they believe that the forces of good and evil, of angels and demons, wage wars constantly in the spiritual realm, but they believe that demons can possess and influence human beings, even Christians. African

17. Theodore O. Wedel, "Ephesians," *Interpreter's Bible* (New York/Nashville: Abingdon, 1953).

18. Michael Perry, ed., *Deliverance: Psychic Disturbances and Occult Involvement*, 2nd ed. (London: SPCK, 1996).

Christians believe these spirits or demons are the harbingers of disease and other inexplicable misfortunes or habits. In the present Ghanaian pastoral scene, for example, fascination with demons and the attribution to them of all inexplicable calamities border on a form of divination. By constant reference to them and to the power they have to inflict harm through disease or bondage to certain habits, Christians give demons center stage.

African Christians have become sensitized to the idea of demons and their effect on them through experiences of possession or oppression. They attribute all forms of disease or unusual and inexplicable occurrences to possible demonic possession or oppression. They further assume that behavior patterns that resist change have demonic undertones and require deliverance to effect change. Sometimes they presume witchcraft spirits are behind any such behavior. What Western society recognizes as addiction is, in the African context, commonly attributed to demonic forces. Thus the great pastoral need is to prevent these demons from possessing and taking control of a human life.

It is pertinent, therefore, to examine the biblical accounts of possession by demons, as well as the common understanding that demons are the root cause of disease and addiction. We turn our attention first to demon possession as we encounter it in the biblical narratives. A judicious reading of these texts against the backdrop of the contemporary culture, with its political, psychological, and social tensions, might yield a more nuanced interpretation which, if incorporated into pastoral practice, would be liberating for the African Christian.

Demonology in the Old Testament

Research in biblical theology and ethics gives us valuable insight into the role of demons or demonology in the Scriptures. According to Werner Foerster, demonology and demons are peripheral to the Old Testament.[19] Occasionally in stories and in cultic usage, the word *demon* plays a part, but demons and demonology have no great influence in the Old Testament. In fact, only rarely does the Old Testament make mention of demons. Foerster notes that there is a reference to "demon," for instance, in the account of the destruction of Babylon (Isa. 13:21). But these are merely descriptions

---

19. Werner Foerster, "Daimon," in *Theological Dictionary of the New Testament,* vol. 2, ed. Gerhard Kittel (Grand Rapids: Eerdmans, 1994), 11.

and give no indication that demons were commonly accepted as an agent in the destruction of peoples (2 Chr. 11:15). Furthermore, the only implicit reference regarding protection from demons is in Psalm 91:6. It is only the Septuagint, however, that allows for this interpretation. The Old Testament generally does not emphasize demons or their place in human affairs, "not even for the purpose of warding them off."[20] In his studies in biblical demonology, Merrill Unger arrives at a similar conclusion regarding demons in the Old Testament — and further asks whether human beings should probe issues on which God is apparently silent.[21] Since the biblical narrative as well as biblical scholarship support these assertions, the insistence on drawing affinities between current African cosmologies and an allegedly biblical worldview begins to break down. Most of the arguments supporting such an affinity are based on an erroneously assumed correspondence between the African worldview and the Old Testament narratives.

Unlike the vague Old Testament depiction of demons, the Greek conception was more elaborate and embraced forces that mediated between God and human beings. In the Greek translation of the Old Testament, these forces were normally called messengers, or *Angelos*. They brought both good and bad tidings, blessings and destruction, to peoples and nations. The Old Testament ascribes the destructive powers to God that the Greek world attributed to demons. God is the ruler of all, and evil spirits are at his disposal. He calls forth hail from its house and it obeys (Ps. 147:17). The Old Testament attributes all good and evil to the one and only omnipotent God of Israel and the whole earth. It was only in this way that the monotheism of the Old Testament was maintained. Any other thinking created the impression that there was another God in the universe and suggested that the God of Israel was not completely in charge. The present African Christian scene, with its fascination with the powers and with the influence of demonic forces, gives the impression that there is a power struggle between God and the ruler of demonic forces — Satan. However, we do not find this idea in the Old Testament. The idea of spirits outside of God's domain is found mainly in the intertestamental writings, such as the Book of Tobit, which attributes the destruction of human beings to evil and envious spirits.

The Tannaitic or Rabbinical Judaism that developed after the first

---

20. Foerster, "Daimon," 11.

21. Merrill F. Unger, *Biblical Demonology: A Study of the Spiritual Forces Behind the Present World Unrest* (Wheaton, Ill.: Van Kampen, 1952), 2.

century bases the concept of spirits on that of angels. Not much is known about the function of these spirits, but Rabbinical Judaism, which follows the Old Testament view, professes that magicians were able to have contact with them. Rabbinical Judaism normally referred to these spirits as spirits of uncleanness, a fitting description since it held that an individual could become unclean by walking around their dwelling places. This belief was partially behind the practice of hand- and foot-washing that date to the first century. Significantly, this belief is similar to current African Christian belief regarding contamination by demonic forces. While in Tannaitic Judaism visiting certain places could open one to contamination, in the African understanding most of the contamination comes through food or other gifts. The strong link with witchcraft in the African conception is missing, however, from Tannaitic Judaism. Since the main function of these demons is to inflict harm, sickness is commonly attributed to them.[22] Other Tannaitic names include "demons of sickness" and "seducing demons." Again we may draw some parallels between these names and the African belief that malevolent spirits, including demons, cause sickness, and that these demons can also entice people to sin. It is in the Tanakh that demons are brought into "firm connection with Satan either now or later."[23] Therefore, while Satan exists and can inflict harm on people through his demons, the Jews were confident that God and his angels, along with the study of the Torah, were able to protect against them.[24]

The belief that demons are minions of Satan that can be warded off through confidence in God and his angels and through Torah study takes on clearer expression in pseudepigraphical Judaism, which produced a number of writings between the Old Testament and the Rabbinical period. Not only do we find reference to demons as subordinate agents of Satan, but we also find evidence that the influence of surrounding cultures, especially the Babylonians, stimulated belief in demons.[25] Because pseudepigraphical Jews were convinced of the presence of demons at work in the Gentile world, from this period forward they no longer traced all evil back to the rule of God. While God still sent punishing angels, "there [was] a stench of evil in the world that could only be accounted for by the evil of demonic powers."[26] And since they no longer attributed all evil to God, some occur-

22. Foerster, "Daimon," 13.
23. Foerster, "Daimon," 13.
24. Foerster, "Daimon," 14.
25. Foerster, "Daimon," 15.
26. Foerster, "Daimon," 16.

rences were out of God's control. "This way a linguistic and material basis was given for dualism within the spirit world and the way was prepared for its later development."[27] Indeed, by the New Testament era, the concept of a dualistic spirit world was in place.

Demonology in the New Testament

It is with the New Testament that African Christians claim the most demonological continuity. The New Testament view of demons is very akin to that of later Jewish thought. Here, as in the Old Testament, there is not as much fascination with demons or demonology as we might assume. According to one biblical scholar, even though there is more recorded activity of demons in Jesus' time, we find "only eight case studies of actual encounters."[28]

Though the word "demon" is hardly mentioned in the New Testament, Christ's contemporaries believed in their existence and activities. It is possible that the term "demonic" applied to various illicit spiritualist enterprises during the first century. St. Paul, for instance, conceived of witchcraft activities as meddling with demons (Gal. 5:20; see also Rev. 9:21, 18:23, 21:8; 22:15). When we consider the bulk of the New Testament and its message versus the small percentage devoted to demons and spirits, we could say that there is a restraint on the part of the New Testament authors regarding demons and their activities. This apparent restraint is because the New Testament lacks "the general interest in the powers of darkness which is so palpable in the pseudepigrapha. It is also due to the fact that there is no relative autonomy of demons as in the latter Judaism as a whole."[29] There is also a lesser presence of demons in the Epistles and Acts than in the Gospels. A. Scott Moreau suggests that

> The relative paucity of the overt examples of demonic confrontation is
> one indication of a shift from a form of direct power encounter with de-

27. Foerster, "Daimon," 16.

28. A. Scott Moreau, "Demon," *Evangelical Dictionary of Biblical Theology*, ed. Walter A. Elwell (Grand Rapids: Baker Books, 1996), 163. He cites as examples Jesus' temptation in the synoptic Gospels (Matt. 4:1-11 and parallels), the healing of the mute man (Matt. 9:32-33; Luke 11:14), the blind and mute man (Matt. 12:22-23), and others. In all, it is a small percentage in comparison to forty healing miracles.

29. Smith-Christopher, "Daniel," 18.

mons to a focus on knowing and correctly applying the truth to thwart demonic influence.[30]

In this comment we find at once some indication of differing attitudes toward demons and a key factor for the apparent lack of fascination with demons in the Epistles. The purpose of the early church was not to engage demonic forces in a power struggle, because they had learned through the death and resurrection of Jesus Christ that all the powers of darkness were subject not only to him but to all who belong to him. Therefore the way to fight demonic powers was no longer to have a toe-to-toe engagement with them but to know and embody this truth.

There is yet a further difference between the New Testament conception of demons and that of the African Christian. The New Testament, interestingly, does not speak of individual, seducing spirits, as some pastors teach. On the contrary, Jesus and the Apostles taught that evil thoughts come from the heart (Matt. 15:19) or that God has given people up *eis adokimon noun*, "to a reprobate mind" (Rom. 1:28 — KJV). When the evil desires that come from the heart are fully grown, they bring forth sin, which leads to death (James 1:13-15). While the Bible does speak of a spirit of jealousy (Num. 5:14) or the spirit of fear (2 Tim. 1:7), it also speaks of a spirit of grace (Zech. 12:10), a spirit of truth (John 14:17), and a spirit of glory (1 Pet. 4:14). If we can understand the latter group as personifications of the work of God's Spirit among God's people, then we can see the former examples as personifications of the harmful work of the Evil One. We need not always conceive of the language of "spirit" as implying an individual or personal agency.[31] Furthermore, the Bible speaks of no particular kinds of demons responsible for specific sins.

> No demon of lust was expelled from the adulterous woman (John 8), or from the woman of ill-repute mentioned by Luke (ch. 7), or from the incestuous people of Corinth (1 Cor. 5). No demon of avarice was expelled from Zacchaeus, no demon of incredulity from Peter after his triple betrayal. No demon of rivalry was expelled from the Corinthians whom Paul had to call to order.[32]

---

30. Moreau, "Demon," 164-65.

31. Perry, *Deliverance*, 103-4.

32. Léon Joseph Suenens, *Renewal and the Powers of Darkness* (London: Darton, Longman & Todd, 1983), 17, cited in Perry, *Deliverance*, 104.

Sometimes, however, certain addictive behavior may cause us to wonder if there is not an evil or demonic power behind it. Most addictive behavior stems from a desire for a particular substance which becomes compulsive until it eventually dominates and controls a person's life. The effect of addiction on the individual, as well as on friends and family who seek to help, has often been likened to the influence of a demon.

In *God the Spirit,* Michael Welker discusses modern demon possession and calls attention to the fact that what we read of demonic possession in Jesus' day has its modern corollary in addictive behavior. Jesus' encounters with demons demonstrate that "the free formation of the will of the possessed person is suspended in the cases described. Without the free contribution of the affected person, he is controlled to his own harm and to his own endangerment."[33] Furthermore, these demonic powers make it impossible for the individual to seek or receive help, and the tenacity of the demons' hold on the individual renders helpless those who seek to help.[34] Asking where we can find modern examples of such demonic presence, Welker points to places

> where *situations of individual and collective suffering* are present that are perceived as agonizing and disintegrative, but at the same time are stabilized and stubbornly defended. For instance, addiction, drug problems, epidemic greed, . . . ecological exploitation, and excessive debt politics call attention to such "demonic forms" of human persons and human societies endangering and destroying themselves.[35]

In the face of human powerlessness against addictive behavior, the African assumes the presence of a seductive spirit that constantly lures the individual to such self-destruction. The truth is that addictive behavior may simply be an illness that has a demon-like hold on an individual. A program for addiction rehabilitation coupled with prayer may be a preferable approach to dealing with the problem than the prayer of deliverance alone. Long-term recovery also requires a change in behavior. In Jesus' own examples of healing, which includes forgiveness, he sometimes cautions the person he has just restored to be careful of how he or she lives (John 8:1-11). Therefore,

---

33. Michael Welker, *God the Spirit,* trans. John F. Hoffmeyer (Minneapolis: Fortress, 1994), 198.

34. Welker, *God the Spirit,* 199.

35. Welker, *God the Spirit,* 202.

while casting out demons from the oppressed is one of the biblical injunctions to the church, it is not the only way that God makes a person whole. Even after a miraculous healing, the individual needs a life of God-centered prayer, Bible reading, fellowship with other believers, and participation in the Eucharist to grow in a life of grace, free from fear of the past.

There is yet another dimension of Jesus' healings that bears mention. We find often in Scripture that when Jesus cast out a demon from a person, he forbade the demon from acknowledging who he was.[36] Demons recognized their fate in his presence and came out of people at his command. However, Jesus never did anything to give undue attention to the demons, and was never interested in their acknowledgment. For instance, when the disciples jubilantly return from their mission in Luke 10, Jesus tells them that the true cause for celebration is in something far greater than the feats of power they had just witnessed. Luke records this exchange for us, and it is important to look at it in its entirety to understand what was important in Jesus' mission:

> The seventy returned with joy, saying, "Lord, in your name even the demons submit to us!" He said to them, "I watched Satan fall from heaven like a flash of lightning. See, I have given you authority to tread on snakes and scorpions, and over all the power of the enemy; and nothing will hurt you. Nevertheless, do not rejoice at this, that the spirits submit to you, but rejoice that your names are written in heaven." (Luke 10:17-20)

To Jesus, witnessing the fall of Satan from heaven and demons submitting in his name is not the same cause for joy as seeing people enter the Kingdom.

Principalities and Powers

Ever since Christianity's introduction to the Gentile world, the multiplicity of gods and other spiritual beings has posed a problem. The approaches African theologians have employed over the years to solve this problem have proved futile. While some, following Western missionary style, tried to impose monotheism on the African Christian scene by imputing a certain unity of gods to African Traditional Religion, others, like the more

---

36. Mark 1:34 and parallels.

radical African Independent Churches, have just replaced the multiplicity of African gods with a multiplicity of spirit beings (such as angels and demons) from the Bible. Neither of the approaches meets the authentic need of the African Christian, whose world is filled with spiritual beings. And yet because the Bible itself speaks of the spirit world and cautions Christians to live as though they were aware of these unseen foes, we cannot ignore the issue. The practical task facing the African theologian is to help the African Christian understand what the Bible means by the "principalities and powers" in the world all Christians are called to live in. By examining how first-century Christians understood the language of power, we may discover new interpretive possibilities for contemporary African Christians.

In his comprehensive studies on the language of power in the New Testament, Walter Wink helps us to consider other meanings of power apart from the spiritual. While his approach subordinates the spiritual aspects of power to socio-political understandings, his observations and comments have relevance for understanding power in the present African pastoral context. He points out difficulties that the average reader meets when trying to understand the language of power in the New Testament. This difficulty lies largely in the fluid way that the word is used throughout Scripture. Drawing synthetically on usage throughout the New Testament, he identifies certain characteristics of power. His conclusion is that power has both physical and spiritual dimensions and that sometimes both dimensions may be operative in any given situation.

In the first place, though the language of power pervades the New Testament, the word occurs in several forms with different nuances in meaning. In several places, we encounter the pair "principalities and powers." We also see "authority and power" (Luke 4:36), "power and name" (Acts 4:7), "kings and rulers" *(archontes)* (Acts 4:26), and "those in authority" *(Hoi exousiazontes)* (Luke 22:25). "Not only do expressions for power tend to be paired, they also attract each other into series or strings, as if power were so diffuse and impalpable a phenomenon that words must be heaped up in clusters in order to catch a sense of its complexity."[37] Consider this passage from Romans 8:38-39:

> For I am convinced that neither death, nor life, nor angels, nor rulers, nor things present, nor things to come, nor powers, nor height, nor

---

37. Walter Wink, *Naming the Powers: The Language of Power in the New Testament* (Philadelphia: Fortress, 1984), 8.

depth, nor anything else in all creation, will be able to separate us from the love of God in Christ Jesus our Lord.

Power, authority, things on earth and in heaven — nothing whatsoever can come between the believer and the God who loves, even unto death. This passage, we will see, emphasizes the relationship of the believer and the Lord and virtually reduces all the powers to *nothing* compared to this relationship. The words used here also tell us that these powers can be earthly as well as heavenly. Wink takes it a step further when he argues that the powers could be earthly governments, political systems, or oppressive sociological systems of any kind. He is careful to stress, however, that we cannot with any seriousness reduce these powers by demythologizing them into categories of modern sociology, depth psychology, and general systems theory.[38] We must attend to the spiritual overtones of these powers while putting them into perspective with their political and social dimensions.

Wink's conclusions about the spiritual aspects of these "principalities and powers" are, however, different from how the African Christians conceive of spiritual power, and more importantly how African Christians understand the biblical depiction of spiritual power. According to Wink, these powers have inner and outer poles, with the inner aspects being the spiritual underpinnings of the outer visible structures. One could almost call it the body/soul relationship on a cosmic level. The inner aspects are the "the spirituality of institutions," the inner essence of outer organizations of power.[39] These inner aspects constitute the "spirit or driving force that animates, legitimates, and regulates its physical manifestation in the world."[40] So whether it is a church or an educational institution or any body that wields power, a spiritual force drives these institutions and determines how they function. If the power "places itself above God's purposes for the good of the whole, then that Power becomes demonic."[41] In this understanding, the demonic is not an inherent quality in some things; it is what a thing becomes when it usurps God's creative purpose for it.

There is some scriptural evidence to support Wink's concept of institutional power. In both the Old and New Testaments, we get the distinct impression that God establishes governments, kingdoms, and authorities.

---

38. Wink, *Naming the Powers*, 5.
39. Wink, *Naming the Powers*, 5.
40. Wink, *Naming the Powers*, 5.
41. Wink, *Naming the Powers*, 5.

In the Old Testament, we often hear Yahweh speaking through the prophets to Israel, assuring them that he has set their neighboring kingdoms in their place also. He also sometimes allows these kingdoms to oppress Israel for a period.[42] A classic example in the New Testament is Paul's Epistle to the Romans, in which he enjoins the Christians to be subject to civil authorities because God places them in these positions (Rom. 13:1; see also Heb. 13:17 regarding Christian authorities). It is God who sets up authorities and rulers and kingdoms, and it is God who deposes them in God's own time.

At the same time we face the fact that the above interpretation eliminates the ontological and objective nature of demonic evil, and does not give us a full picture of the complexity of demonic evil as depicted in Scripture. Scriptural testimony envisions these powers as spiritual beings that are inherently evil rather than as earthly structures that become demonic through behavior or choice. Jesus' own emphasis was on this spiritual dimension. The Scriptures tell us in one instance that the "Son of God was revealed for this purpose, to destroy the works of the devil" (1 John 3:8). The synoptic Gospels give accounts of Jesus' confrontation with evil spirits and demonic powers during his earthly ministry, and Jesus' victory over these powers was demonstrated through exorcism — one of the many signs that the Kingdom of God was invading the devil's territory. According to Luke's Gospel, healing and exorcism were inextricably linked to Jesus' liberating proclamation of the Kingdom:

> The Spirit of the Lord is upon me, because he has anointed me to bring good news to the poor. He has sent me to proclaim release to the captives and recovery of sight to the blind, to let the oppressed go free, to proclaim the year of the Lord's favor. (Luke 4:18)

Later in this same chapter, Jesus tells the crowds that he was sent to preach the good news of the Kingdom (v. 43). Thus, the proclamation and enactment of the Kingdom of God seem to be the primary focus of Jesus' ministry. The question then becomes whether we should understand Jesus' mission as entirely spiritual, or whether there were physical, psychological, sociological, and political implications intertwined. At the risk of giving the impression that we can reduce the Bible, or at least Jesus' mission, to a psychosocial or political agenda, it still bears pointing out that in the con-

---

42. A reading of portions of the major prophets and almost all the minor prophets will show that throughout Israel's history Yahweh has been teaching them this lesson.

text of Israel in the first century, the social and political implications of his ministry were not lost on the crowds or on the authorities. In fact, until his death and resurrection, even the disciples were not sure that Jesus' primary mission was not earthly political power.[43] Our guide, however, should not be the setting in which Jesus lived and ministered, nor even the reaction of the crowds. For our purposes, we need only examine Jesus' intention and attitude toward the different aspects of power on which we have touched.

Many argue that Jesus' primary agenda was spiritual: while he healed and cast out demons, his primary mission was to die on the cross for the sake of our salvation. But this narrow, spiritual soteriology limits salvation to the hereafter. Regarding the Kingdom of God, Donald Bloesch points out:

> While the Old Testament tended to conceive of the kingdom of God as a restored earth and the deliverance which God effects as political-social, the New Testament gave a spiritual interpretation of salvation which did not deny its social implications but pointed beyond history to an eternal kingdom.[44]

Jesus was concerned with a life that was full and complete here on earth. In many ways, he invited people into an attitude and way of life that guaranteed them abundant life. He was explicit about what prevented them from living in the fullness of life that he offered. Nevertheless, his message was focused on intra- and interpersonal relationships rather than on demons and evil spirits. Abundant living comes from being at peace with God, with oneself, and with others.

I am by no means saying that the spiritual dimension of salvation is not of ultimate importance. Barth himself insists that salvation holds conceptual priority over healing, so that the healing of body or mind can be understood as a sign of God's salvation. This spiritual dimension is not an ethereal, wispy, out-of-body experience. The scriptural witness is that the physical dimension is very much a part of the heavenly experience. The parties and banquets depicted in the Bible will continue in an even more resplendent fashion in the fullness of God's kingdom. The physical is as

---

43. After the resurrection and just before the ascension, Jesus gathers his disciples together for what would be his final words to them, and exhorts them to wait in Jerusalem until he sends the Holy Spirit, at which point the disciples ask, "Lord, is this the time when you will restore the kingdom to Israel?" Acts 1:6.

44. Donald G. Bloesch, *Essentials of Evangelical Theology*, vol. 2 (Peabody, Mass.: Prince, 1998), 156.

important in God's scheme of salvation as the spiritual. The two cannot be separated and remain true to a biblical anthropology of "besouled bodies" or "embodied souls."[45] It is not the flesh in its somatic or biological form that God opposes in Scripture. What Scripture stands against are the things that cause the physical body to be corrupted. The Bible decries all of the death-producing effects of conforming to an alien order, and for this reason Christians are urged to crucify "the desires of the flesh" (Gal. 5:16).[46]

In *Unmasking the Powers*, Wink deepens his discussion of the powers and reiterates the point that these powers have both inner and outer dimensions.[47] As in his previous book, Wink makes a distinct effort to balance these inner and outer poles, and in doing so gives us fresh ways of looking at the Bible's understanding of Satan and demons as well as angels, those "principalities and powers" who are assigned to the nations.

According to Wink, it is possible to see Satan as an ally of God rather than as an adversary.[48] He posits that the idea of the devil as an adversary grew over time in Jewish thought. While this idea itself is not original with Wink, his use of it to point out the psychosocial dimensions of these powers is quite intriguing, though not without problems. We often run the risk of reductionism when we subject biblical texts to psychological scrutiny. We see this reductionism often at work in Wink's arguments. Wink's basic thesis regarding Satan is that, rather than seeing him either as God's servant or God's enemy as various biblical texts posit, we might more realistically interpret these two extremes along a continuum, with the perceiver mediating this continuum. That is to say, Satan becomes either an ally of God or an enemy depending on the scope of the perceiver's experience. The problem with such an interpretation is that it makes Satan neutral, and he becomes good or evil relative to the leeway we allow him in our personal lives. While such a view finds support in earlier Jewish thought, to the average reader it makes nonsense of intertestamental literature as well as the bulk of New Testament thought, especially in the light of Jesus' words and attitude toward sin.

---

45. Barth, *Church Dogmatics*, III/2, 327.

46. The New Testament makes a clear distinction between *sarx*, the flesh, and *sōma*, the body. Galatians 5:16-21 tells us of the desires and works of the flesh, which are opposed to God and invariably work against our bodies and souls. The body is made by God and is therefore good; the flesh propels the desires that stem from a misuse of our senses and is therefore evil.

47. Walter Wink, *Unmasking the Powers: The Invisible Forces That Determine Human Existence* (Philadelphia: Fortress, 1986).

48. Wink, *Unmasking the Powers*, 11.

It becomes increasingly clear that we should address these demonological problems from a biblical examination of Jesus' own attitude and example. Jesus took a strong stance against demonic evil, but he did not attribute every sickness to it. His was what we could term a balanced approach, an approach that discerns the presence or absence of evil spiritual beings on a case-by-case basis. If there are evil spiritual beings involved in an ailment, then all of the resources of the church are available through Jesus and should be applied to the sufferer's situation. With a balanced approach, we cannot rule out other causes and sources of illness, but rather must acknowledge them, and in this way we can introduce alternative resources to aid the ailing individual. In this regard some of Wink's comments about Satan bear repeating despite their drawbacks.

Wink suggests that we do ourselves a disservice when we "straightjacket" Satan into rigid doctrinal categories. "Satan is not a fixed, unnuanced figure. The tendency of some Christians to regard Satan as unambiguously evil breeds a paranoid view of reality."[49] And I do not hesitate to point out that the problem with contemporary African Christianity is its paranoia of demonic evil. This is the case to such an extent that people see demons in everything and anything and expend a great deal of energy engaging demonic powers in warfare. We can use an example from witchcraft to illustrate this point.

In chapter two we discussed the belief that all witches have animal familiars and described how these animal familiars operate. In addition to snakes and owls, which are the most common, recent testimonies of ex-witches point to the fact that familiars are numerous and include common household pests. For this reason people fear cockroaches, the common housefly, and ants: witches claim to be able to transform themselves into any of these creatures and inflict harm on intended victims. In one such testimony at a deliverance and revival crusade, the former witch, now a pastor, told the congregation how he had operated in the past. As a fly he would wait until the intended victim sat down to a meal. The fly then hovered around until it landed on the food. If the person ate any portion of the food that the fly had landed upon, then the harm he intended would afflict the individual.[50] While the purpose of the crusade was to bring deliverance to those who felt they were in bondage to spiritual powers, the graphic de-

---

49. Wink, *Unmasking the Powers,* 33.

50. I was a participant observer at the crusade/revival/deliverance at Evangelical Presbyterian Church, Mamprobi, Accra Ghana.

scription of the actions of witches and the fact that even simple household creatures might inflict harm on unsuspecting victims became the focus of discussion among the groups. What made this story more believable was that it was told by a pastor. If such evil exists and can come through creatures such as flies, and if there is no way to tell the difference between a normal fly and one that is an animal familiar of a witch, there should be little wonder that people might see demons everywhere.

But the obverse does not serve us well either. "The rejection of Satan altogether by others has scarcely worked better. It induces blindness to the radicality of evil, trivializes the struggle for conscious choice, and drives the satanic underground, converting the unconscious into a cesspool of erupting nightmares."[51] The present Judeo-Christian understanding of Satan, Wink insists, comes from the "ethicalization" of Yahweh through the course of Jewish and Christian history.[52]

In earlier Judaism, Satan was the adversarial agent of God's divine judgment and wrath. This role changed as Satan increasingly came to be seen as the embodiment of evil in Jewish apocalyptic writings. The theological tension that resulted made it increasingly difficult to imagine Satan as an agent of Yahweh, and this tension eventually gave way, splitting Satan away to become God's rival by the advent of Christianity.[53] The outcome was an autonomous or semi-autonomous Satan, the adversary of God and humankind that we imagine today.

When Satan split from the Godhead, the powers under his control went with him. Early Christians viewed these powers as evil and responsible for inflicting harm on people, which is how Wink explains the biblical understanding of witchcraft. Witchcraft, according to Wink, is part of the repressed unconscious and reflects a "split in the Christian psyche, aggravated by an even more basic split: the repression of women."[54] This claim makes sense of the fact that women are the ones most often accused of witchcraft. They are the ones denied power in the political scheme, and "witchcraft and Satan worship represented an attractive gesture of defiance to a patriarchal God and to a male dominated society. And it provided a means of seizing power against them."[55]

Wink, in his usual psychological and sometimes reductionistic mode,

51. Wink, *Unmasking the Powers*, 33.
52. Wink, *Unmasking the Powers*, 36.
53. Wink, *Unmasking the Powers*, 36.
54. Wink, *Unmasking the Powers*, 37.
55. Wink, *Unmasking the Powers*, 38.

finally invites us to ponder whether Satan is not so much "a person, a being, a metaphysical entity," but rather "a function in the divine economy." For this reason, he enjoins us to move toward "the transformation of Satan as an archetype."[56] This way we arrive at what Freud posits as the goal of analysis, "to move from the unconscious repression of negative elements to the integration of what can be redeemed and the *conscious repression* of what cannot."[57]

To illustrate the above point, I will use Wink's analysis of the narrative of the Gerasene demoniac found in the synoptic Gospels. In this narrative, Jesus and his disciples chance upon a man from the Decapolis who is possessed by demons and living among the tombs. When Jesus confronts the man, the demons speak up and announce that their name is "Legion," and plead that they be allowed to live in a herd of swine nearby. Jesus grants their request, and the herd of swine rush down the cliff into the sea and drown. While many might see this as an account of a real incident, Wink reads the story of the Gerasene demoniac as myth. Wink writes,

> Here mental illness becomes metaphor: the Decapolis was possessed by legions! But through the scapegoat, aggression against the Romans has been transferred to the demons. In Gerd Theissen's words, the demons "speak Latin, present themselves as a 'legion' and like the Romans have only one wish: to be allowed to stay in the country." Mythological language and bizarre pathology act as a screen to mask political unrest that cannot be safely expressed.[58]

In the Western world of the former Roman Empire, this institutionalization of demonic powers may be a real avenue for interpreting pathology. We could thus label some of the biblical stories of deliverance from demonic possession as such. Could we say this of contemporary Africa? Of what "institutional" powers could our present pathologies/demonic possessions be indications? Could we lay them at the door of former colonial powers or despotic post-colonial dictatorships? Is it possible that with ancient social systems in limbo and modernity not yet fully in place, Africans feel themselves floundering as if suspended between these two opposing traditions? For most Africans caught at the crossroads of modernity and tradi-

56. Wink, *Unmasking the Powers*, 40.
57. Wink, *Unmasking the Powers*, 40.
58. Wink, *Unmasking the Powers*, 46-47.

tion, life is increasingly stressful. This stress may contribute to the dreams and sometimes pathological disturbances reported by some parishioners. Though the conscious mind cannot readily understand the metaphorical language of dreams, with help we might come to understand what Morton T. Kelsey refers to as "the dark speech of the spirit."[59] We can interpret these phenomena within a psychological framework that makes sense of the complex factors that people in Africa struggle with. Possible psychological interpretations are the subject of chapter five.

While Wink helps us probe the language of power in the biblical narratives and suggests alternative understandings, his interpretation leans more toward reductionism, seeing demons and evil spiritual powers as socio-political structures rather than as inherently evil spiritual beings. The Bible does present us with both types of evil, but the Gospel narratives seem to indicate that the weight of interpretation should fall to the spiritual side. And it is also clear that, at least in the New Testament, Satan is not a neutral force but an enemy of God and God's people.

Michael Perry's point about how Satan evolved from his position as court prosecutor in the book of Job to an antagonist in the New Testament might help sort out some of the confusion regarding how to understand Satan from biblical as well as extrabiblical sources. Perry suggests that Satan was originally Yahweh's court tester, especially when we see Yahweh give him permission to send evil as a test of Job's godliness (Job 1:6-12; 2:1-10). "It is not long, however, before the Satan begins to get defiled with the pitch he is touching, and his cynicism and eventual opposition to Jahweh begin to show."[60] In the incident in Zechariah, when Satan stands and accuses the high priest Joshua, he is not as neutral as he was in the Job narrative, and Yahweh rebukes him for his accusations (Zech. 3:1-2). Satan is also depicted in 1 Chronicles 21:1 as the one who incited David to count the people of Israel. From here on Perry concludes,

[B]y the time of the New Testament, Satan has become a name of God's archetypal enemy. This is his role throughout the New Testament, from Matthew 4:1 where he tempts Jesus in the wilderness and is told to "get thee hence," to Revelation 20:2, where the "dragon, the old serpent,

59. Morton T. Kelsey, *Dreams: The Dark Speech of the Spirit: A Christian Interpretation* (Garden City, N.Y.: Doubleday, 1968). This was republished as *God, Dreams, and Revelation* (Minneapolis: Augsburg, 1974).

60. Perry, *Deliverance*, 101.

which is the Devil and Satan" is bound and cast into the abyss for a thousand years.[61]

While Satan may have begun as part of God's court, he eventually becomes God's opponent. His aim is to wage war against God's kingdom, but the New Testament conviction is that the war has been fought and won in the advent of Christ and in his victory over sin and death. In the Gospels we read accounts of head-on clashes between Jesus and Satan in healings and other works of power. Such an emphasis is limited in the Epistles, not because Satan is no longer at war with the Kingdom of God, but because as some of the writings indicate, Paul needed to stress "that the battle is within the human soul and that it requires human consent and human struggle to accept the salvation that God has provided."[62]

Thus far we have explored biblical understandings of the demonic and the use of the language of power in the New Testament. We can draw the conclusion that not all diseases are attributable to demons, and that not all power implies spiritual power, but that some afflictions are the result of socio-political oppression. With that understanding, a balanced approach to viewing and understanding demons and other spiritual forces is more in line with the Bible's own witness.

Spiritual Forces in the African Context

The approach that would be most beneficial in the present African context is one that recognizes the place of spiritual and other forms of demonic power to both explain and help with Christian counseling. We must note that African Christians believe that there is a unique ingredient mediating their existence that makes them more susceptible to demonic attacks, whether through possession or oppression. This, in sum, is the idolatry of their forebears and the ensuing generational curse upon their lives. African Christians who advocate and participate in deliverance have offered reasons for the peculiarity of the African situation.

Evangelical Christians believe strongly that, willingly or unwillingly, all Africans participate in the sins — the idolatry — of their ancestors. Whether Christian or not, the power of the ancestral sin and its repercus-

---

61. Perry, *Deliverance*, 101.
62. Perry, *Deliverance*, 139.

sions follow Africans throughout their lives. According to this teaching, accepting Jesus as Savior and Lord is not enough to break the yoke of bondage produced by these curses on the Christian's life. It takes a special kind of prayer — what is usually termed deliverance, prayed by people specifically anointed by God to carry out works of deliverance — to free Christians from this bondage.

We need to ask why the sins of the Christian's ancestors follow him. Why isn't baptism in Christ sufficient to negate all past sins? Again, African Christians claim that in the Scriptures, curses linger on through generations, and that they need special prayers, as well as particularly gifted people for these deliverances. Here we note Jesus' injunction to the disciples about the kind of prayers required to cast out demons. On one occasion a man brings his son to the disciples of Jesus to cast out a demon, but they could not. After Jesus casts out the demon from the boy, the disciples wonder why they could not do it. Jesus responds, "This kind can come out only through prayer" (Mark 9:29). Matthew's account says that it is because the disciples lacked faith (17:20). The Ghanaian church interprets these verses to mean that there are different kinds of demons and that some require special kinds of faith and power to deal with them. Thus, only some believers have the gift to deal with these special kinds of demons. Yet it is also possible that Jesus might be teaching his disciples that the power to cast out demons does not inhere in them, but comes only through prayer. Their prayer then would be an indication of their faith, without which they could do nothing. But what is important about this account is that Jesus enters into the situation and heals the boy. Jesus still heals people today, even when the person who needs healing has little faith.

There is some biblical support for belief in lingering curses, as well as for the idea that the punishment for sin may fall upon the next generation. However, there are within the same passages teachings that people will be punished only for their own sins (Jer. 31:29-30; Ezek. 18:1-32). Moreover, in the new covenant, in the Christ event, the one who has become a curse for us takes away our curse and all its effects. Barth puts it well when he says that in Christ the sinner is at once judged and restored. There remains no other sacrifice for us to offer except this, which has already been offered and which is efficacious for all time. Baptism ushers us into God's life, which means that we belong to God forever.

> Through His Holy Spirit He has begotten me again, me who was in sin, unto a lively hope that I may recognise myself as His child — in my sin,

my lost condition, my earthliness, may recognise myself as righteous before Him. Not because I am that in myself, but because in Christ He has called and chosen me, has promised these His gifts to me through the Holy Spirit, because He has sanctified me, that is, singled me out so that I need not regard myself as lost, but as held by Him, comforted by Him, led by His Hand. And the meaning of Baptism is just this — that we have this promise of participation in this inconceivable life of God. God's life for us in Christ — in us through His Holy Spirit — that is the Christian life.[63]

If African Christians would believe this fact of God's love for them and God's life in them, they would experience less apprehension about sin and its effects, and more joy and freedom in their lives.

Gentile Christians in the New Testament came from a background similar to Christians in Africa. They had multiple gods, worshiped idols and emperors, and dabbled in astrology and magic. If they did not have peculiar demonic problems that required a certain extra-supernatural intervention, then it could be argued that African Christians, who come from a similar background, should not need this extra-supernatural intervention either. Moreover, the first-century Christians from the Gentile world lived closer to the idolatrous ways of life than the third- or fourth-generation Christians in twenty-first-century Africa have. For them, Christ and his redemptive work were new. For the twenty-first-century African, however, the time-less truth encapsulated in the Scriptures is still available. If demonic evil was the primary concern of those early Gentile Christians and the Apostles who ministered to them, they would have devoted a greater portion of the Epistles to those issues, especially because early church practice included the performance of exorcisms on new believers before they were baptized.[64] But a reading of the Epistles shows that their interest was in helping believers live their lives in a way that embodied what they believed, both in public and in private. In light of this, for African Christians to insist on the uniqueness of their situation can only mean one thing: it would imply that the African gods, demons, or evil spirits are more powerful than they were in the first century or at any other time.

What then shall we say about the role of special prayers and specif-

---

63. Karl Barth, *The Christian Life*, trans. J. Strathearn McNab (London: Student Christian Movement Press, 1930), 14.

64. See for instance *The Shepherd of Hermas* or *The Life of Anthony*.

ically anointed people to deliver those who labor under ancestral curses? While Jesus himself taught his disciples on one occasion that certain demons could not be cast out except through prayer and fasting, he did not single out any particular disciples for the task of casting out demons. The power to cast out demons does not inhere in the one who casts them out, but rather in the One in whose authority they are cast out. When we focus on who casts out demons and invest our belief in the people God uses to do God's bidding, we run the risk of setting up spiritual hierarchies within the body of Christ. Furthermore, such focus often results in a cult around a particular "man of God," and the repercussions affect thousands of people.

In chapter two we examined MacNutt's discussion about who is qualified to pray for deliverance, and we maintained that the biblical teaching instructs that all individuals in the community of believers are granted grace to pray such prayers through their union with Christ. At the same time, we also recognize in light of St. Paul's teaching on various gifts within the church as discussed in 1 Corinthians 12-14 that some of the early church fathers read into this list of gifts of the Spirit the special ability to cast out demons, or the gift of exorcism. The overall thrust of the Scriptures, however, leads us to the conclusion that while some may have a special gift in this area, other Christians are not precluded from praying for deliverance.

African Anthropology in the Light of
Barth's Theological Anthropology

What we have seen so far in this dialogue between the African worldview (and its claim to biblical continuity) and Barth's theology shows that human beings can live in the cosmos in the fullness of life that God grants them. The African worldview posits a tripartite constitution of the human being as body, soul, and spirit, with the spirit having precedence over the other two. Things that occur at the level of the body and soul have already happened at the spirit level. At this point we need to reconsider the anthropological data explicated in the previous chapter, and ask: Does the way African Christians understand human beings and their place in the cosmos promote the freedom for which they were made and for which such a high price was paid? Or does their present worldview leave them in further bondage?

As we discussed in chapter two, in both the Anlo and Akan language groups, there seems to be an unclear distinction between soul and spirit. The biblical understanding fleshed out by Barth's theological anthropology resolves some of the apparent contradiction in the terminology and usage of the words as they appear in the Anlo and Akan understandings. Sometimes they use the words that describe the soul and the spirit interchangeably. For instance the Ewe refer to the life soul as *gbogbo,* which is the same word for spirit, so that in translating the Bible into Ewe, the Holy Spirit was translated as *Gbogbo Kokoe.* It is possible to conclude, at least among the Ewe, that the idea of the human being as tripartite does not have a very strong basis, considering the interchangeability of the words *spirit* and *soul.* What seems clear is that the human being has a tangible (physical) part and an intangible part. Barth's claim, supported with scriptural evidence, that human beings are "embodied souls" and "besouled bodies," souls undergirded by God's spirit, offers a viable alternative to understanding and responding to the human being from a pastoral perspective. Moreover, if Jesus is a man and he is man for us, then his constitution would be patterned after ours. Since he is a "besouled body" and an "embodied soul," we can assume that that is what human beings are. To bridge the gap, we must let the spirit that undergirds Christ undergird us also, so that we are always led in the way of Christ.

The most troubling aspect of pastoral theology in Ghana is its understanding of the demonic and how it manifests itself and affects both believers and unbelievers. What, for example, do we make of demon possession or some demonic cases we have witnessed and to which we can testify? What of the dreams, visions, and trance-like stupors that loved ones or we ourselves have had? How do we reconcile them with our discussion so far? How do we distinguish what is spiritual from what is not? Alternatively, is it the case that one flows into the other? It is important to emphasize the unity of body and soul, which is undergirded by the spirit. However, we also need to recognize and make room for a differentiation within the unity. Especially with regard to diagnosis in the African context, how do we determine what is truly demonic from what is psychological or sociological pathology?

Barth's explication of demonic possession and how to deal with it is helpful for understanding and perhaps curtailing the Ghanaian Christian tendency to demonize and spiritualize all ailments. Barth's attitude toward the demonic is based on New Testament examples as well as his study in *Church Dogmatics,* IV/3, of the exorcism of a young woman in the parish of Pastor Johann Blumhardt. In Blumhardt's account of the exorcism, during which the woman was finally freed, the demons cried out "Jesus is Victor!" as they left her body. We note that the demons cast out by Jesus also make similar assertions about Jesus' power and authority over them.[65] Barth devotes an entire section of the *Church Dogmatics*, IV/3, to demonic possession and Jesus' victory over demons, but he doesn't limit the meaning of the phenomenon to the spiritual realm alone. As Daniel J. Price points out, Barth delineates three aspects of demonic phenomenon in his approach.[66] According to Barth,

> the occurrence during which Blumhardt heard this cry: "Jesus is Victor," has three aspects. On the first, it is realistically explained in the sense of ancient and modern mythology. On the second, it is explained in terms of modern psychopathology, or depth psychology. On the third, it is not explained at all but can only be estimated spiritually on the assumption that the two former explanations are also possible and even justifiable in their own way.[67]

Barth's own interest is in the third perspective, the spiritual approach, but he does not ignore or belittle the other two. In the African Christian community, the first and the third perspectives are operative; African Christians realistically understand and treat the demonic from a spiritual perspective. The danger is that with only a realistic explanation of the demonic, they ignore more nuanced and varied aspects.

The Barthian approach does not ignore or label unscientific (as others might see it) the realist explanation, but there is room to offer other plausible explanations that take in all facets of demonic possession. Barth's understanding and treatment of the demonic allow us to use it in tandem with depth psychology to explicate and treat cases that have demonic undertones. As Deborah Hunsinger points out, there is a sense of "psychopathological and spiritual complexity" evident in Barth's treatment of the demonic.[68] Such a balanced approach ensures that the individual suffering from demonic possession receives complete care from both a theological and a psychological perspective. From a biblical perspective, and as explicated by Barth, we get an understanding of the demonic that subjects

---

65. Examples abound in the Gospel accounts; see especially the healing of the boy gripped by seizures (Matt. 17:14-20).

66. D. J. Price, *Karl Barth's Anthropology in Light of Modern Thought* (Grand Rapids: Eerdmans, 2002), 303.

67. Barth, *Church Dogmatics*, IV/3, 170.

68. Deborah van Deusen Hunsinger, *Theology and Pastoral Counseling: A New Interdisciplinary Approach* (Grand Rapids: Eerdmans, 1995), 203.

demons and their influence to the finished work of Christ. In Christ all demonic powers are subject to the one who believes, and the simple prayer of faith can bring freedom.

When the simple prayer of faith does not bring the desired relief, then we need to turn to other plausible explanations. Turning to other explanations and other helping professions is not a defection from or lack of faith. We can incorporate other explanations and approaches within the third dimension of the spiritual approach; that is, prayer for healing can continue while psychological counsel is sought. We should view such prayer as a celebration of the various gifts and avenues for healing that God has granted human beings.

I must stress that I am making a distinction here between the limits of the theological, or spiritual approach, and God. When I say that theology has possibilities and limits in addressing human ailments and advocating that in some cases psychological insights might also prove beneficial, I am not saying that God has limits and possibilities. Theology as a human construct, however revealed and inspired, is not a replica or substitute for God and, like all human undertakings, is imperfect. Our Christian belief is that our imperfect attempts at understanding and apprehending God and gaining insights for our lives are always mediated by grace and by "a great high priest" (Heb. 4:14) who is "able for all time to save those who approach God through him, since he always lives to make intercession for them." (7:25). While I support the place of prayer and discernment in the quest for healing, I also want to suggest that psychological tools, when used with discretion, can help in distinguishing what is purely spiritual from what is a combination of spiritual, psychic, and somatic causes.

CHAPTER FIVE

African Theological Anthropology:
A Jungian Perspective

Introduction

In the preceding chapter, I raised a series of questions that we could answer only partially by using strictly theological insights. These questions had to do with how we are to understand the reported presence of the demonic in dreams and other psychic phenomena, especially when they prove resistant to prayer. As I have argued, African theological anthropology emphasizes the unity of spiritual, somatic, and psychic occurrences to such a degree that there is little differentiation among them. Whatever happens in the body or the soul has already taken place in the spirit. Ghanaians, for example, interpret both the causes and purposes of illness or misfortune in a framework that is spiritual. They believe that witchcraft, demons, and malevolent powers are the spiritual forces that all persons must contend with. One consequence of this belief system is that when prayers are not answered, even more emphasis is put on the need for deliverance from demonic forces.

Contemporary Ghanaian society is in a state of flux. There is tension between old ways of life, which are being disrupted by imported, modern ways, which have not been fully grasped. The old tribal support system is inadequate to meet the new challenge of modernity in the urban centers, and yet there is no firm structure to take its place. This situation puts added pressure on a people living under harsh economic conditions. Attempting to preserve the old while embracing the new, as most Ghanaians do, results in high levels of stress and fragmentation. The situation is especially precarious for women, who are most responsible for household work and for nurturing the family. It is little wonder that women are the ones who are more likely to frequent churches and move from pastor to pastor, seeking deliverance from demonic forces that they believe are threatening their very lives. The search of the fragmented self for wholeness and integration drives people to seek out help. In this environment pastors are the primary source of help, not only because their services are free, but also because the problem is perceived to be of a primarily spiritual nature.

As I mentioned in earlier chapters, pastors in the Ghanaian Independent Evangelical/Charismatic churches use a basic questionnaire to determine the causes of their parishioners' problems. The intent behind these questions is to discern whether demons or witchcraft spirits are indeed the cause of parishioners' complaints. The questions range from what parishioners experience in dreams and visions, to what unusual scents they smell (especially if they cannot detect the source of the odor), to whether they find personal articles mysteriously missing from their homes. The underlying assumption of these questions is that the dreams and visions, the unusual smells, and the loss of personal articles indicate evil spiritual activities against them. Our earlier discussion noted that this pattern of ascribing particular occurrences to evil spiritual forces is directly related to how Ghanaians perceive the world in which they live. Pastoral counseling is, therefore, completely focused on providing a spiritual cure for what is assumed to be a spiritual problem. But not all the problems brought to the pastor's office are of a spiritual nature needing a spiritual cure. For example, in a Church at Pig Farm, Accra, I was introduced to a woman who was brought for deliverance because she was behaving abnormally. She had apparently had more than one deliverance session since her return from England, where she had been living, and she was about to return to London because the pastors of her church judged that she had been cured of her ailment. The woman, however, appeared to me to be dazed and looked more like someone who would benefit from psychological counseling, if not psychiatric care, than one who was able to board a plane and travel to a distant country where she probably had little or no emotional support. Unfortunately, this was not an isolated incident. Recall, for instance, the woman mentioned in chapter one who had come for prayer for an enlarged, probably cancerous, breast. While prayer and spiritual care are certainly needed in times of distress, sometimes psychological and physical intervention is essential. Therefore, for the purposes of pastoral diagnosis and counseling, we must pay proper attention to the psychological aspects of a person's condition, and it is to these psychological dimensions I will now turn.

What would African pastoral theology look like if it were to differentiate the strictly spiritual from the psychological? Could the African pastor helpfully use insights from psychology, so that he need not diagnose all difficulties as evidence of malevolent spiritual powers, or recommend only prayer and deliverance as remedies? Is it possible to distinguish between psychological explanations and spiritual ones? And how may we proceed in this regard so that the individual seeking help receives the best help that the pastor can give, utilizing all available resources? The following observation by James Dittes is a good place to start.

> Psychology, philosophy, and theology may all be concerned with the same phenomenon, such as a particular belief or a particular ritual, but they ask different questions about the phenomenon. Psychological analysis is concerned with the psychological development and the functions of the belief or ritual. Philosophy is concerned with the correspondence between the belief or ritual and some criterion of truth, logic, or goodness, and theology, with its correspondence with such criteria as the will of God and other given norms of faith. The answers to the psychological questions do not necessarily imply or presuppose answers to the philosophical or theological questions. Even a thorough assessment of the psychological history and functions of a particular belief carries no ordinary implications for the "truth" or "faithfulness" of the belief; these still must be ascertained by the criteria appropriate to philosophy and theology.[1]

Thus theological insights address theological issues, and psychological insights apply to psychological issues raised by a particular phenomenon, although I would argue that the most comprehensive truth lies in the realm of theology.

What we know and believe of God from a theological perspective, however, is obviously different from what we know and believe of God from a psychological perspective. From a strictly theological perspective, and particularly from a Barthian perspective, the individual grounds belief in God's self-disclosure and not in any unconscious or even empirical experience. According to Barth, the latter is of no interest to theology because it does not ask the basic questions that psychologists ask. Barth's focus is

---

1. James Dittes, "Religion: Psychological Study," in *International Encyclopedia of the Social Sciences*, vol. 13, ed. David L. Sills (New York: Macmillan, 1968), 416.

on issues of faith and truth, whereas psychologists are usually interested in how religious belief functions in the psychology of the believer.

The pastoral counselor, however, has to be concerned with both of these aspects. The theological and the psychological issues raised by the content of the individual's faith, as well as the processing of that faith, are of interest because they have direct bearing on the pastoral diagnosis and intervention. The key is for the pastoral counselor to differentiate between issues that arise from the psychology of the religious believer, for which she needs psychological insights and answers, and issues of faith, which call for theological insights and answers. Of course, sometimes these issues are intertwined, and the pastoral counselor needs to move back and forth between theological and psychological issues embedded in each case, applying first one insight, then the other, or a combination of the two when appropriate.[2]

Much pastoral counseling in Ghana is concerned with the problem of dreams and their proper interpretation. Currently, counselors treat the causes and interpretations of dreams from a purely spiritual, or theological, perspective. We can, no doubt, gain spiritual insights from dreams and visions. The Bible, as well as church history, attests to the fact that God speaks through dreams and visions, and in the Old Testament we find several allusions to God speaking to the prophets and patriarchs in such a manner. Daniel's dreams and visions, for example, comprise the bulk of the book of Daniel, and in Genesis 37, we read of Joseph's dreams. The writers of the Old Testament assume that dreams are a means by which Yahweh communicates desires and warnings, and we find this same assumption in the New Testament:

> Christianity brought with it various minor amplifications of the traditional Jewish approach to dream interpretation. . . . Church fathers such as St. Clement, St. John Chrysostom, and St. Augustine viewed dreams as pathways to a more intimate grasp of God. These Church leaders pointed out that the origin of dreams is in the depths of the human psyche, placed there by God for purposes of instruction and edification for the dreamer.[3]

2. For a fuller discussion of this method, see chapter four of Deborah van Deusen Hunsinger's *Theology and Pastoral Counseling: A New Interdisciplinary Approach* (Grand Rapids: Eerdmans, 1995).

3. Robert Weathers, "Dream Theory and Research," in *Dictionary of Pastoral Care and Counseling*, ed. Rodney Hunter (Nashville: Abingdon, 1990), 310.

We also need to understand, however, that there are somatic as well as psychic reasons for dreams. Research in sleep and sleep deprivation reported by experimental psychologists shows us the importance of dreams to normal waking life. In one study, students who were prevented from falling into rapid eye movement (REM) sleep for a period were unable to function normally during the day. While these students had slept during the night, their inability to dream affected how they coped with daily tasks. Another study found that REM sleep affects learning of certain mental skills: people taught a skill and then deprived of non-REM sleep could recall after sleeping what they had learned, while people deprived of REM sleep could not. Our physical and mental health seem to benefit from our dreams. But we need to make room for somatic and psychic explanations in our interpretations of those dreams.

Jung, Religion, and Africa

Carl Jung's psychology of the unconscious offers a conceptual framework for understanding paranormal phenomena as psychic occurrences that have their own intrinsic psychological meanings. But his work is especially helpful in the Christian context that we are examining because his basic premise about the psyche, which he never hesitated to call the soul, makes room for a religious component in therapy that is concerned with bringing wholeness to the soul. In her introduction to a collection of Jung's essays, Violet Staub de Laszlo summarizes the core of Jung's therapeutic agenda:

> Psychology and religion — the cure of souls through the care of the therapist and by the grace of redemption, as well as by the self-healing and recreative faculties inherent in the psyche: these themes form the therapeutic aspect of Jung's research.[4]

Both psychology and religion aim at bringing wholeness to the human being, though their means of doing this are often different. African pastoral theology is in a position to facilitate a collaboration between these two fields, as has already occurred in the West, and by doing so it will bring much needed healing to ailing people. Jung is more helpful than many oth-

---

4. C. G. Jung, *Psyche and Symbol,* ed. Violet Staub De Laszlo, trans. R. F. C. Hull (Princeton: Princeton University Press, 1991), xx-xxi.

ers in this regard because he affirms religious aspects of healing, or what De Laszlo terms "the grace of redemption."[5] From a Christian perspective we can utilize Jung's theories to understand the "self-healing . . . faculties inherent in the psyche" as one way that God's work of grace operates in the lives of individuals through physical and psychological care.

Further, Jung is the depth psychologist whose thoughts and research are best suited for exploring the cultural factors that contribute to the psyche's growth towards wholeness. His theory draws upon vital aspects of culture such as fairy tales, myths, stories, and folk tales, some of the vehicles through which cultural norms are transmitted. Because Jung's theories are born out of his examination of those cultural themes with which all peoples are familiar, the concepts may have wide applicability and can be useful for probing the religio-cultural issues raised in Ghanaian pastoral counseling. To this end, I will examine the central concepts of Jung's analytical psychology and draw on their applicability to pastoral counseling in Africa. These concepts include the archetype, the collective and personal unconscious, the self (as distinct from the ego), the persona, the shadow, the anima and animus, and the overarching or central concept of individuation.

First a word of caution: the psychologizing of Christianity has caused many theologians, especially evangelical theologians, to be suspicious of employing psychology in Christian counseling. Nevertheless, the misuse of a discipline should not require its wholesale rejection. Theologians, especially, ought to be aware that a discipline can be misused because theology itself has been and continues to be misused to oppress and dehumanize people. Yet we do not throw the discipline away for that reason. While it is true that some psychologists minimize religious affects and attempt to ridicule religious belief, there are also those, such as Jung, who attempt to interpret religious phenomena according to their implications for the psychology of the believer.

The word psychology can be broken down into its two basic Greek components, *psyche* and *logos,* "the soul" and "words about the soul," respectively. Taken a step further, we might even say that the soul has its own internal logic, its own way of living within the world that it seeks to convey to us. We could learn a lot about the soul and its life if we employed psychology properly. Not all psychic occurrences have exclusively spiritual meanings. When we understand the psyche on its own terms, we can make meaningful connections among otherwise mysterious events.

5. Jung, *Psyche and Symbol,* xx-xxi.

Jung's understanding of the psyche and how it manifests itself in conscious and unconscious life opens up possibilities for interpreting certain paranormal behaviors that we cannot explain from a purely theological perspective. When we offer only theological explanations for paranormal behaviors, then parishioners naturally expect a spiritual cure. In the present African pastoral context, where pastors address paranormal phenomena from a theological perspective, pain, doubt, and sometimes confusion arise when prayers for a cure go unanswered. This pain grows more acute when people assume that the individuals seeking a cure do not have enough faith to receive the required healing or that sin in their lives causes their ailment. The situation is not unlike Job and his three "friends" who tried to counsel him through his sufferings (Job 2:11ff.). His friends brought little comfort and actually left him feeling worse. They were convinced that some unconfessed sin caused his predicament. At one point Job asks, "How long will you torment me, and break me in pieces with words? . . . if it is true that I have erred, my error remains with me" (Job 19:2, 4).

Assuming that God has failed them, the images that such individuals acquire of God and self over time compound their bondage to fear. Not only are they afraid of the demonic forces, they also assume that God is unable or unwilling to help them. These assumptions are detrimental to the persons seeking help. If such individuals continue to be a part of the worshiping community, they will experience a tension between their internal God-image and the God-image presented to them by the tenets of the church. This tension will only increase those emotional problems for which they sought help.

Jung's attitude toward spiritual phenomena is complex. On the one hand, he interprets spiritual events as the activity of unconscious conflicts. On the other hand, he recognizes that psychological explanations come up against their limit in certain inexplicable spiritual phenomena. Jung himself experienced the paranormal activity of the psyche innumerable times throughout his long life. He thus brought to his theories not only an objective psychological approach to spirits as unconscious complexes, but also the knowledge that, from the perspective of feelings and subliminal perceptions, belief in the independent existence of spirits is reasonable. If the problems that Africans attribute to spirits come from unconscious complexes as well as from genuine demonic sources, then Jung's theories about the psyche offer a viable and more nuanced pastoral tool for therapy than is currently available.

There are three further reasons why Jung's psychology may prove useful. In the first place, both a medical and an ecclesiastical heritage enriched his approach to analytical psychology and religious phenomena. He was not a detached objective theoretician but a man who brought his own faith journey to bear on the processes he explored. While some scholars might find this subjectivity questionable, Jung developed a critical method of engaging with his own subjectivity, subjecting his dreams and ideas to a rigorous process of analysis and self-examination.[6]

In addition to this dual heritage, Jung twice visited Africa, not only to study its people but also to better understand himself. Marianna Torgovnick, a cultural critic, notes that Jung's journey to Africa had a tremendous impact on the formulation of his theories:

> When Jung formulated his theories of the human psyche, he did so with his journey to Africa behind him; this was, for men of his generation, the equivalent of the European Grand Tour. To Jung as to many other moderns, Africa is the quintessential locus of the primitive.[7]

Primitive, in this sense, does not carry the pejorative connotations often associated with it.[8] Rather it refers to the vitality of life that comes from being in touch and living with one's affects and emotions. Jung comments on the distinction between European and African ways of life, seeing in the African pace of life, as well as the effusive display of feelings, something the European might emulate. It is primarily the African's natural tendency to live, or, as it were, have their being in their feelings that Jung refers to as "primitive." He explains:

---

6. Contrary to what we might expect, this subjective element can actually foster critical thinking for the very reason that our convictions are influenced by the assumptions and conclusions we arrive at in the course of scientific work. Nevertheless, we must also be aware that human subjectivity can skew our interpretation of facts, and thus the theories we propound. Therefore, extra caution is necessary in projects in which the subjective element, such as religious belief, is an integral part.

7. Marianna Torgovnick, *Gone Primitive: Savage Intellects, Modern Lives* (Chicago: Chicago University Press, 1990), 11, cited in Michael V. Adams, *The Multicultural Imagination: "Race," Color, and the Unconscious* (London: Routledge, 1996), 60.

8. While I have retained the use of this term for its psychological sensibility, there is a caveat. The term *primitive* as employed here may not be technically pejorative, but it is still a racially coded term. Jung's travels should be understood in their historical context: Europeans were producing reams of "scientific" anthropological studies in colonial Africa, a cultural project that produced and codified whiteness through the cipher of the African primitive.

I use the term "primitive" in the sense of "primordial," and . . . do not imply any kind of value judgment. Also, when I speak of a "vestige" of a primitive state, I do not necessarily mean that this state will sooner or later come to an end. On the contrary, I see no reason why it should not endure as long as humanity lasts.[9]

Here the psyche is viewed in its natural, undisturbed state and is in closer contact with what the European is alienated from: the psychic roots of his being. Jung found in his experiences in Africa an opportunity to "reflect psychologically on the European self from the perspective of a non-European other."[10] Africa also afforded him the much-desired opportunity for his "own psychological self-reflection."[11] Since Jung's theories stem in part from his observance of the people of Africa, it is hoped that some of the insights and the theories from his findings may be illuminating in the present African situation.

Finally, Jung's work speaks to the "human condition of doubt and distress, of the search for meaning, of the joyful recognition of universal human sentiment and of the contemporaneous formulation of abiding truths."[12] In short, Jung's work speaks to us in the places where we hurt and hope and search for meaning. These are the places where we seek wholeness and try to become fully human in spite of our brokenness. The people who flock to pastors in the African churches are people in pain searching for meaning and seeking God's intervention. Jung's psychology explicitly addresses the very things Africans — indeed, all people — seek: wholeness, meaning, freedom, and integrity.

Tied closely to the process of becoming whole is the understanding of *spirit* or *the spiritual* that Jung brings to his therapy. By *spirit* Jung does not mean something supernatural or something born of faith. "Spirit" in Jung's thought is simply the inner drive, that which spurs creativity and all

9. C. G. Jung, "Review of the Complex Theory," in *Collected Works,* 2nd ed., vol. 8 (Princeton, N.J.: Princeton University Press, 1969), para. 218. Hereafter cited as *CW.* Again I need to indicate that such phraseology can be viewed as racially coded — it recapitulates the imperialistic, "scientific" knowledge of Africans that is found in earlier writings of Linnaeus, Kant, and Hegel. It does not need to be pejorative to be racialized: the problem is with the kind of knowledge of the universally human that such methods produce, rather than with any implied value judgment.

10. Adams, *The Multicultural Imagination,* 60.

11. Adams, *The Multicultural Imagination,* 60.

12. Jung, *Psyche and Symbol,* intro. by V. De Laszlo, xv.

that contributes to the intrinsic self-healing capabilities of the soul, thus affecting the relationship between the psyche and the soma. Jung is careful to avoid simplistic diagnostic models. Thus, while he asserts the importance of psychic phenomena and explores the growth of the psyche towards wholeness, he is cautious about reducing all inexplicable affects to psychic terms. He believes that we run certain risks when our worldview leads us to believe that "all life processes are psychic."[13] In the first place, such approaches over-generalize and too often lack demonstrable evidence to support their claims. Human beings daily face the possibilities of causes other than the psychic and the pneumatic. When we claim that all things have spirit behind them, we are using the word "spirit" too loosely. The tendency to see all life processes as pneumatic (which is the case in the African situation) or psychic enlarges the boundaries of the psychic to proportions that render it essentially meaningless. Jung argues that "concepts that are too broad usually prove to be unsuitable instruments because they are too vague and nebulous."[14] Thus, he limits the term *psychic* to only those occurrences where it is clear that there is a "will capable of modifying reflex or instinctual processes."[15] When we limit the term *psychic* to those occurrences where there is a clear indication of volition, we can more easily separate true psychic phenomena from the plethora of occurrences that some now categorize as psychic, thus facilitating the therapeutic process.

Jung's Analytical Psychology

Jung based his analytical psychology largely on his understanding of the *archetype*. This theory evolved out of his own self-analysis as well as from his work with psychotic patients in Zurich's Burgholzli Hospital in the early years of the twentieth century.[16] Through this work, Jung discovered that the imagery we experience during dreams falls into perceptible patterns — patterns that are also found in myths and fairy tales in diverse cultures and which are not readily accessible to consciousness or memory. To Jung, these patterns seemed to express "universal human modes of experience and be-

---

13. Jung, *Psyche and Symbol*, 4.
14. Jung, *Psyche and Symbol*, 4.
15. Jung, *Psyche and Symbol*, 4.
16. Andrew Samuels, *Jung and the Post-Jungians* (London: Routledge & Kegan Paul, 1985), 24-25.

haviour."[17] These universal images became known as primordial images. While the particularities of the images change from culture to culture, the underlying patterns remain constant. Thus the archetypal form is universal, though the content is borrowed from the particular culture. Jung hypothesized that the human mind has certain modes of perception that organize the world into these archetypal or collective patterns. All human beings are born, have a mother and a father, experience the sun, moon, and wind, and die. Thus the experience of birth, parenting, natural phenomena, and death is part of our universal human experience, though the meanings attributed to these experiences may be culturally specific. Nevertheless, the psychic apparatus that organizes these experiences falls into particular perceptive patterns. Jung coined the term *collective unconscious* to denote the inherited propensity to perceive reality through these primordial forms.

Prior to the development of the concept of the collective unconscious, Jung hypothesized a more particularized *personal unconscious*. Jung expressed this distinction as follows:

> Certain complexes arise on account of painful or distressing experiences in a person's life, experiences of an emotional nature which leave lasting psychic wounds behind them. . . . All these produce unconscious complexes of a personal nature. . . . A great many autonomous complexes arise in this way. But there are others that come from quite a different source. While the first source is easily understood, since it concerns the outward life everyone can see, this other source is obscure and difficult to understand because it has to do with perceptions or impressions of the collective unconscious. . . . At bottom [these complexes] are irrational contents of which the individual had never been conscious before. . . .[18]

Here Jung distinguishes between two kinds of complexes: (1) portions of consciousness that have been split off and repressed in response to a trauma or some other factor that is related to the individual in a personal way, and (2) psychical entities that have never been in consciousness previously, which are related to the individual in a more impersonal way. Jung retained the term *complex* for the former and applied the terms *primordial image* and *archetype* for the latter. He defined archetypes as "*a priori,* inborn forms

17. Samuels, *Jung and the Post-Jungians,* 24.
18. Jung, "The Psychological Foundations of Belief in Spirits," *CW,* vol. 8, para. 594.

of 'intuition' . . . the . . . determinants of all psychic processes."[19] Thus, the major distinguishing characteristic of an archetype is that it is unconscious and exists in the individual through heredity.[20] Jung was later to refine his concept of the archetype and make a distinction between what he called the archetype as such, that is, how it is in itself, and the archetype as represented, that is, how it manifests itself. He characterized the archetype as such by the term *psychoid*, meaning "soul-like" or "quasi-psychic," due to its irrepresentable nature.[21]

Jung believed that the psyche in its natural state tends toward wholeness, that is to say, each individual strives toward becoming whole, individuated, undivided. His practice sought to bring forth the inherent drive of the psyche toward wholeness by drawing on the psyche's own resources. Jung identified three such inherent capacities of the psyche: (1) the psyche's intrinsic healthiness in its natural state, (2) its compositeness, that is to say, its undivided wholeness, a capacity evidenced in its ability to hold together opposing elements such as its dark and light sides, and (3) its collective nature, which transcends any individual experience. These qualities bind all humankind into one family with one common denominator — a psyche with an inherent capacity to work for its own health and wholeness.

The Archetypes

Archetypes are fundamental to Jung's understanding of the psyche and the human journey to wholeness. Generally, the archetypes consist of the *persona* (the role or function one has in the social world), the *shadow* (the "dark side" of the personality that individuals normally try to hide from the public), the *anima* and *animus* (the male and female contrasexual archetypes respectively), and the *self* (both the goal and center of the personality). According to Jung, the self is the central archetype: "The self is not only the center but also the whole circumference which embraces both conscious and unconscious."[22] This strong emphasis on the centrality of the self has led some of Jung's followers to order the archetypes hierarchically. Some contemporary Jungians have subscribed to this approach and argue

19. Jung, "Instinct and the Unconscious," *CW*, vol. 8, para. 270.
20. Jung, "The Concept of the Collective Unconscious," *CW*, vol. 9, para. 88.
21. C. G. Jung, *Memories, Dreams, Reflections* (New York: Vintage, 1961), 397.
22. Jung, "A Study of the Unconscious Processes at Work in Dreams," *CW*, vol. 12, para., 44.

that there are four types. Jungian theorist Andrew Samuels, for instance, quoting Violet Brome, delineates these four types as the "'shallow' archetypes such as persona and shadow, then 'archetypes of the soul' (animus and anima), then 'archetypes of the spirit' (wise old man and woman), and, finally, the self."[23] Jungian therapy also often proceeds in that order, from the shallow (that is, the processes more accessible to consciousness) to the deeper (the more unconscious processes and less accessible parts of the psyche). Work with the patient progresses in a more or less sequential way from the surface structures to the deeper structures. Samuels, however, thinks that this strictly hierarchical treatment of the archetypes arises out of an "over-literal adoption of Jung's adage that the archetypes are usually dealt with in analysis in a predictable order — persona, ego, shadow, animus/ma, self."[24] Samuels believes that a better approach is to conceive the archetypes as "interrelated planes of imagery" having a definite goal (in this sense the wholeness of the individual).[25]

I believe that Samuels's conception of the archetypes, if employed in the African context, would facilitate pastoral therapeutic work. This is because Jungian therapy is usually a long process, and if the work were to progress in the basic predictable order, it could not be contained in the context of pastoral counseling. The counselee-to-counselor ratio is too high for pastors to devote such extensive attention to any single parishioner. If, however, the archetypes are conceived of as "interrelated planes of imagery," all working toward the wholeness of the individual, then we can hope that extensive work done with one part would in turn benefit the others. In my research I found that most of the presenting problems in Ghanaian pastoral counseling sessions have psychic undertones that arise from the repression of the dark side (the shadow), as well as of the unconscious contrasexual archetypes (the anima or animus). For this reason, the discussion of the import of Jung's theory for African counseling will emphasize Jung's contributions that help individuals understand and come to terms with these two archetypes, showing how they might be integrated into the personality. Rather than repudiate them as frightening and malevolent spiritual presences, we might interpret psychic phenomena as disowned parts of the self that the person needs to become conscious of and integrate.

23. Violet Brome, *Jung: Man and Myth* (London: Macmillan, 1978), 276-77, quoted in Samuels, *Jung and the Post-Jungians*, 32.

24. Samuels, *Jung and the Post-Jungians*, 32.

25. Samuels, *Jung and the Post-Jungians*, 32.

The Psyche

The focus of Jung's interest was the human *psyche* in its totality, in both the conscious and unconscious components. He was most interested in the unconscious processes of the psyche, those portions that are not under the control of the ego. Jung believed that the psyche expresses itself through its imaginative activity, individually or collectively, by means of its own symbols. For example, Jung identifies the *mandala* as a central and culturally widespread symbol of wholeness, which is often represented as a square surrounded by a circle. Mandalas are found in cultures throughout the world, including both Anlo architecture and Akan symbolism.

The goal of the psyche is to attain wholeness by integrating both the conscious and the unconscious through a process known as *individuation*. For Jung, individuation "implies becoming one's own self [or] . . . 'coming to selfhood' or 'self realization.'"[26] However, we should not confuse this understanding of individuation as "the coming of the ego into consciousness."[27] Such an understanding is nothing more than "ego centredness and autoeroticism."[28] Thus individuation is not egocentrism, as one might think, but rather a process that leads the individual to realize that the self is made up of more than a mere ego. The self comprises "as much one's self, and all other selves, as the ego. Individuation does not shut one out from the world, but gathers the world to oneself."[29]

We can see Jung's concept of individuation as analogous to Jesus' admonition to his followers that they can only find themselves if they lose their lives for his sake. Those who make Christ the center of their lives will become all that they were created to be. But those who close in upon themselves are attempting something alien to their own being and will lose their created potential. The psychological corollary in Jungian terms is the ability of the ego — the center of personal consciousness — to lose its autonomy to the self, which is the center of the whole psyche. This does not mean that the ego gives up its responsibility for making choices; it only means that it recognizes that it is not the center of the personality, and it allows the center, which is the self, its rightful place. In this sense the ego, which is in touch only with conscious material, will be better served if it submits to the self,

---

26. Jung, "The Function of the Unconscious," *CW*, vol. 7, para. 266.
27. Jung, "On the Nature of the Psyche," *CW*, vol. 8, para. 432.
28. Jung, "On the Nature of the Psyche," *CW*, vol. 8, para. 432.
29. Jung, "On the Nature of the Psyche," *CW*, vol. 8, para. 432.

which encompasses both conscious and unconscious material. The psyche has its own ways of prompting the ego toward submission. Sometimes these promptings take place as dreams, the content of which compensates for the one-sided life of the ego by interjecting elements that the individual has consciously rejected or unconsciously repressed. Other psychic manifestations include unconscious wishes, fears, and fantasies.

Jungian therapy sometimes seeks to channel these fantasies through what Jung calls "active imagination," in order to align them with the views of the patient's ego perspective. Based on his study of the unconscious mind, Jung showed how fantasy material has its own clear pattern of organization, almost as if there were an unconscious intention of the psyche to manifest certain motifs to compensate for an imbalance in the ego. Through active imagination, we allow our fantasies to reveal the emotions that are concealed in the images. If we can stay with the process, as Jung discovered through his own experience with active imagination, we can continue the process of individuation and work toward attaining wholeness without the help of a therapist.[30]

For Jung, play, fantasy, and imagination are the building blocks of all creativity. Jung discovered that during play, aspects of ourselves that are normally outside of awareness begin to emerge. Jungian analyst Joan Chodorow writes,

> The great joy of play, fantasy and the imagination is that for a time we are utterly spontaneous, free to imagine anything. In such a state of pure being, no thought is "unthinkable." Nothing is "unimaginable." That is why play and the imagination tend to put us in touch with material that is ordinarily repressed.[31]

Ordinarily non-assertive people may exhibit normally unseen streaks of violence, for example, while playing or watching their favorite sports, and we wonder if they are the same people we know. Inhibitions seem to be lifted for the moment, and ego gives way to a part of the repressed unconscious.

Alternatively, when we watch children at play we may also witness some of the therapeutic effects of imagination. Chodorow points out that during play children have the opportunity to write different endings to traumatic situations in which they may have been involved:

30. Jung, *Memories, Dreams, Reflections*, 176-77.
31. Joan Chodorow, ed., *Jung on Active Imagination* (Princeton, N.J.: Princeton University Press, 1997), 5.

> In the spontaneous dramatic play of childhood, upsetting life situations are enacted symbolically, but this time the child is in control. The child gains a sense of mastery by playing out little dramas voluntarily with a doll, a stuffed animal, or perhaps an imaginary companion, or a pet, sibling, or friend. Unlike the original experience that may have been overwhelming, in play the child gets to imagine all kinds of variations and creative resolutions; for example, an imaginary companion may bring courage, strength, magical powers — whatever is needed. . . . The key to the transformative healing process is — play is fun. In a seemingly magical way the life-enhancing emotions (joy and interest) modulate and transform the emotions of crisis. It seems that symbolic play is based on an inborn psychological process that heals emotional pain. . . . Whether we are children or adults and whether we are conscious of it or not, imaginative activity goes on all the time. It is expressed in many ways including play, dreams, fantasy, creative imagination and active imagination.[32]

As counselors we can capitalize on this inherent tendency of fantasies to lend themselves to being organized to help individuals become aware of their fantasies in a way that brings wholeness to them.

According to Jung, the psyche has its own aims and goal for wholeness. While a person may not always achieve perfect harmony or perfect psychic balance, the psyche naturally propels itself toward psychic homeostasis. Samuels offers examples of this drive toward psychic balance, which Jung understood as a kind of self-regulation of the psyche. Examples of the compensatory function of the unconscious to the conscious state would include a very "macho" man discovering that parts of his personality are very feminine, or a comparatively independent person realizing that he secretly loves to be babied. Those who are very meek in their conscious personality may have dreams of being aggressive and find that aggression, when mixed with the gentleness, would give more of a balance to their personality.

The Persona and the Shadow

The *persona* and the *shadow* are concepts that are fairly easy to grasp. The persona is the aspect of the personality we first encounter when meeting someone new. In such encounters in Western cultures, people usually in-

---

32. Chodorow, ed., *Jung on Active Imagination*, 5-6.

troduce themselves by what they do: "Hello, I am Dr. Wadewor, your cardiologist." The word "persona" derives from Roman theater and denotes the mask that an actor dons and doffs at will during a performance. The persona is therefore the front individuals put on, the public image they present, the socialized image that makes living with others possible, helping them to act in a manner befitting their status or the immediate social setting. The persona ensures that we function in our various roles and fulfill social as well as individual expectations. Each profession, for example, has a typical persona. Interaction with people on a professional level reveals the persona, not the whole person. What we perceive is the adaptation of the person to the professional role. If a person unconsciously identifies with his persona, he has mistaken a part for the whole and radically constricted his personality — he will not have access to its full breadth and depth. He will think that the sum total of who he is is simply what he does.

The shadow, by contrast, is the dark side of the personality that the individual consciously or unconsciously tries to hide from the public. In a certain sense, its contents are opposite to the persona. We do not allow the shadow to appear and be subjected to public scrutiny precisely because it contains what we fear, despise, and regard as unacceptable in ourselves. It takes considerable effort for us to recognize our own shadow as a present reality and to face its primitive darkness. By primitive darkness I mean the uncontrollable, untamed, uncultured aspects of human nature. Yet, we can be brought to acknowledge the presence of our shadow as a first step in the long journey toward integrating it into the ego-personality. Some individuals can achieve this without therapy. However, this is not an easy process, because the individual typically puts up a lot of resistance. According to Jung,

> These resistances are usually bound up with *projections,* which are not recognized as such, and their recognition is a moral achievement beyond the ordinary. While some traits peculiar to the shadow can be recognized without too much difficulty as one's own personal qualities, in this case both insight and good will are unavailing because the cause of the emotion appears to lie, beyond all possibility of doubt, in the *other person.* No matter how obvious it may be to the neutral observer that it is a matter of projections, there is little hope that the subject will perceive this himself. He must be convinced that he throws a very long shadow before he is willing to withdraw his emotionally-toned projections from their object.[33]

33. Jung, "The Shadow," *CW,* vol. 9:2, para. 16.

Since *projections* (the automatic process by which we perceive contents of our own unconscious in others) are not under conscious control, by definition the individual is not aware of them. If the individual is unaware of his projections and assumes that he is relating to people or to the environment as they really are rather than how he perceives them to be, then he unknowingly lives in isolation from his environment. The world he relates to is not the real world, but an illusory one. For example, if a man projects onto another his own feelings of hatred and fantasies of murder, thereby assuming that the other person hates him and wants to kill him, he will relate to the person as though she really had those evil intentions against him. But since in reality the other person has no such feelings or intentions toward him, the man is in fact relating merely to his own projections and not to the other person. Not only are his perceptions of the other distorted, but he also remains completely unaware of his own feelings.

Jung's attitude toward the shadow makes it potentially helpful in understanding and providing counsel for the psychic problems prevalent in the African church. Unlike Freud, Jung objected to overemphasizing the dark side of the psyche without giving equal attention to the light, creative, and intrinsically wholesome side. He did not repudiate the dark shadow side, but he saw it as integral to the whole and inseparable from the light side. He argued that the health of the psyche was linked to how these two opposing sides were held together.

The work toward wholeness can only take place on an individual basis. Jung defines *individuation* as the "process by which a person becomes a psychological 'in-dividual,' that is, a separate, indivisible unity or 'whole.'"[34] Because African pastoral counselors work primarily with individuals who seek wholeness in one form or other, they are in a unique position to help in this process.

Anima and Animus

The *anima* and *animus* are the unconscious contrasexual aspects of the male and female psyches respectively. They express what is psychologically feminine in a man and psychologically masculine in a woman. For Jung, "[t]he animus corresponds to the paternal Logos," while the "anima

34. Jung, "Conscious, Unconscious, and Individuation," *CW*, vol. 9, para. 490.

corresponds to the maternal Eros."[35] He uses the terms *Logos* and *Eros* as "conceptual aids" to describe what he conceives of as the "connective" or relational quality of Eros and the "discriminating and cognition" quality of the Logos.[36] The anima and animus act as a link between the individual conscious and the collective unconscious. As such, they promote images that represent what any given culture perceives as the inherent qualities of men and women. While the *content* of the images that appear in dreams and visions might be culturally determined (because the anima and animus develop in relation to cultural norms), nevertheless the forms as contrasexual elements themselves are transcultural. That is to say, the form but not the content is transcultural. The universality of these contrasexual images is discussed in Jung's description of the anima:

> [E]very man carries within him the eternal image of woman, not the image of this or that particular woman, but a definite feminine image. This image is fundamentally unconscious, an hereditary factor of primordial origin engraved in the living organic system of the man, an imprint or "archetype" of all the ancestral experiences of the female, a deposit, as it were, of all the impressions ever made by woman. . . . Since this image is unconscious, it is always unconsciously projected upon the person of the beloved, and is one of the chief reasons for passionate attraction or aversion.[37]

These inherent contrasexual components of the psyche are portions of the self that are normally shut out or unrecognized when people function consciously. They are parts of the self that are considered *not* to be the self because they are characteristics usually assigned to the other gender. For example, in Ghanaian culture today, gentleness and meekness are seen as "feminine" qualities, while aggressiveness and assertiveness would be seen as "masculine." Therefore, a meek or gentle man would try to suppress any gentle affects and tendencies, and a naturally assertive woman would try to hide any aggressive or assertive tendencies. Furthermore, these contrasexual images are often strange and mysterious and sometimes even frightening, yet at the same time attractive. They are also loaded with potential to lead the psyche to health and wholeness. If men and women can assimilate

---

35. Jung, "Syzygy: Anima and Animus," *Psyche and Symbol*, 14.
36. Jung, "Syzygy: Anima and Animus," *Psyche and Symbol*, 14.
37. Jung, "Marriage as a Psychological Relationship," *CW*, vol. 17, para. 338.

the various aspects of their contrasexual psyche into their conscious personality, they will live more integrated lives.

Jung discovered in his therapeutic sessions with patients that images from dreams and fantasies were frequently the opposite gender of the dreamer. This is not to say that his patients did not dream about people of the same gender, but rather that the troubling dreams, those that were laden with psychic difficulties, invariably contained the images of the opposite gender of the dreamer. He attributed the contrasexual nature of the images to the fact that, for instance, a male will tend to project onto the female gender that which is foreign and strange to him, and vice versa. Jung thus saw the anima and animus as projection-making aspects of the psyche. That which is undesirable, denied, unconscious, or consciously suppressed is then projected onto the other. However, the anima and the animus not only express themselves in dreams at night, they can also manifest themselves in conscious, waking life.

According to Jung, it is difficult to acknowledge the presence of these projection-forming archetypes without overcoming "certain moral obstacles such as vanity, ambition, conceit, resentment, etc."[38] Added to these obstacles are intellectual difficulties, such as a lack of ability to understand the nature of the projections or how to cope with them. Yet it is possible for people to come to terms with their inner man or woman, and each of us becomes a more integrated person when we do so.

The Ego

The *ego*, which is not to be confused with the self because it forms only a part of the self, is the conscious component of the psyche. Jung calls the ego "the complex factor to which all conscious contents are related," the "centre of the field of consciousness" and "the subject of all personal acts of consciousness."[39]

While the ego rests on unconscious factors, it is itself a conscious factor. It is acquired in the individual's lifetime, first "from the collision between the somatic factor and the environment," and then subsequently through personal acts of consciousness within the individual's given en-

---

38. Jung, "Syzygy: Anima and Animus," *Psyche and Symbol,* 17.
39. Jung, "The Ego," *Psyche and Symbol,* 3.

vironment.[40] Culture thus plays a vital role in the formation of the ego. But the ego is not the full personality; it is only the *"conscious personality,"* and thus only a partial person.[41] Since the unconscious is difficult to grasp cognitively, it is very easy to mistake the ego for the full personality, a mistake that prevents us from knowing the whole person. To know the full individual, what Jung calls the self, we must also attend to the unconscious.[42]

While in theory we can conceive of the ego as limitless because we cannot place boundaries on the field of consciousness, empirically it "finds its limit when it comes up against the *unknown*."[43] The unknown that confronts us comes both from outer sources, which we experience through the senses, and inner sources, which we experience via images and emotions. Jung designated this inner world the *unconscious,* and he saw the content of consciousness resting on both somatic and psychic bases. That is to say, sometimes the things that the ego experiences arise from conscious as well as from unconscious sources. The ego is also concerned with action, and thus human free will and willpower are moderated by the ego.

The various autonomous complexes interact with the ego as they come into consciousness. Jung called the process the *transcendent function.* When a conflict is unconscious, the ensuing tension can manifest itself in physical symptoms, often in the stomach, the back, or the neck. We normally experience conscious conflict as a moral or ethical tension. In acute cases of conflict, especially ones based on honor or love, the conflict arises out of the tension between what our hearts and minds are saying. We can resolve a conflict only if we are conscious actors in what is going on. We have to consciously own the conflict:

> The objection is at once advanced that many conflicts are intrinsically insoluble. People sometimes take this view because they think only of

---

40. Jung, "The Ego," *Psyche and Symbol,* 5.

41. Jung, "The Ego," *Psyche and Symbol,* 5.

42. It is likely that Africans understand this concept, which is why the two people groups under review have such an extensive and sometimes confusing understanding of the soul. Africans know that human beings are more than what is readily observable. It is for this reason that they posit different types of souls. However, the tendency to see all things from a spiritual perspective causes them to interpret manifestations of the unconscious or the psyche pneumatically. The Anlo, for instance, call an aspect of the soul *amea nnuto,* "the real person or the owner of the being."

43. Jung, "The Ego," *Psyche and Symbol,* 3.

external solutions — which at bottom are not solutions at all. . . . A real solution comes only from within, and then only because the patient has been brought to a different attitude.[44]

Jung had a strong belief in the ultimate goodness of conflict because he saw it as the avenue for the self-regulation of the psyche. If the tension between the opposite feelings within the individual can be brought to consciousness and held there, then something will eventually occur to naturally resolve the internal conflict. The transcendent function is born out of the tension that exists between the conscious and the unconscious as the individual deals with the conflict. "It is called 'transcendent' because it makes the transition from one attitude to another organically possible,"[45] and because the new attitude transcends and encompasses both sides of the conflict.

The transcendent function is the psychic bridge between ego-consciousness and the unconscious as one practices active imagination or dream interpretation. It brings together opposites in a new way in a reconciling effort to regulate the psyche. This change is primarily a newfound attitude toward oneself and others. The original feeling of being "stuck" gives way to a freedom to proceed in a purposeful manner.

Jungian analyst Ann Belford Ulanov recounts an extended clinical example that demonstrates this idea. She describes the case of a young woman who entered analysis in her early twenties because of what she felt was a dead space inside her, a space caused by an "early and deep wound — a feeling that her mother did not love her."[46] This dead space felt like a deep hole, one into which she might eventually fall and "disintegrate. It was this feeling that threatened her with madness." Through therapy she was able to arrive at the place where she could face "that abyss and engage it in active imagination." The depth of her pain could only express itself in the image of the *Mater Dolorosa*. Ulanov interprets this image of the Virgin weeping tears of blood as the transcendent reaching out to this young woman, informing her "that through her personal pain she was touching everyone's pain, the pain of the world." At this point in her therapy, the young woman recalls a dream in which

---

44. Jung, "Some Crucial Points in Psychoanalysis," *CW*, vol. 4, para. 606.

45. Jung, "The Transcendent Function," *CW*, vol. 8, para. 145.

46. Ann Belford Ulanov, *The Functioning Transcendent: A Study in Analytical Psychology* (Wilmette, Ill.: Chiron, 1996), 9.

She circles a pool and thinks of escaping the scene through a back door, but decides against it. When she returns to the pool area, she is drawn to her knees before a red, gold, and blue statue of the Virgin.[47]

For this young woman, the task was to remain with this image and yet not fall into unconscious identification with it, which would result in ego inflation (that is, the ego becoming over-accentuated). "Accordingly, she continued crossing back and forth from her conscious position to that of the *Mater Dolorosa* archetype — the work of the transcendent function persisted."[48] With the transcendent function acting as a bridge supporting her and her own ability to withstand identification with the image, her personal ego was enlarged. Ultimately,

> the limitless tears of blood expressing the pain of this dead space in her turned into limitless human tears and finally found their limits. They stopped. The dead space now filled with personal human feeling. She felt in immediate contact with the Suffering Mother, the Theotokos Virgin of her earlier dream, but she felt her own small human identity too which had digested and integrated her portion of the world's sorrows. A dream summed it up: "I dreamed I have found the place of truth, far away from civilization, in the mountains. This is what matters. Everyone sees the mountain from their own perspective."[49]

This is the transcendent function at work. Here the opposites are the dead space inside her on the one hand, and the image of the Virgin Mother on the other. The dead space is the original, consciously held attitude, whereas the Virgin filled with endless pain is the unconscious archetype. The ego is torn between these two opposites, trying to keep to the middle ground. She crosses back and forth between them and draws energy and a sense of being from the compassionate mother. She is able to do this by neither identifying with the real mother (whose lack of love for her could have turned her into a cold and lifeless human being) and thereby falling into the abyss of non-being, nor by identifying with the image of the *Mater Dolorosa*, the all-compassionate mother. By moving back and forth between the conscious attitude and the unconscious archetype, she allows both images to work on her.

---

47. Ulanov, *The Functioning Transcendent*, 9.
48. Ulanov, *The Functioning Transcendent*, 9.
49. Ulanov, *The Functioning Transcendent*, 9-10.

The result is a new attitude, a well-grounded, feeling person who is neither larger-than-life (the archetype) nor egoless (the former conscious attitude). She is in touch with her human limits: she is not dead and unfeeling, like the dead space inside her, nor does she have the endless compassion of the *Mater Dolorosa*. The transcendent function acts as a support system, uniting the opposites at work in her so that the end result is a grounded human being who can feel and give love within the limits of finitude. What has occurred is not an answer or solution to the problem, but rather a movement from "either/or" to "both/and"; it provides an opportunity for the individual to make a choice, a choice which ultimately proves beneficial.

In order for the ego to hold two opposites in tension so that a third entity — the mediatory symbol — can come through, discrimination is required. The ego must be able to distinguish ego from non-ego, what is acting from what is acted upon, what is positive from what is negative. It is only after such discrimination that the ego can hold together and balance the various antitheses that ultimately produce the new synthesis. This ego function is thus important in the process of individuation, since individuation entails the conscious realization and integration of the individual's entire potential. The individual can bring forth and work on the less-developed sides of her personality that she would typically hide. The result is a fully-rounded, more multi-dimensional person. There is a balance to the personality that did not exist before.

The Self

The purpose of Jungian analysis is more than strengthening the ego; it is to form a *self* that is fully individuated. As the ego is the center of the conscious aspect of the human being, so the self is the core of both the unconscious and the conscious. Thus, the self transcends the ego. Jung differentiates the self and ego further:

> The ego stands to the self as the moved to the mover, or as object to subject, because the determining factors which radiate out from the self surround the ego on all sides and are therefore supraordinate to it. The self, like the unconscious, is an *a priori* existent out of which the ego evolves.[50]

50. Jung, "Transformation Symbolism in the Mass," *CW*, vol. 11, para. 391.

The relationship between the ego and the self might be understood as analogous to the Barthian relationship between the body and the soul. We see the body and soul as a differentiated unity, an asymmetrical order in which the soul has logical priority over the body. Similarly, while the self transcends the ego, it nevertheless cannot exist without it. The transformation of the ego comes about through the ego's ability to integrate both the light and the dark sides of the archetypes, including this central archetype, the self. Samuels interprets Jung's vision of the self as "the potential for integration of the total personality."[51] This integration includes all "psychological and mental processes, physiology and biology, all positive and negative, realised and unrealised potentials, and the spiritual dimension."[52] In other words, the self holds together all that we are physically, emotionally, and spiritually in the past, present, and future. Because of this past and future nature of the self, the individual has the potential to live hopefully and meaningfully.

There is a deep purpose to each person's life, a *telos* toward which all activities point. When life does not make sense, when there is no *telos,* the self flounders and seeks to redress the situation. Since the self automatically seeks to integrate all aspects of life, it will work to synthesize all the archetypes to achieve an equilibrium that will sustain it. If we develop one aspect of the psyche over others, pathological imbalances occur, throwing the self out of joint. This self-regulating characteristic of the self makes it the central archetype of the personality, because the wholeness of the individual hinges on the capacity of the self to integrate all aspects of the personality. Jung called this self-regulating capacity *compensation.* In compensation, the self automatically corrects any imbalance or one-sidedness in the psyche. The unconscious compensates for the one-sidedness of consciousness. Balance is, however, not easy to achieve, and initial attempts are often fraught with difficulties. The imbalance shows up somewhere in the psyche and makes itself known through symptoms such as anxiety, disturbing emotions, or physical discomfort.

Several types of imbalance manifest themselves in the psyche at different times. For instance, in an ego/self imbalance, either the self may overwhelm the ego, endangering it, or the ego might resist subordination to the self and identify with it. If the self overwhelms the ego and does not allow it to come into being, it hampers the conscious integration of the

51. Samuels, *Jung and the Post-Jungians,* 91.
52. Samuels, *Jung and the Post-Jungians,* 91.

shadow into the psyche. We need the ego for this work because the shadow is, by definition, the shadow of the ego. On the other hand, if the ego usurps the role of the self, which can be equated with wholeness, then the whole person is lost. For wholeness to be achieved, the ego must be subordinated to the self.

Identification with the self can occur in two ways. First, the self can assimilate the ego by the self, in which case the ego falls under the control of the unconscious. When the ego falls under the control of the self, the individual lives in a dream-like state. Second, the ego can control the self, and the ego thus becomes over-accentuated. In both cases the result is inflation, producing disturbances in adaptation. According to Jung,

> In the first case, reality had to be protected against an archaic . . . dream-state; in the second, room must be made for the dream at the expense of the world of consciousness. In the first case, mobilization of all the virtues is indicated; in the second, the presumption of the ego can only be damped down by moral defeat.[53]

In Ulanov's example above, if the young woman had identified with the psychic image rather than drawn energy from it in order to live her life more fully with human limits, ego inflation would have resulted. She would probably have conceived of herself as the Virgin Mother, feeling as though she carried all the pain of the world within her own being. On the other hand, if she had resisted subordination to the self and lived only at the conscious level, she would have internalized the bad mother and lived as a cold, dead being, closed off from all relationships.

An ego/persona imbalance brings about confusion between the real identity and a person's social role. The individual cannot differentiate between being a whole person and having a function. If the particular function or role no longer exists, the individual feels lost. When people identify with their jobs or their roles, for example, they lose all sense of identity upon retirement. Similar disorientation can occur when a woman who identifies herself solely as a wife suddenly becomes widowed or divorced.

In ego/anima or animus imbalance, the ego may completely reject its contrasexuality, subjecting the individual to stereotypical, one-sided behavior. Often such behavior is an exaggeration of what the society sanctions for each gender. A woman may go out of her way to be submissive, even

---

53. Jung, "The Self," *CW,* vol. 9:2, para. 47.

self-effacing, in circumstances that require that she take a stand and speak out; a man may not cry even if he loses a beloved child. Other times the ego might identify completely with the contrasexual archetype, resulting in behavior that in any given culture might be termed "womanish" in a man or masculine in a woman.

Usually in ego/shadow imbalance, some vital part of the personality is repressed. For example, sometimes people will repress their sexual or aggressive tendencies because they see them as dangerous or evil. But these tendencies are not necessarily evil in themselves. If we deny or repress them, we cut them off from consciousness, but they grow all the more powerful. We no longer experience them as a part of the self but rather project them onto others. As long as we project these "undesirable" aspects onto others, we do not have a real self or a real relationship. We live with an illusory self and an illusory other. If we integrate the split-off aggression or sexuality into our psyche, we live a much fuller life with its foibles and weakness. We live within the limits of our humanity rather than try to be something we can only fail to be — perfect. Integrating the split-off aggression or sexuality thus allows us the freedom to be truly human with the possibilities and limitations that come with humanity. In other words, integration will give balance to our personality. Sometimes, however, we identify with the shadow. In such an instance, we see no good in ourselves, constantly beat ourselves down, and make ourselves and those around us miserable.

The self can only be fully individuated — made whole — and come into its own when the psyche is allowed to embrace all its contradictory realities. As Jung puts it, both the conscious — things that occur by day — and the unconscious — those revealed by night — must be integrated. But integration can occur only "when its double aspect has become conscious and when it is grasped not merely intellectually but understood according to its feeling-value."[54] The individual must be willing to give both intellectual and emotional assent to the contents that need to be integrated.

A remarkable characteristic of the self is its drive toward wholeness. The self seeks wholeness automatically. In fact, whether the individual desires this wholeness and works toward it or not, "wholeness is . . . an objective factor that confronts the subject independently of him."[55] It is as if the self has its own agenda and works relentlessly toward it, pushing aside anything in its pathway that would prevent the self from attaining wholeness.

54. Jung, "Self," *Psyche and Symbol*, 30-31.
55. Jung, "Self," *Psyche and Symbol*, 31.

Jung on Wholeness of the Self within Christianity

Jung offers an interpretation of the wholeness of the self by means of the imagery and concepts of the Christian tradition. Drawing on resources from Scripture as well as writings of early church fathers, Jung explains from a psychological perspective the meaning of the Christian injunction to "be transformed by the renewal of your minds" (Rom. 12:2). Jung begins his discussion with the theological premise that since the "God-image in man was not destroyed by the Fall but was only damaged and corrupted ('deformed')," it can be restored by grace.[56] Theologically, humanity receives the grace that restores the God-image in all its fullness "in the descent of Christ's soul to hell" — the traditional *descensus ad inferos*.[57] Jung understands that the transformation process can also be described from a psychological perspective. From this point of view we achieve wholeness through the transformation of the mind as enjoined in Romans 12:2: "and do not be conformed to this world, but be transformed by the renewing of your minds, that you may discern what is the will of God." Jung understands this as the process by which the God-image is restored in human beings:

> The totality images which the unconscious produces in the course of an individuation process are similar "reformations" of an *a priori* archetype. . . . As I have already emphasized, the spontaneous symbols of the self, or of wholeness, cannot in practice be distinguished from a God-image. Despite the word *metamorphousthe* ("be transformed") in the Greek text . . . the "renewal" *(anakainosis, reformatio)* of the mind is not meant as an actual alteration of consciousness, but rather as the restoration of an original condition, an *apocatastasis*. This is in exact agreement with the empirical findings of psychology, that there is an ever-present archetype of wholeness which may easily disappear from the purview of consciousness or may never be perceived at all until a consciousness illuminated by conversion recognizes it in the figure of Christ. As a result of this *anamnesis* the original state of oneness with the God-image is restored. It brings about an integration, a bridging of the split in the personality caused by the instincts striving apart in different and mutually contradictory directions.[58]

56. Jung, "Christ, A Symbol of the Self," *Psyche and Symbol,* 39-40.
57. Jung, "Christ, A Symbol of the Self," *Psyche and Symbol,* 39-40.
58. Jung, "Christ, A Symbol of the Self," *Psyche and Symbol,* 40.

Jung is not trying to address the spiritual concept of sanctification so much as to describe the self's coming to wholeness by using Christian symbolism, interpreting it psychologically, and in this regard he has some insights worth considering.

Jung goes on to say that "[t]here can be no doubt that the original Christian conception of the *imago Dei* embodied in Christ meant an all-embracing totality that even includes the animal side of man."[59] Since redemption is total and complete, it automatically includes both the good and the bad, even the aspects of our nature that we would rather hide. In addition, while we are saved by the finished work of Christ, we are nevertheless invited to work out our salvation in fear and trembling. It is possible that one aspect of working out our salvation entails allowing the suppressed dark side to come into the light as well. Thus, salvation of the total human being must also include psychological healing.

African Anthropology in Light of Jungian Analytical Psychology

For many people, the inner and outer worlds are so split that the individuation process becomes stunted. Some are flooded by their inner world and pay too much attention to it, while others, who hardly recognize the presence of their inner world, need help to pay attention to it. The aim of therapy is to help the individual build a bridge between the inner and outer worlds so that the self attains the balance that is necessary for wholeness. Jungian therapy by its nature enlarges on the data clients present and invites individuals to perceive connections, motivations, and feelings of which they are hardly aware.

Much of what Jung discovered in therapy with his patients has relevance for African pastoral counseling today. When we consider the numerous reports by both parishioners and pastors regarding the presence of demonic activity that seems to persist in spite of prayer, we wonder whether the reasons or causes for such "demonic" activity have not been misdiagnosed. Psychologically, when unconscious content is not allowed to manifest itself, whether through repression, suppression, or social prohibition, the repressed unconscious will find an outlet in one form or another. As we have seen several times, the psyche works its way toward growth — at all costs. This growth entails dealing with both conscious and unconscious processes.

---

59. Jung, "Christ, A Symbol of the Self," *Psyche and Symbol*, 41.

Much of the psyche's work toward wholeness as Jung envisioned it depends on how it is able to incorporate and balance contradictory elements, especially the contrasexual anima and animus. In a society where there are clearly defined roles and expectations of behavior, however, parishioners suppress the contrasexual, complementary aspects of the psyche in more intense ways. In Ghanaian culture, for example, men and women are assigned strict masculine and feminine roles from which they are not allowed to deviate. Not only are there guidelines for acting, there are even prescribed norms for thinking and feeling. Ghanaians often ridicule effeminacy or any slight tendency toward female characteristics or mannerisms in a man, and a man will go to great lengths to suppress such behavior in himself. In pre-colonial days, male initiation rites expunged any traces of feminine qualities, and child-rearing practices handed down through generations also fostered the rejection of all that is considered feminine in men. Similar guidelines exist for girls and women. Any tendency toward the masculine in a woman, ranging from having a masculine physique to being verbally and mentally astute (especially in the presence of men), is socially unacceptable. Many proverbs and myths warn of the ill effects of stepping out of socially prescribed female roles, mapping a social and moral landscape that prevents women from transgressing the prescribed boundaries.[60]

Under such circumstances, the repressed contrasexual side often finds expression through behavior forbidden by society, or such behavior will manifest itself in dreams or in "demonic" possession accompanied by displays of unusual strength. During an exorcism, it sometimes takes a couple of strong men to hold down an average-sized woman. From a Jungian perspective, we can interpret these manifestations as the psyche's way of embracing the opposite side to achieve the balance that is needed for wholeness. We could say that such a woman is "animus possessed." If, on the other hand, a woman is free to be assertive and aggressive when the occasion calls for it, and does not feel self-conscious or embarrassed by such behavior, then she has integrated the contents of her animus. Her masculine side becomes an acceptable part of her ego-attitude and strengthens it.

Some parishioners report dreams in which they are engaged in sexual activity, and such dreams may be evidence of the psyche's search for completeness through this most intimate of human expressions. But *incubus*

---

60. For examples of these proverbs and myths and the adverse effects they have on women, and thus the whole society, see Mercy Oduyoye's *Daughters of Anowa: African Women and Patriarchy* (Maryknoll, N.Y.: Orbis Books, 1995).

and *succubus* experiences bring enormous concern in Ghanaian pastoral counseling. Many pastors report parishioners who have dreams in which they feel they are being sexually molested and on waking they find evidence of sexual activity on their bodies, such as semen. Stories like these are not new in Christian history. In their history of pastoral care in the church, William Clebsch and Charles Jaekle document similar cases. In the early church, the sexual act that occurred to women in dreams was imputed to an incubus; when the person molested was a male, the spirit was a succubus.[61] In the section on sacramental medicine, the authors draw on a large body of literature from early church practice that deals with the activities of these spirits and how the church responded to the reported molestation. They also show that the medieval church believed causes other than spiritual ones explained sexual experiences during dream states.

As we have already seen, contemporary Ghanaian culture, with its prescribed gender roles and expectations, as well as its interpretation of biblical injunctions on female subordination, makes Ghanaian women especially susceptible to the complexes that may result in such dreams. In all of the pre-counseling interviews that I observed, a significantly larger number of women than men reported suffering from the incubus as well as other demonic possession states. As I investigated these situations closely, I found evidence that many of the reported incidents arose from the repression of natural instinctual drives. If, in a marital conflict, the cultural as well as religious norms forbid the woman to act in what might be termed an aggressive manner, she is likely to suppress her opinions and any behaviors that might express them. The result is very likely the disturbed dreams, often of a sexual nature, that parishioners report. A Jungian would see the contrasexual animus drawing its sword of power and demanding to be joined to Eros in this most fundamentally intimate manner.

From a Jungian perspective, sexual images in a dream could represent the basic instinct of sexual desire itself or, at the spiritual end of the spectrum, the ultimate image of connectedness and a union of opposites. While some dreams have a sense of the numinous, lifting the dreamer into a deeply felt sense of the spiritual, strong sexual dreams, especially the so-called wet dream, can be the means of bringing the dreamer back to the body. Instead of lifting the dreamer into the spirit, the dreams embody the dreamer. When such dreams are overspiritualized, as is often the case in

---

61. *Malleus Maleficarium* (1486), quoted in William A. Clebsch and Charles R. Jaekle, *Pastoral Care in Historical Perspective* (New York: Jason Aronson, 1983), 194.

Ghanaian Christian communities that believe that such dreams are an indication that one has a "spiritual spouse," people live in excessive fear of sexual dreams. The fear is more than a common fear of nightmares; it is also a fear of the social implications of having a spiritual spouse. Those who have spiritual spouses are unable to marry or maintain an existing marriage. When these occurrences lead to impotence in men or infertility in women, there is added social stress due to the centrality of child-bearing and bloodlines in African cultures. Fear of sexual dreams may also lead to insomnia, which can in turn cause numerous other social, physical, and psychological difficulties. When these difficulties are then blamed on spiritual causes, the cycle of misdiagnosed suffering continues.

The only possibility of breaking the cycle lies in a proper diagnosis and dream analysis so that the most effective therapeutic approach can be identified and brought to bear. The simple prayer of faith uttered by the lowliest of believers can indeed relieve problems that are truly spiritual in nature. But when spiritual resources alone do not bring the required relief, we may be overlooking or ignoring important psychological issues. This is not to say that prayer is not important, or that exorcism is a hoax. Rather, we ought to regard prayer and deliverance not as the end of healing but rather as a beginning, as that which opens the individual to receive healing from whatever source it may come.

Possession States and Other Paranormal Behavior

Previous discussion notwithstanding, demonic possession is a real possibility that pastoral counseling must be prepared to address. When parishioners exhibit abnormal bodily movements, such as foaming at the mouth, falling, or discomfort during prayer, these must be considered as possible signs of possession, with the severity of the behavior indicating the power of the demon present in an individual. During exorcisms, which invariably follow the exhibition of the signs mentioned, the demons act out their identity or say their names, and often engage in long conversations with the exorcist.[62] While we cannot discount the possibility that some of these signs may be indications of actual demonic activity, the frequency of the

---

62. Francis MacNutt describes several such instances; see his *Deliverance from Evil Spirits: A Practical Manual* (Grand Rapids: Chosen Books, 1995). While the contexts differ, I have concerns regarding the observations and inferences he draws.

occurrences, as well as the resistance of some of the possession states to the prayer of faith, prompt us to ask whether there may also be psychological and sociological factors at work. It is likely that there is more to the "demonic" than the merely spiritual, even from a biblical perspective. As we noted in the previous chapter, Scripture sometimes uses the word *daimon* rather than *demon*. Ulanov points us to psychological explorations of these two terms, both used to describe "a *numen,* a working of a higher power, a greater than human power."[63]

According to Ulanov, the demonic, which always presents itself to us as an "other," has two principal meanings — demonic and daimonic. The daimonic "calls to mind the daimon of Socrates, which inspires, guides, and confirms a source of value beyond human conventions,"[64] like a muse. We know many instances in which people have acted in ways beyond their capabilities or normal way of doing things and wondered what came over them. People say, "I don't know what possessed me when I did this or that." Thus:

> The daimon, in this understanding, is also seen as a helpful fate urging self-realization and realization of the truth, as a bridge between the human and the divine, as that which drives us beyond our narrow limits, beyond the hedges of conventional points of view. In Latin, the daimonic is associated with the word "genius," from the verb "to generate" or "beget." Thus the daimon has been thought of as . . . that energy that fights against apathy, boredom, rigidity, and even death.[65]

The daimonic is a creative force that ought to be embraced, not repudiated. It is life-giving and affirming and draws us out of placid, vegetative states, bringing purpose and meaning to life again. The second term, demonic, is "a destructive power, an evil spirit in the New Testament sense, that works moral destruction on human personality."[66] These are the spirits that Jesus confronted in the helpless victims he healed.

Both "spirits" are adversarial, but one we can transform to be our advocate, to work with us rather than against us, while the other sets itself against us, aiming at our ultimate destruction. The former enlarges our

---

63. Ann Belford Ulanov, "The Psychological Reality of the Demonic," in *Picturing God* (Cambridge, Mass.: Cowley, 1986), 127.

64. Ulanov, "The Psychological Reality of the Demonic," 127.

65. Ulanov, "The Psychological Reality of the Demonic," 128.

66. Ulanov, "The Psychological Reality of the Demonic," 128.

horizons and stands with us to attain our potential. The latter comes to steal, to kill, and to destroy. Our task is to see the "spirits" as other, but to differentiate between them and discern which is the adversary and which the advocate. Ulanov suggests that first we approach the spirit with an attitude of "respect," that is, "to observe it, to give it close attention . . . and not to become this other and fall into identification with it, nor run away from it, or repress it."[67] We must also listen to our instinctive responses in the face of danger to help us decide whether this is something to run from or to embrace. We can also do what the New Testament enjoins us to do for our enemies: when we face a demonic other, we can love it, feed it, and generally take care of it. If it gives back to us, then we know we have met an advocate; if on the other hand it merely fattens itself at our expense, then we do the obverse: "give nothing — no libido, no interest, no attention . . . no life."[68]

Ulanov illustrates the usefulness of this kind of attentiveness to a demonic other by means of a series of dog images in a man's dreams. In the first of these dreams, the middle-aged man was threatened by wild dogs. In the early dreams, the man always turned and ran away. Then he experienced a set of dreams in which the dogs were leashed and, though he was afraid, he stood his ground. In the next set of dreams, a single dog was tied to a tree, and the man was encouraged to explore why the dog might want to make contact with him. Through this encouragement the man began to respond to the dog, and over the following months the size of the dog began to diminish. In the last dream of the series, the dreamer suddenly walked up to the dog and barked back. To his surprise, "the dog-figure underwent a remarkable metamorphosis in response to the transformation in the dreamer's attitude: it changed into a little boy."[69] Using this dream series as an instructive model, pastors could help their parishioners learn to confront their frightening dream images rather than merely label them as evil and repudiate them. Instead of fighting their way back to consciousness from terrifying dreams, they could benefit from staying with the dream and paying attention to the content. They might discover a lost part of themselves that would help heal whatever pain brought them to counseling.

In addition to the possible psychodynamic individual benefits we can attain through attentiveness and respect to the demonic other, there are psychosocial benefits to the individual as well as the community. In *Power,*

---

67. Ulanov, "The Psychological Reality of the Demonic," 141.
68. Ulanov, "The Psychological Reality of the Demonic," 142.
69. Ulanov, "The Psychological Reality of the Demonic," 142.

Pathology, Paradox, Marguerite Shuster points out the psychosocial under-pinnings of possession states:

> Whether a culture officially approves or disapproves of states called "possession," having the category available makes possible the interpretation and the relief of certain stresses that could otherwise threaten the social structure. Such a category provides sanction for cathartic expression of intense emotional excitement. It gives room for the acting out of socially unacceptable behaviors such as role reversals and those associated with hostile impulses and sexual feelings. Thus, internal psychological pressures find an outlet.[70]

Anyone who has witnessed a deliverance session would agree with Shuster's observation. We notice that in some of these sessions, an otherwise timid and well-mannered individual may use foul language, act out in lewd ways, and ridicule those who are casting out the demons from her. In this case Africans believe that the demon has taken over her personality, and so she is not really conscious of what she is doing. While we may blame her actions on the presence of the demon, she, as well as those who hear her, may benefit from the cathartic effect of such an outburst of outrageous behavior.

Apart from the psychological benefits, social tensions also find expression through mass trance performances. In such cases, the pressures may be transformed "into a common struggle against the external sources of malevolence."[71] Sometimes participants in worship services in Africa demonstrate behavior that fits the description of a mass trance performance. During these church services people dance vigorously; they lift their arms into the air, sway their hips, and get in touch with and express their emotions. The songs of praise and worship, the great oratory and emotional appeal of the leader of worship, the pastors' emotional and sentimental messages — all contribute to an experience that is fully physical, emotional, social, and spiritual.

There are also obvious psychic and somatic benefits from the atmosphere the worship setting creates, and there is a general cathartic effect for the congregation. The worship moment, which incorporates low-impact

---

70. Marguerite Shuster, *Power, Pathology, Paradox: The Dynamics of Evil and Good* (Grand Rapids: Academie, 1987), 70.

71. Shuster, *Power, Pathology, Paradox,* 70.

aerobics and emotional release through shouting and weeping, carries the people through until the next meeting time. Normally, meetings take place twice a week, since there are mid-week services as well as those on Sundays. Sometimes, however, a whole week is dedicated to revival in the congregation. These revivals usually end with a deliverance session in which people are freed from demonic and other spiritual powers. Shuster suggests further that sometimes group possession and deliverance might be used much like group therapy. Within the spiritual setting, however, where belief in a higher power helps give meaning to life, the problems can be given over to these "'powers' for resolution instead of remaining the responsibility of individuals or the group."[72] She contends that some of the phenomena generally termed possession are actually altered states of consciousness. A close look at what occurs during these deliverance sessions and the trance-like behavior displayed by devotees of fetish shrines supports Shuster's observation.

According to Shuster, altering brain states often induces some of the phenomena generally referred to as possession. This can be accomplished through drugs, rhythmic dancing and drumming, hyperventilation, or other biochemical means. Some follow a "period of fasting and physical stress, joined with an intense expectation of receiving a vision, revelation, or some special sign."[73] In most of the Independent Evangelical churches, activities such as those described above form part of any church service. While there are no drugs per se, Roman Catholic, Anglican, and African Independent Churches burn incense, which many believe to contain spices with hallucinogenic properties. Coupled with that, Ghanaian dishes, for example, often contain a variety of spices, and certain combinations of those spices ingested with food at home, and later inhaled as incense within a worship setting, could induce altered brain activities resembling a possession state.

Apart from the possible use of hallucinogenic drugs or spices/herbs, we can see how loud music, rhythmic dancing and drumming, and hyperventilation could result in extreme forms of behavior. Shuster, drawing from a large body of research, reports that innocent bystanders watching such occurrences have become affected by what was going on and copied the behaviors they observed. Some people acted out as though they were possessed after being touched or rubbed against by one possessed.[74] In several of the Ghanaian Independent Charismatic churches, deliverance ses-

72. Shuster, *Power, Pathology, Paradox*, 71.
73. Shuster, *Power, Pathology, Paradox*, 69.
74. Shuster, *Power, Pathology, Paradox*, 70.

sions are characterized by people falling one after the other when they are touched on the forehead (usually with a gentle push). In addition, falling or momentary loss of balance (what in American Pentecostalism is known as being "slain in the Spirit") is seen as an indication that the individual has been touched by the power of God or is at least open to the work of the Holy Spirit. While I do not doubt that the awesome presence of God can produce such a powerful effect, it is also possible that the charged emotional atmosphere and group dynamics can induce the falling phenomenon.

Apart from the group phenomena just described, the individual deliverance sessions in which a pastor tries to bring healing to a troubled person have certain peculiarities that indicate psychological underpinnings. Sometimes the power of suggestion is at work, as when characteristics of demonic possession appear in an individual only *after* confrontation by the exorcist. The suggestion to the individual that he may be possessed by a demon sometimes seems to induce the possession state. The authoritative command to the demon to manifest itself and to exit, usually attained by a word of knowledge (that communication by deep impression and conviction from the Holy Spirit), works to convince the individual that he has a particular demon. In addition, the length and intensity of the exorcism seem to accord with the expectations of both the exorcist and the possessed. In this case, faith plays a vital role in the process of deliverance. Shuster points out that in "cases where individuals believe that exorcisms will be long and arduous, they are; whereas some people of a simpler faith just read their Bible, pray a bit, sing a few songs, and the task is done."[75]

In this regard, I recall an occasion in which characteristics of possession abated in an individual when I ignored them. On several occasions this person had kept a group of us praying through the night in an attempt to cast out what we believed to be demons. On this particular night, I was the only group member present when the individual fell into a possession state. I got out of bed and began to pray. However, I felt a strong urge to ignore what was going on; it was almost a direct order *not* to pray. I remember telling the individual, "I'm going to sleep now. You tell the Lord you want to sleep too." The signs of possession ceased instantaneously and we both slept through the night. Whether exorcism will work or not sometimes depends finally on whether the individual wants to be cured.

Another area of concern that psychodynamic theory helps us to explicate is the idea that thoughts, whether our own or another's about us, have

75. Shuster, *Power, Pathology, Paradox*, 76.

the power to affect us. No doubt there is a religio-magical underpinning to this idea that has found its way into the African Christian heritage. Whatever an individual thinks or says is called into being; what others say to him or think about him is also believed to happen. On the effect of thoughts and drawing from her research on paranormal phenomena, Schuster says:

> if thoughts are the sorts of things that may or may not, depending on circumstances, penetrate others' screening devices, then thoughts have a sort of reality about them. That is, wholly apart from actions or verbal communication, they in themselves impinge in some way upon the rest of the universe. The rather sobering conclusion follows that "what anybody thinks has some tendency to come about in fact, just because it is thought of; and it still has that tendency even when the thought is no longer in anybody's consciousness."[76]

This understanding of the power of thoughts, normally linked with curses, is one with which the Ghanaian identifies, believing that evil thoughts or wishes can be made to materialize. This in turn is viewed as according with assumed Old Testament belief that life and death are in the tongue (perhaps based on Proverbs 18:20-22), so that what one says can literally come true. In effect, words are like the Logos bringing forth what is called into existence. If this is the case, we can use the same idea in counseling to counter the effects of earlier thoughts. We can help parishioners to begin thinking positive thoughts, the kind that produce fecundity in living (Phil. 4:8).

In addition to the psychic, there are sometimes purely somatic reasons for paranormal behavior. From a biochemical perspective, lack of calcium in the water source of particular areas has caused clairvoyance in some people. Shuster notes that we might see colors by looking at flowers, but may equally see colors by pressing on the eyes. Other biochemical effects in the body, which suggest a somatic basis for certain paranormal occurrences, include such phenomena as "getting high" after prolonged exertion. In addition, "[f]lickering or strobe lights, dancing, pounding drums, or reiterated syllables can induce an altered state of consciousness."[77] We need only watch people at a rock concert, where all these features are present, to substantiate this point.

---

76. R. Heywood, *Beyond the Reach of Sense* (New York: Dutton, 1961), quoting H. H. Price in Shuster, *Power, Pathology, Paradox*, 57.
77. Shuster, *Power, Pathology, Paradox*, 21.

Summary

While pastors and parishioners within the African church may attribute certain paranormal phenomena to spirits and so seek spiritual intervention as a cure, Jungian analytical psychology allows us to see those phenomena a different way, understanding the operations of the psyche or soul and its drive towards wholeness. Wholeness entails paying attention to the unconscious as well as conscious processes of the psyche, and can only be achieved if individuals are willing to examine their psyches in depth.

Thus, from a Jungian psychodynamic perspective, we find that we can legitimately adduce psychic reasons for some of the paranormal behavior witnessed in Ghanaian and other African churches. The struggle of the self to come to birth and optimum functioning, a desire that is frustrated by a restrictive cultural atmosphere coupled with an undue emphasis on the cosmos and its role in human affairs, accounts for many of the phenomena encountered. However, by far the most useful contribution of this approach is its understanding of how the repressed or suppressed unconscious, especially the shadow and the anima/animus, can rear up in manifestations that have generally been labeled as demonic.

There are drawbacks to Jungian therapy. Its greatest limitation is the length of time that therapy requires and its cost. The present proposal, however, is for African pastors to use Jungian concepts in pastoral counseling, which they currently offer as a free service to their parishioners. Moreover, what I advocate here is not full-scale Jungian therapy, but rather a program in which pastors incorporate certain helpful analytical psychological insights of Jung's findings, especially the application of archetypes, in order to help resolve some of the problems that commonly arise. If healing is to come to the total human being, then a therapeutic approach that works with the natural propensities of the self toward wholeness is essential.

CHAPTER SIX

Toward a Model for Pastoral Counseling

Introduction

As we have seen, given that both pastors and parishioners in Africa believe that there are profound similarities between biblical and African worldviews, and that the Bible itself adduces spiritual causes for a host of problems, it is understandable that pastoral theology rests on the assumption that most problems presented in counseling are spiritual in nature. Following Karl Barth, however, I have argued that the Bible uses a variety of worldviews to make its theological points, owing allegiance to none, and that therefore African theological anthropology cannot claim kinship between an African worldview and a *single*, uniform biblical view. Nevertheless, if African Christians can perceive that it is possible to use worldviews without becoming captive to any, they might discover a new freedom to borrow from a wider range of resources that will make theological anthropology and pastoral care in Africa more effective and relevant to parishioners' needs.

I have argued that African theological anthropology is currently embroiled in African cosmological ideas rather than in the word of God, despite what most pastors believe. In so far as it is based on what Barth would call a "speculative philosophy," or a way of understanding humanity from the framework of a human pattern of thinking rather than from the word of God, its anthropology and soteriology are inadequate for a viable approach to pastoral counseling. What the church in Africa needs, therefore, is a conceptual framework with which to refine and sharpen its theological anthropology, so that instead of supporting a cosmology that perpetuates a climate of fear and bondage, pastoral theology might better bring the promised freedom and healing of Christ to ailing people. Such an anthropology with strong scriptural and Christological dimensions can, I believe, be found in Barth's theological anthropology.

Consequently, I have sought to base a new African anthropology on Barthian Christology, arguing that we need to pay attention to *each component* of the human being in pastoral practice. For while many Africans conceive of the human being as composed of body, soul, and spirit existing in an almost *undifferentiated* unity, I would argue, following Barth, that the human being is rather a besouled body and an embodied soul, existing in a *differentiated* unity and undergirded by God's spirit. Unfortunately, when a belief in the undifferentiated nature of body and soul is coupled with a belief that spiritual causes are sufficient to account for all inexplicable phenomena, the treatments that result usually address only the spiritual dimensions of the problem. Counselors, therefore, need to consider three points: first, that we should tend to the body and soul in their particularities, paying attention to individual components, recognizing separate somatic and psychological causes, and approaching diagnoses in a more differentiated way. When we can pinpoint the primary source of a problem, therapy will be more focused and effective. Second, we should acknowledge the interconnectedness of body and soul (they exist as a unity), and thereby understand that somatic factors do not affect only the physical and that psychological elements do not affect only the psyche. And third, we should note that when the Scriptures employ the word "spirit," they do not refer to a separate entity inhabiting a human being (the word is also a synonym for soul or the inner parts of a being) and thus not everything should be subsumed under spiritual categories. The real strength of the African emphasis on unity is that it provides a basis for a holistic approach to therapy; the drawback is that it may miss the real source or cause of a presenting problem and thereby pay insufficient attention to that component.

From a Christian theological stance, we can only undertake anthropology from a Christological perspective that rests on the belief that the real human being cannot be known apart from Christ. Moreover, Christ's death, resurrection, and ultimate victory over death and all satanic forces cannot be negated by ancestral curses, nor the spells of witches, nor all the powers of hell combined (Rom. 8:31-39). While the devil can have a foothold in the Christian's life through habitual and unconfessed sin, he cannot take ownership of a life that was created and redeemed by God. Ultimately, therefore, the bondage that African Christians suffer is not so much imposed by demonic forces outside them, but rather is a result of their cosmological ideas about malevolent forces. When bondage arises out of internalized distortions of God's truth, it needs to be addressed with the word of God itself. That is to say, pastors would take a better path if, instead of focusing so much on delivering parishioners from demonic spirits, they concentrated on Scripture itself as a means to critique a worldview that keeps people in fear. St. Paul cautions Christians about the bondage that arises from false teaching when he warns the believers at Colossae not to be taken in by the "elemental spirits" and the "doctrines of men" that result in rules and laws about what to touch and eat and on what days they can worship (Col. 2:20-21). While African Christians are familiar with this passage, they mistakenly believe St. Paul's mention of "elemental spirits" refers to spirits of the air and sea and so on. Therefore we can hardly be surprised at the hysteria of the 1980s when the Ghanaian Mami Water Spirit, who inhabits the sea in the form of a mermaid, was linked to a depiction of a woman carrying a water jar and wearing an anklet found on the "Queen of the Coast" brand of canned sardines. Christians were warned not to buy the cans and to avoid anklet-wearing women for fear of possession! Instead of thinking about elemental spirits as spiritual or demonic beings, we should heed biblical and extrabiblical texts that approach such entities from a different perspective, emphasizing their physical and psychic components.

Focusing on these features is certainly far more beneficial than steering clear of objects perceived as connected to evil. And this is where Jung's analytical psychology is both beneficial and illuminating, offering valuable insights for addressing many issues found in pastoral counseling. By understanding, say, how social pressures and strict gender roles and expectations can cause people to suppress their contrasexual side in such a way that symptoms of illness emerge, or how dreams and other paranormal phenomena (from which decisions are made about the presence of demonic forces) are likely to arise from psychic as well as somatic causes, pastors and parishioners can work on identifying aspects of their psyche and move towards integrating them into their personality. Rather than repudiate and suppress these components as intrinsically evil or negative, we can encourage individuals to embrace them as much needed complementary aspects of their being human.

Theoretical Framework for Counseling

What would pastoral counseling look like if informed by insights from Barth's theological anthropology and Jungian analytical psychology? In the first place, pastoral counselors informed by the insights of Barth would see the individuals who come for help as belonging primarily to God (not to the devil nor even to themselves), and thus all the resources of God are available for the healing needed, regardless of past deeds, or beliefs, or even ancestral behavior. Pastoral counselors can make these assumptions because they believe that in Jesus Christ a work has been done in and for parishioners that transcends any other work. Christ has died for them and has purchased salvation for them, a salvation that includes healing in all aspects of life. The efficacy of Christ's redemptive work does not inhere in the parishioner's belief, but rather in the power and integrity of the God who redeems.

Pastors informed by Barth's theological anthropology would also understand the interplay between culture and the word of God. From a Barthian perspective, pastors are not likely to allow the cosmos or any cosmology that arises from the culture to hold greater sway in the counseling situation than the power of God. Pastors would understand the liberation that comes from subordinating the cosmos to the transcendent word of God, and from that stance they would be able to help free parishioners from the cosmological fears that threaten to paralyze them. Furthermore, the African fear of ancestral curses, chieftaincy lineages, and the repercussion of the sins of one's forebears would be rendered impotent with the knowledge that, in Jesus Christ, the Gentiles have been made heirs of the promises made to Abraham and his descendents (Gal. 3:29).[1] The power of God's word and promise to God's people is far greater than these lesser evil powers. Moreover Christians have all the protection and care on this earth that they would have in heaven. All (not just some) of God's omnipotence can protect them because their lives are truly hidden with God in Christ and seated with him in the heavenly places (Eph. 2:6-8).

God calls all those who believe in Jesus God's very own and invites them to be in relationship. The true meaning of the natal name and its possible effect on Christians' lives are negated by the ultimate name that God gives to God's people in Christ. As Christians, they have a new name through their adoption by God, and pastors can encourage them to focus

---

1. This by no means discounts the importance of "family of origin" issues in counseling. Our ancestors have a big impact on our fate even if we remain unconscious of what happened in their lives. An emphasis on what we can learn from their mistakes and foibles, traumatic events in the past, addictive habits and what caused them, etc., might be more beneficial in counseling individuals than the emphasis on curses, which then leads to "a spiritual cure" that does not really address the issue at stake.

on the implications and privileges of that new name. They are forever loved, accepted, and favored by the God and Father of us all. Barth sums up this great privilege of a child of God in these words:

> What remains is the unsurpassable honour done to man when the commanding God who is his Father calls us as His own child not just anywhere or to any great or small achievements and activities, but to Himself. To be with this Father as the child of this Father is freedom.[2]

The individual need not perform any act except to come into relationship with the Father, whose mercy is so large that even those who do not know or own him as their Father can seek and expect his intervention. The pastor who understands that God's mercies are boundless can expect the same intervention even on behalf of nonbelievers and those with little faith. There is no need to expect people who are hurting to first make a confession of faith in Jesus Christ, nor to insist that they renounce their implication in ancestral sins before God can help them. These may form part of ongoing care and Christian nurture after the immediate suffering has been attended to.

The concept of the human being as body and soul existing in differentiated unity is vital to bringing about needed changes in pastoral counseling, and so Barth's explication of this concept from a biblical perspective is helpful in reformulating a theological anthropology. I believe that if African pastors understood that the constitution of the human being is an embodied soul undergirded by God's spirit — in which the body and soul are interrelated and yet distinct — their approach to pastoral diagnoses would change drastically. If human beings are besouled bodies and embodied souls undergirded by God's Spirit, then human beings do not really have what is normally referred to as spirit. If what undergirds human beings is the Spirit of God, it would be preposterous even to suggest that evil spiritual powers can affect human beings through their spirit.

If they understood this, pastoral counselors would not base their diagnoses entirely on spiritual causes. Pastors would look for psychic and somatic causes of presenting problems because these would be the problems derived from what constitutes human beings — body and soul. They would only secondarily look for what may come from evil spiritual powers because human beings live in a spiritual world. They could thus more readily differentiate between symptoms that are only spiritual, psychic, or somatic on the

---

2. Karl Barth, *Church Dogmatics* III/4 (Edinburgh: T&T Clark, 1960), 648.

one hand, and those that exhibit all these components on the other. From this assessment, they could use the most appropriate counseling approach for greater benefit to the parishioner. Realizing the interplay between the body and the soul as both interconnected and differentiated would help the pastoral counselor probe the complaints of parishioners in a way that spans all aspects of their lives. Counseling would thus take account of the possibility that presenting problems may arise from the normal problems of living in the world.

The importance of the finished work of Christ manifested in the Christ event and its implications for human life past, present, and future stand out in Barth's theological anthropology. Pastors who truly understand the scope of the work of Christ for the whole cosmos and understand Christ's rule over all principalities and powers, things that are and things that are to come, would be free from undue preoccupation with these spirit powers. They would also understand that God's grace extends to all people, not just those they characterize as saved, or as belonging to the household of faith, because God lets the sun shine on both the just and the unjust and shows mercy to those God wills (Matt. 5:45). Moreover God comes to all who are in need and, as Jesus stressed throughout his earthly ministry, he came to heal those who were sick. The Gospel accounts confirm that people brought their sick to him and he healed them. Barth, commenting on the activities of Jesus, says,

> It is the man with whom things are going badly; who is needy and frightened and harrassed. . . . The picture brought before us is that of suffering. . . . For human life as it emerges in this activity of Jesus is really like a great hospital whose many departments in some way enfold us all.[3]

The Bible asserts that while we were yet sinners Christ died for us (Rom. 5:8); therefore, getting right with God is not a prerequisite for God's intervention in human suffering. In fact, the obverse is the case: God first addresses the need of the suffering human being and then encourages the human being to live in a way that retains that healing. Pastors who fully understand this reality do not demand, for example, that parishioners require their parents to repent and renounce certain ancestral practices before deliverance can be effected. The freedom that individuals will experience from such good

---

3. Barth, *Church Dogmatics* IV/2, 221.

news — that their or their forebears' past mistakes need not hinder God's blessings — lies at the core of the gospel message.

Guidelines for Practical Application

The pastoral counselor equipped with insights from Barth's theological anthropology and Jungian analytical psychology has tremendous advantages in bringing healing to troubled souls. A great deal of the success in using this combined theoretical framework depends on how the counselor handles both the theological and psychological concerns in any given counseling situation. While most of the proficiency will come with practice, the following guidelines are helpful for thinking through the issues at stake.

An excellent multidisciplinary model for use in a pastoral counseling context is one provided by Deborah Hunsinger in *Theology and Pastoral Counseling,* in which she employs the insights of Barth's Christological anthropology and the theories of depth psychology to address a variety of counseling situations.[4] Some of these situations call for assessments that are complex, where both theological and psychological concepts are needed and pastoral counselors must speak, as it were, two languages, interpreting a counselee's material in either a theological or psychological theoretical framework. Instead of a paradigm that reduces theology to psychology, or vice versa, Hunsinger proposes a paradigm that holds both theology and psychology in asymmetrical relationship, whereby the disciplines are united, differentiated, and ordered in such a way that theology holds conceptual priority over psychology. This paradigm is attentive to the possibilities and limits of both conceptual frameworks while granting basic integrity to both theology and psychology.

Hunsinger bases her framework for relating psychological and theological concepts upon the formal pattern of thought in Karl Barth's Christological anthropology and Barth's interpretation of the Chalcedonian definition of the complex relationship between the two natures of Jesus Christ. In A.D. 451 the Council of Chalcedon declared that the person Jesus Christ was to be understood as "complete in deity and complete in humanity"; they further declared that his two natures, human and divine, were to be related "without separation or division" and at the same time "without confusion

---

4. Deborah van Deusen Hunsinger, *Theology and Pastoral Counseling: A New Interdisciplinary Approach* (Grand Rapids: Eerdmans, 1995), 213-36.

or change."[5] Barth interprets the Chalcedonian definition on the two natures of Christ to mean that they exist in "inseparable unity," yet at the same time in "indissoluble differentiation," but with conceptual priority assigned to the divine nature over the human nature. George Hunsinger writes,

> [T]he two natures are not . . . ordered according to a scale whereby they would differ only in degree. [They] are rather conceived as asymmetrically related, for they share no common measure or standard of measurement. Although there is a divine priority and a human subsequence, their asymmetry allows a conception which avoids hierarchical domination in favor of a *mutual ordering in freedom.*[6]

Since we understand divine nature to have nothing in common with human nature, it would be almost blasphemous to conceive of a hierarchical ordering of the two natures. The two natures belong to different planes and yet are mysteriously united in the one man Jesus, each maintaining its own integrity. He was never one without the other fully present. Each nature kept to its assigned place. The human nature did not seek to dominate the divine nature, nor did the divine nature diminish or overshadow his human nature.

When pastoral counselors see theology and psychology existing in inseparable unity, in indissoluble differentiation, and with asymmetrical ordering — with theology having conceptual priority over psychology — they have a valuable conceptual map for diagnosing and bringing healing to troubled persons. They can use the model for both paradigmatic and nonparadigmatic cases. Paradigmatic cases are those in which the person seeking help has both theological and psychological questions. The parishioner therefore seeks out a pastoral counselor for the reason that the issues are so closely intertwined with each other that it is difficult to sort them out. In nonparadigmatic cases, hurting persons may not necessarily seek theological or psychological insights for their situation. Nevertheless, the counselor's stance and belief about human beings, derived from the word of God and especially the finished work of Christ on behalf of the whole human race, allow for a level of hope and confidence in the process. Even if

5. For a complete account of the deliberation of the Council of Chalcedon, see *The Oecumenical Documents of the Faith,* ed. T. H. Bindley and F. W. Green (London: Methuen, 1950).

6. George Hunsinger, *How to Read Karl Barth: The Shape of His Theology* (New York: Oxford University Press, 1991), 286-87, n. 1.

the counseling session only reaches the psychological level, theology nevertheless gives the work a hopeful and constructive orientation.

Based on the Christological anthropology that this theory advocates, psychological insights are thus undergirded by the larger theological framework of who this human being is before God in light of the Christ event. While pastoral counselors are most concerned with addressing the immediate causes of suffering, they also see healing through the larger picture of salvation, though they should take care not to turn counseling sessions into evangelistic crusades. Thus the counselee's predicament becomes the focus of attention, while at the same time the counselor understands the ultimate goal to be the person's salvation in Christ, both for the present time and for eternity.

African pastors and counselors could benefit from such a paradigm because there is a tendency to simply let theological insights answer all questions, whether they are theological or not. Often there are implicit psychological questions woven into the theological questions parishioners present, and these psychological questions are left completely unaddressed. Furthermore, there are often questions of a purely psychological nature that need psychological insights to answer them (and of course physical issues that need somatic responses). If African pastors could differentiate between those situations that call for purely psychological insights and those that call for theological insights (as well as those that call for a combination of the two), they would more finely tune their diagnoses to meet a variety of unaddressed needs. Finally, the whole situation can be placed within a larger theological frame of reference in order to help parishioners understand their place in the larger Christian drama.

As I have already mentioned, salvation is the ultimate end, that to which the present act of healing or intervention points. Most Ghanaian pastors, for example, attempt to focus on the immediate problem of the parishioner through the prayer of deliverance, and then ask questions that probe the background of the individual for possible familial or demonic causes. These questions can lead to a discussion of parishioners' spiritual states: whether or not they are born again, the nature of their church affiliation and relationship with God, their expectations about miracles, and so on. The impression on the sufferer, then, might be that a right relationship with God is the pastor's primary focus, thus putting salvation in the foreground of the pastoral intervention. In this case, what occurs then in counseling is a hierarchical ordering of healing and salvation where salvation takes priority over healing and healing is rushed through the one-shot prayer for deliverance. As a result, pastors currently allow insufficient room for the psychological needs of the religious believer.

We can use the example of God-image or God-representation to illustrate the distinction between the psychology of the believer and issues of faith. Based on an extensive investigation into the origin, development, and functions of a person's belief in God, Ana-Maria Rizzuto, a psychiatrist with a background in object relations psychology, concludes, as Freud did, that humans piece together an internal image of God out of their relationship to primary objects, especially significant figures from early childhood such as parents or primary caretakers.[7] She hypothesizes that there is a significant correlation between our internalized primary objects and our unconscious images of God.

To test her hypothesis, she conducted a longitudinal study, administering a questionnaire to twenty people — ten women and ten men — who came from various backgrounds and who were hospitalized in a psychiatric care unit. These individuals took part in the interviews assuming that the questions were part of the normal data collected for the care provided in the psychiatric center. Rizzuto used two parallel questionnaires — one to elicit family of origin information and the other with complementary questions to elicit information about God — in order to focus on fundamental attitudes, images, and feelings. Each of the participants also drew a family picture as well as an image of God. From these data, Rizzuto correlated the two sets of feelings — that is, about God and family — and concluded that there was a close correlation between a person's God-image and his or her internalized "primary objects."

Children unconsciously create a God-image out of daily experiences with significant others, forming the image from hopes, fears, and longings, as well as the fantasies and sometimes actual characteristics of these significant others. They then use this God-image formed from the "matrix of facts and fantasies, wishes, hopes, and fears, in the exchanges with those incredible beings called parents."[8] Throughout their lives these images provide psychological stability, balance, and some form of relatedness to others, especially those who contributed to the warp and woof from which the image was created. The God-image also provides a sense of self-esteem and hope for daily living.[9]

While these God-images are based partly on fantasies — fears, wishes,

7. Ana-Maria Rizzuto, *The Birth of the Living God: A Psychoanalytic Study* (Chicago: University of Chicago Press, 1979).

8. Rizzuto, *The Birth of the Living God*, 7.

9. Rizzuto, *The Birth of the Living God*, 89, 199, 202.

and dreams — the fantasies do not in any way detract from the reality of the God-image. Rizzuto asserts that due to their psychological significance for the owner of the image, the role of fantasy is even more important than the actual characteristics of the parents or primary caregiver. Along with the God-image, children also form a certain self-image from the interaction between themselves and significant others, again building it out of fantasies and using it to provide psychological support and equilibrium throughout life. These images are not static, however, but undergo changes as an individual matures and experiences crises and significant life passages. While both God- and self-images are based in fantasy and termed illusory, they are no less real to the one who created and owns them. Rizzuto argues for the place of "illusion" in psychic life but differentiates her use of this term from Freud's use: "Illusory transmutation of reality . . . is the indispensable and unavoidable process all of us *must* go through if we are to grow normally and acquire psychic meaning and substance."[10]

We can build on Rizzuto's insights by turning to Deborah Hunsinger, who proposes that we can view any psychologically- or theologically-shaped God-representation through its own set of norms. We can also simultaneously view any God-representation from the perspective of both disciplines. While there could be various possibilities for relating the norms of the two disciplines to any God-representation, Hunsinger suggests a logical classification scheme illustrated in the grid below.[11]

Theological Norm (Θ)

		Adequate	Inadequate
	Functional	#1 Ψ Functional Θ Adequate	#2 Ψ Functional Θ Inadequate
	Dysfunctional	#3 Ψ Dysfunctional Θ Adequate	#4 Ψ Dysfunctional Θ Inadequate

Psychological Norm (Ψ)

---

10. Rizzuto, *The Birth of the Living God*, 228 n.4.

11. Hunsinger, *Theology and Pastoral Counseling*, 131.

Within the limits of this classification, there are four possible logical God-images from a theological and psychological perspective, and pastoral counselors would naturally seek to work toward both theological adequacy and psychological functionality.[12] A theologically adequate and psychologically functional God-image is one that is wholesome both theologically and psychologically. Theologically, it is based on God's own self-revelation, consonant with God's word. Psychologically it promotes emotional equilibrium and reservoirs of hope.

In the second logical possibility, the psychology is functional but the theology is inadequate, so a person's God-image may confer psychological benefits, but it is not based on the God that is revealed in Christ.[13] Hunsinger imagines situations that might arise in which one's God-image is psychologically functional but theologically inadequate, cases in which the respective norms would, in other words, be in a kind of "tragic conflict" with each other:

> Perhaps in some instances there are [such cases]. The particular circumstances of a person's life might make it psychologically necessary that God be pictured in a certain theologically inadequate way. . . . The work of the church would not be understood as giving someone "a direct experience of God" but, rather, providing the conditions (in so far as is possible from the human side) for Christian nurture, conversion, and sanctification: Scripture, prayer, fellowship, worship. In, with, and under the simple act of human witness, God may bear witness to himself.[14]

In the third category psychological dysfunction meets theological adequacy. Ordinarily we would assume that if an image is theologically adequate, it will also be psychologically functional. But this is not always the case. In this instance, Hunsinger invites us to ask whether it is the images themselves or the use of the images that are dysfunctional; it is often the case that the *use* of the images produces the dysfunctionality.[15] For example, the image of God as Father is a theologically adequate image but could be used in a dysfunctional way, depending on the individual's internalized

---

12. Hunsinger, *Theology and Pastoral Counseling*, 130ff.
13. Hunsinger, *Theology and Pastoral Counseling*, 136.
14. Hunsinger, *Theology and Pastoral Counseling*, 137.
15. Hunsinger, *Theology and Pastoral Counseling*, 142-43.

image of his or her father. In the present African cultural scene, we need to ask this question with more urgency and supply answers that can relieve the burdens that people carry. Child-rearing practices and the relationship of many fathers with their children may be reason enough to probe whether the image of God as Father, for example, is being used in a psychologically dysfunctional way by an individual seeking help. Does the individual feel that God is remote and uncaring based on the relationship with a male parent? In this case a pastor's constant reference to trust in a heavenly Father might do more disservice to the individual than provide the emotional support the pastor intended. And yet the image of God as Father is grounded in Scripture and demonstrated by Jesus Christ, making it a unique tradition of the church that should not be discarded. As Hunsinger points out, such occasions when theological adequacy meets psychological dysfunctionality should be viewed by the church as opportunities to determine "whether the image has been received as intended by the church but also for the church to question whether it has properly understood and communicated the image in accordance with Scripture."[16]

The worst possible logical relationship is one of theological inadequacy and psychological dysfunction. While "[e]ven the most apparently dysfunctional God representation has the capacity . . . to meet some vital emotional need,"[17] the stakes are too high to allow it to persist, and a pastoral counselor needs to help the individual work toward some adequate and functional images. Unwholesome images about God can leave the individual stuck without growth or meaning to life.

Hunsinger's categories give us hope that even theologically inadequate images can lead to healing. We know that Jesus first heals and only then tells the individual to "go and sin no more" (John 8:11, New King James Version). Sometimes, however, pastors seem as though they are trying to protect God by focusing on right doctrine rather than healing, even though the concrete issues of the counselee are the more urgent need. This is not to say that right doctrine and correct images of God are irrelevant. Yet focused attention on what is assumed to be a "correct" image of God can actually add undue stress to the burden the parishioner already bears. Hunsinger's model can help pastors enable parishioners to reveal all dimensions of their feelings and thus facilitate counseling. In other words, freedom can only come when pastors nurture a counseling environment that welcomes truth in all of its complexity.

16. Hunsinger, *Theology and Pastoral Counseling*, 143.
17. Hunsinger, *Theology and Pastoral Counseling*, 143.

Hunsinger's categories and guidelines provide clarification from theological and psychological perspectives on pertinent issues regarding God-images that might encourage pastors to stay with and provide support for their parishioners during moments of crisis, even when their God-image is theologically inadequate. These categories and guidelines might also help African pastors address the issue of psychological functionality, helping them look beyond questions of theological adequacy, concerns about achieving a proper understanding of demonic activity, and anxieties about uttering appropriate prayers of deliverance. If pastors can give their attention to ordinary needs for healing, they might be willing to allow individuals to express themselves and grow through their theologically inadequate but psychologically functional images of God. Of course when images are both theologically inadequate and psychologically dysfunctional, pastors need to take steps to help the individual correct them. Yet how is this best done? It is certainly not by forcing a particular kind of direct experience of God upon individuals seeking pastoral help, an experience that is mediated by the pastors' own subjectivity.

As I have already shown, the current emphasis on right spiritual diagnoses and on pointing out to the ailing individual the exact causes of spiritual bondage shifts the focus away from the psychological to the theological, but it also raises issues about correct doctrine. Pastors, then, need to understand that all our images and knowledge of God are tentative at best. None of us has a perfectly adequate image of God, for all human understanding of God is limited by our created finitude. Not even in the incarnation can we say that we know God fully. Even in the incarnation of God in Jesus Christ, God is both revealed and hidden: how can what is human fully contain the divine? Thus, if parishioners see that God's sovereignty and grace are able to mediate even inadequate God-images, they will not be pressured into anxiously conveying what they consider the correct image of God at the expense of the health of the counselee. When diagnosis is a collaborative effort between the pastor and the counselee, without a set agenda or the need to find and neatly label the underlying spiritual causes of problems, counseling can then proceed more freely.

Nancy Ramsay, a pastoral theologian, suggests that an appropriate pastoral image in diagnosis and counseling is that of a midwife, because it envisions the pastoral relationship as relational and collaborative rather than unilateral: "Labor suggests the careful interdependence of persons who share a common goal — empowerment of the one in travail in behalf of new life and new possibilities that are uniquely his or hers to offer."[18] Guided conversations in which the pastor invites troubled persons to talk about their situation and the circumstances that brought them to the pastor's office would yield a wealth of information for addressing the need of the moment as well as offer helpful resources for addressing future situations and shaping their lives.

In the area of pastoral diagnosis, Paul Pruyser's guidelines and questions are also useful for the kind of collaborative approach needed in pastoral counseling. Pruyser sets forth what he considers the key features of any pastoral diagnoses:

> They should produce empirical differentiations, both to the helper and the helped. They should be amenable to interview situations. They should span *conscious* and *unconscious levels* of organization where possible. They should have phenomenological aptness, richness, and diversity to capture personal idiosyncrasies. They should *yield a picture of the person, even if only a sketch or telling fragment,* from which pastoral strategies for intervention can be developed, for that is the obvious goal and basic justification of all diagnosing.[19] (emphases added)

An effective diagnostic tool should cover all counseling situations and be applicable to all individuals who seek counseling. It must aim at determining who this troubled person is that seeks help from a pastor; it ought to be able to tap into her dreams and hopes, where she has been, and where she is going with her life.

Since troubled people who seek help from a pastor do so because they want a theological perspective on the problems that plague them, it makes sense to have a theological approach to diagnoses.[20] But theologies (and here I am using the word to mean one's knowledge of God, or "God talk") are as diverse as human beings. Theology is not limited to a body of knowledge handed down in church tradition, nor is it an objective knowledge of what exists "out there," but it is a subjective, experience-laden knowledge. For example, local communities may have "local theologies," but even within those theologies are individual operative theologies, theologies that

18. Nancy Ramsay, *Pastoral Diagnosis: A Resource for Ministries of Care and Counseling* (Minneapolis: Fortress, 1998), 119.

19. Paul Pruyser, *The Minister as Diagnostician: Personal Problems in Pastoral Perspective* (Philadelphia: Westminster, 1976), 61.

20. Pruyser, *The Minister as Diagnostician*, 43.

are always in a process of flux as the work of God unfolds in each person. Therefore, it is important for pastoral counselors to be aware of an individual's personal sense of God over and above that of a faith community.

Another dimension of belief that is important in pastoral counseling is what Pruyser terms the sense of God's providence in an individual's life, which can manifest itself as a feeling of hope when the individual feels surrounded by God's mercies and has a sense of gratitude and faith in a higher power.[21] In Africa, where a sense of fate or destiny is readily acknowledged among people who ascribe both good and bad events to God, it is easy to assume that there is a widespread belief and trust in God's providence. However, it is important to distinguish between what might be called destiny or fate and Christian providence, and so a pastor should probe for which type of belief the sufferer holds.

A good clue as to whether a parishioner believes in fate or providence is whether resignation or hope undergirds the individual's approach to a problem. If it is resignation, there is a good chance that a belief in destiny or fate is at work, a belief that whatever will happen will happen. Where there is hope, however, there is more likely to be persevering patience that is more than a passive waiting for things to turn around. A counselee demonstrates this kind of active waiting upon God in a willingness to work toward ameliorating the problem. Ability to distinguish between faith and fatalism is thus key in any counseling enterprise, since it is the best indicator of how a parishioner feels about and understands what is happening, and what the parishioner hopes for. The ultimate question then becomes whether God is near at hand and responsive to need, or far away and unconcerned.

If Christians understand that God is working on their behalf, then they are more likely to know the kind of contentment in all circumstances that Paul speaks of in Philippians 4:11. With this contentment comes gratitude, a spirit of thanksgiving in all circumstances, which bears spiritual, psychological, and somatic benefits. When Christians face crises but know that they are participating in the will of God, the psychological and somatic benefits may include a serenity that mitigates the stress of the painful situation. Pastors must therefore be able to distinguish between resignation and true contentment, for true contentment continues to seek and work for the best outcome. It is not despairing, fatalistic, or resigned to whatever may come, but is filled with hope in the face of adversity.

Pruyser's questions also illuminate the issue of sin and forgiveness

21. Pruyser, *The Minister as Diagnostician*, 64-69.

in pastoral diagnosis. In the African context, sin is more than a matter of individual choice — it is also understood as punishment for taboos broken in previous generations. When a taboo is violated, whole clans can be wiped out by the gods, and punishment for these sins can last for generations. Thus it is understandable that some Ghanaian pastors, in their effort to help their parishioners overcome the possible curses in their lives as a result of a parent's sin, might request that the parents be present at their deliverance sessions. For this reason, the pastor needs to discern the counselee's attitude toward repentance, as an understanding of repentance is crucial to the well-being of the counselee. Pruyser mentions three things that the pastor can look for in this regard.[22] Does the counselee accept and rightly appropriate the gift and grace of repentance, or resist it? Is there genuine repentance, a mingling of godly sorrow and the joy of forgiveness? Or is there resistance to the grace and forgiveness of God, as evidenced by constant reference to past wrongdoing and an inability to move forward with life as a result of the sin? More crucial still is the pastor's own attitude toward repentance and forgiveness. If the pastor has a healthy balance of godly sorrow and the joy of forgiveness and can leave the past behind, this can be a positive element in the counseling situation. From Jesus' teaching we know that not all diseases or ailments come as a result of one's sin or the sin of one's parents (John 9:2-3), and so pastors would do well not to dwell on the failures of a troubled person and the failures of that person's ancestors. Trouble and suffering will fall on all people regardless of their degree of righteousness.

Another diagnostic variable is the counselees' sense of vocation, a sense of the calling of God. Do they have a sense of calling and thus a sense of self-worth? Do they have a sense of fulfillment at the end of each day knowing that they have done their best? In a culture where gender roles are clearly defined, some people might feel out of place if they are not performing certain tasks according to what the culture demands. If a man grew up believing that he must provide for his family and therefore that he has to be the sole breadwinner, he might develop feelings of insecurity if his wife has to work, and this may affect his sense of self-worth and further affect the atmosphere in the home, especially if there are no avenues available to address the issue. If his wife makes more money than he does, a man may feel so threatened by her economic position that he stays at home sick rather than going to work and risk bringing home less income than his spouse. As a result, the wife may have to do more work than is traditionally required

---

22. Pruyser, *The Minister as Diagnostician*, 72-73.

of her. Thus the woman finds herself in a double bind: if she does not go beyond the prescribed traditional role, her family suffers, and she may feel as if she is not fulfilling her maternal role. At the same time, however, she jeopardizes her relationship with her husband if he feels that she is usurping his role as provider, and marital conflict can ensue when the husband feels that his wife does not respect him. Globalization and industrialization have dramatically changed the culture and economy so that many families can no longer afford to live on one income. If both husband and wife work outside the home, the husband might need to share in household chores, a situation that was unthinkable until recently. The astute pastor can find a way to defuse what could be a potential crisis by leading a couple through role renegotiation in the light of Scripture and both their present circumstances.

The idea of communion, the sense of "us" rather than "I," is not alien to the African concept of being human. For the African, human beings are always beings-in-relation. Since a sense of being in communion is vital to health and well-being, the individual's sense of herself as either isolated or as part of a community is an important clue to who she is. However, the African's sense of "us-ness" might work against wholeness if it curtails individuation, a necessary prerequisite for living in true relationship. If individuals are enmeshed in unhealthy relationships and find themselves unable to function well on a day-to-day basis, but nevertheless feel that they need to stay in those relationships because the family requires it of them, they need to be encouraged to take a stand on issues in a way that fosters health for themselves as well as for the group. Real communion should be fulfilling for all who participate in it; people should feel enriched by their relationships, not deprived or overextended. The wise pastor will know how to help isolated parishioners connect and seek communion, as well as to help those who feel smothered or enmeshed to find the needed personal space for growth.

Another important aspect of diagnosis is to use a model that, according to Pruyser, allows for "mutual self-examination." This is in contrast to a medical model in which people submit their ailments to a doctor's expertise, or to a priestly model in which lay persons submit their conscience to the probing of a spiritual authority. These authoritarian models tend to ignore important psychological factors.[23] If suffering people are empowered to participate in their own diagnosis and remedy, then their psychological problems are less likely to be overlooked.

Certainly there is a greater need for the diagnostic process in African

23. Pruyser, *The Minister as Diagnostician*, 35-36.

pastoral counseling to be a participatory enterprise, since the authoritarian model now in place fosters a focus on demonic possession, and we would hardly wish to become mired in a medieval model that sees the primary pastoral task as looking for the presence of demons. Sticking the name of a demon on a complex, multifaceted problem may give the illusion of understanding, and may be understandable in a context in which there are a limited number of therapists, psychiatrists, and social workers, but it falls woefully short of addressing the root issues that people really face. It is not enough to ask the counselee to recall dreams or smells or the loss of personal effects. The diagnostic tool needs to probe major life changes as well as possible stress from problems that arise in daily life.

I need to say a final word regarding the use of diagnostic tools. Counselors should not use diagnostic tools as if they were a rigid set of measures to determine the state of the counselee. These tools are merely guidelines and should remain fluid in the hand of the pastor, allowing him or her to use them judiciously as only one means to explore the issues that arise in the unfolding conversation. Pastors should not encumber the pastoral encounter with theological or psychological jargon that might only confuse and frustrate the counselee. Over time and with practice, pastors will learn how to glean vital information that helps them get a feel for the total person, and thus formulate a plan of intervention, without posing questions or responses that are filled with specialized vocabulary.

Therefore, in the pages that follow, I provide as a model a composite text taken from a number of counseling sessions that can serve as an illustration of how pastoral counseling might proceed.[24] The text particularly takes account of the total person and utilizes the insights of theology and depth psychology suggested in this study.

Verbatim

Background

First, a little background is necessary to introduce the pastoral conversation below. The counselee presented here is a young woman (whom we will call Akosua) who was very frustrated when all attempts to bring peace and con-

---

24. Portions have been modified and the name has been changed to disguise the identity of the counselee. I am indebted to her for permission to use this material.

tentment in her marriage through prayer had failed. Akosua had married in her late twenties, but her previous romantic relationships had been dysfunctional. When she loved a man she loved him desperately, but the man would either leave for no reason or the relationship would go cold. When a man loved her enough to contemplate marriage, Akosua was tentative. Talks with pastors had led Akosua to believe that demonic powers or familial spirits were at work against her where marriage was concerned. Indeed, she had been told on several occasions that spiritual forces were against her.

Akosua often had dreams in which she sensed a dark figure attempting to have sexual intercourse with her, and her pastors interpreted these dreams as the spiritual enactment of a marriage that she may have unknowingly contracted with a spirit being. But Akosua had no knowledge of any such occurrence in her life. She found all these things puzzling, especially since she came from a Christian home and had no knowledge of any fetishes with which her people might have had contact. Pastors encouraged her to renounce her complicity in any ancestral worship through attendance at annual festivals and to pray a prayer of deliverance. In these prayers, the demonic forces believed to be blocking her relationships with men were subjected to the blood of the Lamb (that is, brought under the authority of the power believed to inhere in the sacrificial blood of Jesus), bound, and cast into hell in the name of Jesus. While it seemed that Akosua did not outwardly subscribe to what she had been told by the pastors, some inner part of her believed it. She prayed constantly and asked God to remove whatever familial spirit was at work against her.

Eventually Akosua became engaged. Before her wedding, however, she had a series of strange dreams, which she shared with a few close friends. These friends prayed with her and confirmed some of the things she had heard about spiritual marriages being the source of marital problems. Akosua dreamed that she found herself walking through a dark alley on her way home. About a block from her house, someone who looked like her sister poured human feces all over her body. In another dream a few weeks later, she was on her way to her own wedding, but she was on foot and traveled through difficult terrain and weather before arriving at the wedding site. She arrived at the door to the chapel drenched, and only then did she realize that her wedding gown was two colors — white and black. At the entrance to the church she found a memorial service going on while the wedding party was in the church. Friends and pastors told her that the dream was an indication that death was lurking around the corner either for herself or her future spouse, and so they prayed for safety for the engaged couple. They also suggested that since the couple had been pressured into having the ceremony in their hometown rather than in the capital city, as they had initially planned, witchcraft spirits were probably at work. They encouraged Akosua to convince her fiancé to have the wedding in the city. In the end, however, the marriage was held in their hometown.

Since their wedding day nothing had been the same between Akosua and her new husband. Everything Akosua did displeased him; he only found fault with her, and the more Akosua tried to please him, the worse things became. Fasting and praying and several deliverance sessions brought no relief. To make matters worse, the couple was childless after three years of marriage. Akosua had hoped that a child might draw them closer together. Doubt about God's presence in her life brought Akosua to the office of Pastor Asamoah, their new pastor. Akosua had heard that he was very helpful, and she came to him hoping that she would be able to sort out some of her feelings and find peace.

Session Text

Akosua: *(Tentative knock at the door)* Hello.
Pastor Asamoah: Come in. Hello, Akosua. Have a seat.
A: Thank you, and thanks for seeing me.
P: Well, I'm glad you came. How are you today?
A: Quite well; I still have a lot on my mind, but I think I'm doing all right.
P: I'm glad to hear that. Is there anything I can do for you today? You asked to see me at the close of church last Sunday.
A: Actually, there is. I've been going through a difficult time lately and nothing seems to make any sense anymore. I feel my life has come to a standstill but I'm still going on. I seem to be going round in circles, and no one seems to be able to help me.
P: It seems as though you are going through a difficult and confusing time.
A: Yes, and I believe I've done everything I can do to help the situation, but it doesn't get any better. Sometimes I think God is not listening to my prayers anymore. Nothing makes sense with where God fits in with things that are going on in my life. It is not that I don't believe in God anymore. It is just that I wonder if he is listening to my prayers or if he cares about the things that are happening to me. Maybe he's interested in the big things, but I just don't know.

P: Hmm. I see how that can be a difficult thing to grapple with. Could you tell me more about what is making you feel God is not watching out for you on a day-to-day basis and interested in the little details of your life?

A: Well, this has been going on for a while. I've been praying about a particular situation and nothing seems to be happening. The worst part is that I don't even sense that God is listening to these prayers. It's almost as if he's not there or . . . I mean there are times when I have prayed and I know that God is listening to my prayer, but somehow for these prayers nothing seems to be happening.

P: What exactly have you been praying about, and what is it that God is not answering? Could you tell me more?

A: Well, it's like this. Well, basically right now it is about my marriage. It is also about things that happened long before. I got married late in life but long before then it felt like men hardly noticed me at all. I used to wonder if I was not pretty enough or what was wrong with me. If someone came into my life, they left again and I couldn't figure it out. If they loved me, I did not want them. If I liked them, they did not like me. Somehow there was never a click. Well, I went to see a few pastors that suggested that it is obvious that since I was an okay kind of person it is likely that the source could be from my home.

P: Did they tell you why they thought that something in your house could be the reason why you have relational problems?

A: Well, there are a lot of broken marriages in my house, and my grandparents had more than one spouse each. And [the pastors] said that often when things like that go on generation after generation, then there is a spirit behind it. They suggested that the people in my household fast and pray that God would break the cycle and that he would give me a husband and children also. One thing I was asked was whether I experience someone sleeping with me in my dreams. I had on occasions experienced that. I was told that it was an indication that I had a spiritual marriage and that it had to be broken before I could marry or have any children. I believed that God took care of all that after the prayer. After all, it is not my fault and I am his child and I assumed he would take care of me and I had nothing to worry about. But all this was many years ago. Anyway, so now I finally get married and the marriage is not jelling. You know we just live together and [it is] almost as if my husband doesn't see who I am; he doesn't appreciate me; there are always tension and arguments. Sometimes we talk and it looks as if we [are] talking past each other. It's almost as if we can't hear each other. Almost as if we want to say the same things but [are] saying them in opposite ways. And, well . . . I don't know. You could say that we have communication problems, but it seems there's more going on here.

P: You think that what is going on is more than just that you are learning to communicate with each other and it is taking longer than usual?

A: Yes, pastor, yes. And let me share with you a couple of the dreams I've had, some before the wedding and some during the relationship. Just before the wedding, I dreamt that it was almost like it was my own sister and she just dumped this bucket of feces on me. One dark night I was walking through an alley very close to home. I was either on my way home or from home; I can't quite remember. And I woke up and I thought, "What is this?" Later when I shared with pastors they said that dreams like that, where dirty things are thrown on you or at you, there is usually witchcraft activity involved. A witchcraft thing is being put on me or something like that. It is a way of covering up who you really are. It is like you've been dirtied and when people look at you they see the dirty external rather than who you really are. Who you are doesn't really show; when people look at you they see nasty things rather than what is really inside. Well, we prayed about it and I prayed about it quite a bit, but *(pause)* I don't know.

P: So you think that what is happening now in your marriage is a result of a witchcraft spirit or a spell placed on you? That maybe your husband cannot see who you really are because of this?

A: Yes, because of this thing that has been put on me. I guess I had assumed that since I had prayed, God would take that away and that things would be normal, that my husband will see me for who I am and understand how I love and appreciate him and nothing seems to be happening. I don't know, but I think that in many ways I don't believe what I've been told, but I don't understand why all these years of praying have not taken it away.

P: If I hear you correctly, you think that this is the main source of your marital conflict, that something evil is influencing your relationship with your husband?

A: Yes.

P: Let me ask you something, Akosua. Do you think that other people find you attractive, find you a nice person to be with and appreciate who you are and the things you do?

A: Yes, I do. I know that other people appreciate me and other people think, well, I'm okay.

P: So it is just your husband who doesn't?

A: Yes, it's just my husband who doesn't.

P: That is interesting. Why do you think that whatever is covering you is seen only by your husband and not by other people? Why would other people see you as a lovely person and a nice person to be with and only your husband wouldn't see you in the same light?

A: I don't know. That has been a little confusing but sometimes it makes me think that he has been blinded also. I don't know how this thing works.

P: So it seems as though when whatever was put on you through a witchcraft spirit was set in place from this dream that you had, your husband could also at the same time have been blinded to you? Could you tell me more?

A: Well, the way I understand this, the way it works is that since it is witchcraft spirits at work, your husband is also blinded to you. Or maybe that in my husband's own house, people are like that or maybe that he is also married spiritually to somebody, so that he doesn't really belong to me or even to himself. He is not free to be a husband to me.

P: *(Pause. Akosua was looking very perplexed.)* What do you think God's purpose for marriage is? Have you ever considered it?

A: Well, I know that one of the reasons the Bible gives us is so that we'll not be lonely anymore. I know that sometimes we'll have problems and work through them. But what is happening here is like little things that have become so big and they seem unsolvable, and that is one major characteristic of a witchcraft spirit at work. You find yourself fighting over little things for no reason. And that is why people say, *"Yea dani woanim"* [they have turned your face].

P: Do you feel lonely now?

A: Yes. In many ways I do.

P: Do you think that if, as you said, God's purpose for marriage is that we not be lonely anymore that he would want to do something, everything in his power to bring your marriage together because he created marriage so people would not be lonely anymore?

A: Yes, that is what I suppose, but I still do not know why for all these years of praying, nothing seems to have happened.

P: So you seem to be at a point where you believe God is not interested in answering your prayers and putting together your marriage even though he answers other prayers? As you mentioned earlier, you pray about other things and you feel as if God is at least listening, but on this issue which seems very dear to your heart and even possibly in the will of God since he created marriage, God is not listening?

A: Yes, that seems to be the general idea and, like I said, it is very confusing to me why he wouldn't listen.

P: Do you have any reasons why God is not listening or responding to your prayers?

A: I don't know and that is the worst part.

P: Is it possible that you think that the spiritual forces at work maybe are preventing this particular issue?

A: In many ways, but I also know that God is stronger than these spiritual forces, and that is why I can't understand. If it is these spiritual forces, why doesn't he just knock them out? But the other thing that people said to me was that, well, we got married in my husband's hometown, just to please him and other family members. And, well, people were saying that all the dreams and the feelings I was having before the marriage ceremony [were] because maybe I shouldn't have gone and gotten married there because the spiritual forces could have gotten to me or to our relationship and they wouldn't have if we had just gotten married where we were — that is, in the capital, as we had planned. And I'm tempted to believe these explanations and I also know that maybe I didn't pray enough over the whole relationship and this marriage. I mean I was sure that this was what God was asking of us, but the truth is that right now I think I'm more confused than anything.

P: If I hear you correctly, you are saying that the place you got married, the location of the actual ceremony has something to do with what is going on now? It seems as though you're saying that God's power to protect you is more present in one locality than another. Could you tell me exactly what you mean by saying that you believe where you got married could have contributed to the difficulties in your present situation?

A: Well, I think that what I'm saying is that it looked like everything was going on well until the decision to have the ceremony in this particular place was made, and that is when I started having these dreams. I don't know if I mentioned it earlier that part of my wedding dress was white and the other black and that I walked a long time through rain and just bad weather, got lost several times before I arrived at the church and when I got there, a funeral was in front of the door right at the entrance. I even had to ask them if this was the place also for the wedding, and the wedding was inside. And later I was thinking that is a mixture of joy and sadness. My dress itself was like half-mourning, half-rejoicing. And the way people interpreted it to me when I shared it was maybe evil spiritual forces might be trying to kill us or at least are bent on destroying or preventing the marriage. So we concentrated our prayers on asking God for protection and now it looks like it is more like, you know, they were preventing the joy that would come from the marriage. And I know, I hear what you said, it is not as if God's power is more present in one place than another but, well *(laughs),* now that you say it, it doesn't make any sense that I would think so. But I think I've been secretly thinking if only we had gotten married in the capital where we both lived that would have been better. But what I hear now is that God could have had us marry in Fantsiniko or even in the fetish grove and it wouldn't have made a difference because he is God, right?

P: What do you think?

A: Well, in my heart, I believe so, but I think if you are going to do something like that, you really have to pray a lot before, you know, soak the whole place in the blood of Jesus and all that.

P: Could you tell me what else was going on in your life before this relationship started? Maybe a little about how it started and how you came to a decision to marry Frank. Was it a clear-cut decision or were there always doubts in your mind as to marrying Frank? Could you tell me at least as far as you think you remember?

A: Well, I must confess I had moments of doubt. There were times I could tell that I was pondering whether this was the person, but I think that we all go through that. I believe there is no perfect person out there for us. It is possible that is all that was there, but I think that you might have hit on something, that I always had this little doubt in my mind. I'm not sure how much of it I was processing, or you could say that I was not completely relaxed about the relationship. There were lots of moments when I was, and I know that when I came to the decision, that this was it, and I let it go. But I don't know, maybe back of my mind I may have always wondered. But I know that I prayed about it, and I knew this was what I wanted to do, and this is what God would have and so . . . .

P: Did you and Frank ever have premarital counseling with the pastor or any older couple?

A: Not really, but we read a lot and we talked to people. You could say that we had about three sessions of counseling with the pastor. And we were getting on really well, you know. In many ways we complemented each other. In fact you could say that the relationship looked too good to be true. It seemed everything I had asked for had been given to me, even to the last details. What kind of person I wanted and all that, and I guess that is why sometimes I can buy the spiritual conflict idea. It is possible that there is some of it.

P: Yes, it is possible that there is some of it, but could there be something more? Maybe your personalities and different styles of communication that you are still working on? What do you think? Could the dreams you were having be just a replay of the conflict that you were having in your mind as you made the decision to marry Frank? It could be that your doubts were deeper than you allowed yourself to think.

A: That is a possibility; but how come I didn't pick up on it then? Because if I hear you correctly these may be the doubts I was having that were coming up in my dreams.

P: It is possible, and sometimes we don't always pick up on these clues. Often conversations like we are having now help bring them out. But how do you feel now that you think it might not just be evil spiritual forces at work, but that the doubts from the beginning of the relationship could be a factor? Do you think those doubts are still present? I would encourage you to think about these things and maybe look back at the beginning of the relationship and we can meet again next week?

A: Yes, I'd like that.

P: Would you like to share in a prayer?

Dear heavenly Father, we come before you today with our pains, our questions and our doubts and fears, for you say that we can bring whatever burdens we have and you will carry us and them. We thank you for this conversation and for the fact that you were listening to it as well. I bring your daughter Akosua before you and ask that you will calm her fears and assure her of your love and care. Please let her know she is not alone and that you are with her even through these problems. Your promise is that you will never leave us nor forsake us. I pray you will press this truth into Akosua's heart. May she know that you do not reprove her for her doubts and fears, but you wait to see her grow in grace through them. In Jesus Christ our Lord, we pray with thanksgiving. Amen.

A: Amen. Thank you. I'll see you next week.

P: Yes, and have a blessed week. Bye.

The Analysis

From a purely African theological perspective, especially as evidenced in Ghanaian counseling today, Akosua appears to be under intense demonic or spiritual attack from familial spirits. The spiritual forces that attacked her in her dreams prior to her marriage are now entrenched in her marriage and refusing to move. Notably, several prayers on her behalf had not solved the situation, and Akosua continues to live in an unhappy marriage. Since prayer alone has failed to rectify the situation, it is probable that more than just spiritual causes are responsible for the impasse. As the conversation above shows, there might be psychic factors at work as well. For a fuller analysis, we can turn to the Clinical Pastoral Education model of verbatim reporting. Such a model can be helpful to the pastor who needs to formulate clear plans for ongoing pastoral visits until Akosua is brought to a place of healing in herself and in her marriage.

Description

Akosua is a nurse midwife at one of the government hospitals. She is a pretty girl by all standards with an easy smile and a pleasant manner. Sometimes there is a tentativeness about her that suggests she is still finding herself in the world. Today she has on a frock made from an African print. Her hair is in braids tied back with a hair band that picks up one of the many colors in her dress.

THEOLOGICAL

Akosua is a Christian who, due to her present situation, seems to be going through a period of great doubt as to the real presence of God in her life. She constantly wonders if God is with her or hears her. We might say that if Akosua was aware of the providence of God in the past, she is not aware of it now, and it weighs heavily on her. We can describe Akosua's God-image as almost malevolent, though it is still fairly fluid. God seems to be elusive at this time, and if Akosua were forced to voice it, she might say that God was not dependable. At the same time, Akosua holds on to what she has been taught about God and thus continues to pray about this rather baffling situation. A little of the confused distorted image of God comes through when she suggests that God's protective power is more present in one place than in others. There is a perceptible influence of her cultural worldview here. There are different kinds of gods occupying different terrains, and these gods are more powerful on their terrain than on others. What is more troubling is Akosua's tendency toward works righteousness. Much seems to depend on her attentiveness to prayer and fasting and deliverance sessions rather than on the desire and promise of God to protect and love her.

For Akosua, God no longer seems to care, or if he does, Akosua sees no evidence of this fact. God's grace and mercy seem to elude her in her time of need. The problem is compounded by her sense that she must be perfect before her prayers are adequately answered. Underlying all of this is a belief that when powerful spiritual forces are present in a location, a special effort is needed on God's part to effect deliverance. She feels that she must bear all the pain and confusion stoically, and that the only plausible causes for God's unresponsiveness are either her own failure to pray effectively, or sin committed by herself or by her ancestors.

At this point we may ask how a Barthian reading of Scripture might help Akosua gain a scriptural perspective of God's love and care for her. How might Akosua be helped to see that God is interested in her, loves and cares about her, and listens to her prayers for healing and wholeness? Furthermore, how can she be helped to understand God's own attitude toward sin and human suffering? Barth's reading of Scripture offers insights into God's attitude toward human sin and suffering that may be helpful to Akosua in her current situation. In reflecting on the gospel stories of healing, Barth points out that God is involved in human suffering. Jesus' own example demonstrates that God's concern in the face of suffering is not judgment or finding fault, but is rather to mercifully alleviate the pain of the sufferer and restore her to health. A scriptural example that supports this assertion is the healing of the blind man in John 9. To the query of the disciples, "Rabbi, who sinned, this man or his parents, that he was born blind?" Jesus answers, "Neither this man nor his parents sinned; he was born blind so that God's works might be revealed in him" (John 9:2-3). Barth comments:

> [In] these stories it does not seem to be of any great account that the men who suffer as creatures are above all sinful men, men who are at fault in relation to God, their neighbours and themselves, who are

therefore guilty and have betrayed themselves into all kinds of trouble. No, the important thing about them in these stories is not that they are sinners but that they are sufferers. Jesus . . . does not ask, therefore, concerning their sin. He does not hold it against them. . . . The help and blessing that He brings are quite irrespective of their sin.[25]

It is possible that for Akosua, too, the question is not whether she or her parents have done wrong for which she bears the consequences, but rather that Akosua is in pain and that God wants to bring her rest and release. God does not expect Akosua to be without sin or to be perfect before God hears and intervenes. On the contrary, God showers mercy on all, the good and the bad alike, for he causes "his sun to rise on the evil and on the good, and sends rain on the righteous and on the unrighteous" (Matt. 5:45). God is always ready to show his mercy to all. According to Barth,

> The free inclination of God to His creature, denoted in the biblical witness by grace, takes place under the presupposition that the creature is in distress and that God's intention is to espouse his cause and to grant him assistance in his extremity. . . . God's very being is mercy. The mercy of God lies in His readiness to share in sympathy the distress of another, a readiness which springs from His inmost nature and stamps all His being and doing. It lies, therefore, in His will, springing from the depths of His nature and characterising it, to take the initiative Himself for the removal of this distress.[26]

In contrast to what Akosua supposes, God is more than willing to alleviate her pain and end her suffering. In fact, if Barth is right, it seems nearly impossible for God *not* to act on Akosua's behalf, because such a failure would be counter to the very nature of God. Thus God is not indifferent to Akosua's plight, but rather wishes to turn toward her in mercy to alleviate her suffering.

If God is omnipotent, merciful, and just, and Akosua's sin (past, present, and future) and that of her forebears have all been judged and acquitted in Christ and no longer imputed to her, why does Akosua still feel out of sorts and unable to find relief? How might the pastor help Akosua understand and deal with what she feels to be the work of demonic forces in her

---

25. Barth, *Church Dogmatics* IV/2, 222-23.
26. Barth, *Church Dogmatics* II/1, 369.

life and marriage? We cannot dismiss her concerns and fears even though we are aware of God's presence with her. Here Barth's own conception of the demonic, as explicated in previous chapters, may open the door to a psychological interpretation to supplement his theological framework.

PSYCHOLOGICAL

Akosua seems to be floundering in her marital relationship, a situation that is clearly challenging her faith. She has internalized responsibility for maintaining the relationship, thus placing undue stress on herself. Akosua's relational history reveals that she struggles with unaddressed issues with commitment. Why, for instance, is she drawn towards men who do not love her? One possible answer is that Akosua has unresolved issues from her relationship with primary caregivers in her family of origin. But she cannot come to this realization on her own, nor would a pastor using the prevailing Ghanaian counseling framework be able to help her appreciate the value of the dreams she has been having. This is where a pastor with the insights of analytical psychology might provide tremendous help to Akosua.

From a Jungian perspective, we can explain most of Akosua's dreams psychodynamically. If we examine the dreams immediately prior to her marriage, for instance, we notice that they were filled with intensely contrasting images: the wedding dress that is half white and half black, the wedding ceremony with a group of mourners congregated outside the church while the wedding guests were inside. Akosua finds herself at the center of this collision between dark and light, pain and joy. While a pastor interpreted these images as indications of imminent death or some other evil, from a Jungian perspective we could interpret them as an invitation to Akosua to realize that marriage is a process whereby she will discover her full humanity. Through her marriage she will come to realize that human beings are not perfect, but rather have weaknesses and limitations with which they struggle everyday. The opposites of joy and pain, light and dark, will be blended together, for real human existence entails both pain and joy, trying times and peaceful times. If Akosua's own personality leads her to see the world in black and white, perfectionistic terms, then these dreams may provide her with an opportunity to recognize and accept that marriage entails living with an imperfect person. Such an interpretation might help Akosua see that her dreams were not a foreboding omen, but rather a sign of the death of her old self — that is, Akosua as a single person — and the birth of a new person in union with another human being.

We can venture another possible interpretation of the pre-wedding dreams, an interpretation that is by far the most important from a Jungian perspective. This would be to see the dreams as the integration of the shadow into the conscious personality. Since the realization of the shadow is inhibited by the persona, the public image, it is often difficult to recognize the shadow and to allow its integration into the personality. We might interpret these dreams of intense opposites as an invitation to Akosua to integrate the less appealing aspects of her psyche into her personality by allowing them to enter consciousness, thus creating a more balanced person. As Jung puts it,

> [I]t is a therapeutic necessity, indeed, the first requisite of any thorough psychological method, for consciousness to confront its shadow. In the end this must lead to some kind of union, even though the union consists at first in an open conflict, and often remains so for a long time. It is a struggle that cannot be abolished by rational means. When it is willfully repressed it continues in the unconscious and merely expresses itself indirectly and all the more dangerously, so no advantage is gained. The struggle goes on until the opponents run out of breath. What the outcome will be can never be seen in advance. The only certain thing is that both parties will be changed. . . .[27]

Furthermore,

> This process of coming to terms with the Other in us is well worth while, because in this way we get to know aspects of our nature which we would not allow anybody else to show us and which we ourselves would never have admitted.[28]

Theological and Psychological Analysis in Tandem

We can explore the issues underlying Akosua's God-image, showing how, from a Barthian perspective, theological and psychological insights can relate to each other, but with the theological given conceptual precedence over

---

27. C. G. Jung, "Rex and Regina," *Collected Works,* 2nd ed., vol. 14 (Princeton, N.J.: Princeton University Press, 1969), para. 514.
28. Jung, "The Conjunction," *Collected Works,* vol. 14, para. 706.

the psychological. This is also a good point to revisit Deborah Hunsinger's categories and show how they may be used to facilitate the pastoral counseling process.

Recalling Hunsinger's classification grid and the ensuing discussion above, we can say from a theological perspective that Akosua's God-representation is a complex one. Hunsinger proposes that from the point of view of psychology and theology, we can view any God-representation from either particular field by its own set of norms. We can also view any God-representation from the perspective of both disciplines simultaneously. From a theological perspective, it seems that Akosua believes that God is able to do all things, yet she wonders why God is not doing anything about her particular situation. There are only two possible answers to the problem posed in this way: either God is not able to do all things or God does not care about Akosua enough to do something about her situation. And yet we perceive from her confusion that she does not believe in either of these possibilities. Her God-representation does not seem to be inadequate in so far as she knows God to be powerful and loving and able to come to her aid, but the lack of apparent help from God in her situation produces doubt. On the other hand, she reports receiving answers to her prayers at other times even in the midst of difficulty. When she sets limits on God's omnipotence and assumes that God is unable to prevent the evil spiritual forces in a particular locality from attacking her marriage, we have glimpses of a theologically inadequate image of God. It is theologically inadequate because Scripture testifies that God is omnipresent and has power over evil forces, over all principalities and powers.

From a psychological perspective, Akosua's God-representation is dysfunctional because it does not help her in her situation, since she seems to be frustrated by the lack of help from God. At the same time, we find traces of psychological functionality in that Akosua assumes that God and God alone can help her in her difficulty. By continuing to trust God's promise in spite of continuing hardship in the marriage, Akosua continues to have hope, which buoys her up when depression threatens to overcome her. Maybe for the moment it is the kind of image Akosua needs to survive, to avoid drowning in self-pity over her marriage.

The aim of pastoral counseling in this regard is to bring Akosua to the place where her God-image is both theologically adequate and psychologically functional. As Ghanaian counseling is currently practiced, all the attention would focus on the malevolent power of the perceived demonic forces at work. The implicit psychological questions woven into the theological questions would thus be ignored. Operating from a more comprehensive framework, however, a pastor would not feel the need to quickly repair Akosua's God-representation. The pastor's focus would be on helping Akosua find healing for herself and her marriage first, and in and through that journey come to a richer and fuller understanding of God. He would put greater emphasis on trusting God and the mystery of God's ways even when fervent prayers do not seem to bring the desired result. If her salvation is ultimately secure in Jesus Christ, and if Akosua trusts in God's promise, she can lean on her faith to take risks in her marriage and actively work toward her own healing process, both intrapsychically (regarding shadow and animus issues) and interpersonally with her husband.

PLANS FOR NEXT VISIT

The next visit could probe the psychological underpinnings of some of the issues Akosua describes in her dreams as well as any unresolved childhood issues that may be blocking her from giving and receiving love. Exploring these issues psychologically could have the paradoxical effect of assuring Akosua of God's love apart from her works, freeing her from the anxiety of trying to earn love from her relationships.

When Akosua came back for the next appointment, Pastor Asamoah probed a little further into her childhood memories and the possible sources of some of her other dreams. It seems that Akosua was struggling with abandonment issues and lack of love. She wanted more than her husband was willing or able to give. She recalled that her mother was absent on a number of occasions and that she was never sure when her mother was going to come back. It seems likely that in her previous relationships and marriage Akosua was repeating patterns that were rooted in her childhood attachment issues. She was constantly afraid that the love she found would leave unless she did something to keep it there. Her partners understandably felt smothered in this kind of situation and left.

Pastor Asamoah subsequently arranged, with her consent, to speak to Akosua and her husband, Frank, together. He also had a chance to talk with Frank alone later, and Frank shared about his own childhood. As Frank recounted his story, it became clear that he had difficulties attaching in relationships. His own mother had smothered him, becoming so attached to him that she became emotionally dependent on him. While Frank outwardly loved and cared for his mother and was always on hand to meet her needs, inwardly he resented her for her constant need of him and for the shame he felt about needing time for himself. His mother carried him constantly as a baby and never allowed him to go off and explore the world. She always had a watchful eye on him. He was not allowed to make and correct his own mistakes; there were always people on hand to do that for him. Frustrated at several stages in his psychosocial development, Frank grew up a very emotional boy, crying at the drop of a hat, and yet he constantly heard, "Boys don't cry; put a lid on it." He learned over time to suppress his feelings and to be emotionally distant in all his relationships. The distance served him well in many relationships, and the culture even rewarded him for it. Often in the face of emotional situations he would act tough, like a typical "macho man." As an adult, however, Frank's stunted emotional development has left him isolated and apathetic. He has learned to survive by dispensing little emotional energy. The only model of marriage Frank knows is what he grew up with, and since he is unwilling to invest any emotional energy, he has been unwilling to learn new patterns or redefine his relationships, which could chart a productive course for his marriage.

In a sense, Akosua and Frank were both living a lie and were not willing to work on what they needed to make their relationship work. The wall they felt between them was not imaginary, but it was not, strictly speaking, a spiritual wall, as Akosua had been told. It existed on a psychological and emotional level, and was built both through conscious and unconscious behaviors. While they desperately wanted to draw near, their unconscious fears of intimacy only increased their distance from each other.

While this is not an exhaustive analysis, it helped Pastor Asamoah set in motion a plan of intervention that would help the couple first address the individual issues they brought into the relationship and then learn how to live in relationship with each other, working through their interpersonal issues in the context of their marriage.

Conclusion

The approach to counseling demonstrated in this counseling session is different from what currently prevails in Ghana in so far as this pastor utilizes resources from both theology and depth psychology. His knowledge of psychology made it possible for him to discontinue the line of conversation with Akosua that suggested that her problems derived entirely from spiritual sources. Above all, his confidence in God's grace and presence made it possible for him to stay with Akosua through her confusing thoughts about

God without interjecting his own "correct" theology. He was able to guide Akosua to a truth about God's omnipotence that helped her overcome some of her fears. Finally, by bringing both parties together and addressing the issues that were hindering their growth as a couple, he was able to dispel some of the cosmological beliefs that held Akosua in bondage.

The aim of pastoral counselors, after all, should be to work toward an adequate theology that goes hand in hand with a functional psychology. We are willing to give theology logical priority within the counseling situation without failing to address real psychological issues. There are some pastoral situations when it may be beneficial or even necessary to err on the side of psychological reductionism in the difficult work of diagnosis. As Christian counselors we are free to do this because, in the first place, we know that God's grace, mercy, and faithful love are active even in the most imperfect works of healing. Pastoral counseling must finally trust in the overcoming power of Christ's death and resurrection, by which God is forever bound in covenant love to those who suffer and seek relief. Undergirded by the unfailing faithfulness of the God revealed in Jesus Christ, even the most childlike prayer is invested with power to cast out and defeat the truly demonic.

In light of Christ's victory over evil, we might say that the work of individuation is deeper and more difficult than the work of exorcism. We must also be willing to work with God for the total transformation that we need to experience abundant life. God calls us to salvation and sanctification, and sanctification necessarily includes the difficult process of individuation. Thus, psychological healing towards individuation is an integral part of the total healing that the Spirit of God is working in all people, transforming each person into the image of Jesus Christ.

Selected Bibliography

Adams, Michael V. *The Multicultural Imagination: "Race," Color and the Unconscious*. London: Routledge, 1996.

Akesson, Sam K. "The Akan Concept of Soul." *African Affairs* 64, no. 257 (1965): 280-91.

Augsburger, David W. *Pastoral Counseling across Cultures*. Philadelphia: Westminster Press, 1986.

Aulén, Gustaf. *Christus Victor*. New York: Collier Books, 1969.

Awasu, Wilson. "Religion, Christianity and the Powers in Ewe Society." Ph.D. diss., Fuller Theological Seminary, School of World Mission, Pasadena, Calif., 1988.

Baeta, C. G. *Prophetism in Ghana*. London: S.C.M. Press, 1962.

Barth, K. *The Christian Life*. Translated by J. Strathearn McNab. London: Student Christian Movement Press, 1930.

————. *Church Dogmatics*. Edinburgh: T&T Clark, 1960.

Bediako, Kwame. *Christianity in Africa: The Renewal of a Non-Western Religion*. Edinburgh: Edinburgh University Press, 1995.

————. *Jesus in African Culture: A Ghanaian Perspective*. Accra: Asempa Publishers, 1990.

Berkhof, Hendrik. *Christ and the Powers*. Scottdale: Herald Publications, 1962.

Bloesch, Donald G. *Essentials of Evangelical Theology*. Vol. 2. Peabody, Mass.: Prince Press, 1998.

The Book of Confessions, "The Shorter Catechism." Louisville: Presbyterian Church, USA, 1991.

Busia, K. A. "The Ashanti." In Cyril Daryll Forde, *African Worlds: Studies in the Cosmological Ideas and Social Values of African People*. London: Oxford University Press, 1963.

Carlson, Dwight L. "Exposing the Myth That Christians Should Not Have Emotional Problems." In *Christianity Today*, Feb. 9, 1998, Vol. 42, No. 2, online at http://www.christianitytoday.com/ct/8t2/8t2O28.html, accessed December 13, 2000.

Chodorow, Joan ed. *Jung on Active Imagination.* Princeton: Princeton University Press, 1997.

Clebsch, William A., and Charles R. Jaekle. *Pastoral Care in Historical Perspective.* New York and London: Jason Aronson, 1983.

Danquah, Joseph B. *The Akan Doctrine of God.* London: Lutterworth Press, 1944.

Dickson, Kwesi. *Theology in Africa.* Maryknoll, N.Y.: Orbis Books, 1984.

Dickson, Kwesi, and P. Ellingworth. *Biblical Revelation and African Beliefs.* London: Lutterworth Press, 1969.

Dittes, James. "Religion: Psychological Study." In *International Encyclopedia of the Social Sciences,* Vol. 13, ed. David L. Sills. New York: Macmillan and the Free Press, 1968.

Driscoll, John T. "Miracles." In *The Catholic Encyclopedia.* Vol. 10. New York: Robert Appleton Co., 1911. Online Edition 1999.

Ellis, A. B. *The Ewe-speaking Peoples.* Anthropological Publications, Evangelical Presbyterian Church, 1890.

Foerster, Werner. "Daimon." In *Theological Dictionary of the New Testament.* Vol. 11, ed. Gerhard Kittel. Grand Rapids: W. B. Eerdmans Publishing Co., 1994.

Forde, Daryl. *African Worlds: Studies in the Cosmological Ideas and Social Values of African People.* London: Oxford University Press, 1963.

Frank, Jerome D., and Julia B. Frank. *Healing and Persuasion: A Comparative Study of Psychotherapy,* 3rd ed. Baltimore: Johns Hopkins University Press, 1993.

Gaba, Christian R. "Anlo Traditional Religion." Ph.D. diss., University of London, 1965.

————. "Sacrifice in Anlo Religion." In *Ghana Bulletin of Theology,* vol. 3, no. 5 (December 1968): 10-15.

Hanson, Paul. *The Dawn of Apocalyptic.* Minneapolis: Fortress Press, 1986.

Hiebert, P. "Worldview." In *Dictionary of Pastoral Care and Counseling,* ed. Rodney Hunter. Nashville: Abingdon Press, 1990.

Horton, Robin. "African Traditional Thought and Western Science." *Africa,* vol. 3 (January 1967): 53-58.

Hunsinger, George. *How to Read Karl Barth.* New York, Oxford: Oxford University Press, 1991.

Idowu, E. Bolaji. *Oludumare: God in Yuroba Belief.* London: S.C.M. Press Ltd., 1963.

Jennings, Willie J. *The Christian Imagination: Theology and the Origins of Race.* New Haven: Yale University Press, 2011.

Johnson, P. J. "Witchcraft." In *Dictionary of Pastoral Care and Counseling,* ed. Rodney Hunter. Nashville: Abingdon Press, 1990.

Jung, C. G. "Definitions." In *Collected Works.* Vol. 8. 2nd ed. Princeton, N.J.: Princeton University Press, 1969.

———. "Instincts and the Unconscious." In *Collected Works*. Vol. 8. 2nd ed. Princeton: Princeton University Press, 1969.

———. *Memories, Dreams, Reflections*. New York: Vintage Books, 1965.

———. *Psyche and Symbol*. Translated by R. F. C. Hull. Bollingen Series. Princeton: Princeton University Press, 1991.

———. "The Psychological Foundations of Belief in Spirits." In *Collected Works*. Vol. 8.

———. "A Review of the Complex Theory." In *Collected Works*. Vol. 8. 2nd ed. Princeton: Princeton University Press, 1969.

Kearny, Michael. *World View*. Norato: Chalder and Sharp Publisher, Inc., 1984.

Kelsey, Morton T. *Dreams: The Dark Speech of the Spirit*. Garden City, N.Y.: Doubleday, 1968.

Ladd, G. E. *The Presence of the Future*. Grand Rapids: Eerdmans Publishing Co., 1974.

Lartey, E. Y. *Pastoral Counselling in Inter-cultural Perspective*. Frankfurt am Main: Verlag Peter Lang, 1987.

Loder, J. E., & W. Jim Neidhart. *The Knight's Move*. Colorado Springs: Helmers & Howard Publishers Inc., 1992.

MacNutt, Francis. *Deliverance from Evil Spirits: A Practical Manual*. Grand Rapids: Baker House Book Company, 1995.

Meyrowitz, Eva. *The Akan of Ghana: Their Ancient Beliefs*. London: Faber and Faber Limited, 1958.

———. "Concepts of the Soul among the Akan of the Gold Coast." *Africa*, vol. 21, (1951).

Moschela Clark, Mary. *Ethnography as Pastoral Practice: An Introduction*. Cleveland: Pilgrim, 2008.

Moreau, A. Scott. "Demon." In *Evangelical Dictionary of Biblical Theology*, ed. Walter A. Elwell, 163-64. Grand Rapids: Baker Books, 1996.

Newbigin, Lesslie. *The Gospel in a Pluralistic Society*. Grand Rapids: Wm. B. Eerdmans Publishing Co., 1989.

Oduyoye, Mercy. *Daughters of Anowa: African Women and Patriarchy*. Maryknoll, N.Y.: Orbis Books, 1995.

Otto, Rudolf. *The Idea of the Holy: An Inquiry into the Non-Rational Factor in the Idea of the Divine and Its Relation to the Rational*. London: Oxford University Press, 1958.

Parrinder, Geoffrey. *West African Religion*. London: The Epworth Press, 1961.

Perry, Michael. ed. *Deliverance: Psychic Disturbance and Occult Involvement*. London: SPCK, 1987, 1996.

Pobee, J. S. "African Instituted (Independent) Churches." In *Dictionary of the Ecumenical Movement*, 10-13. Geneva: World Council of Churches; Grand Rapids: Wm. B. Eerdmans Publishing Co., 1991.

Price, D. J. "Karl Barth's Anthropology in Light of Modern Thought: The Dynamic

Concept of the Person in Trinitarian Theology and Object Relations Psychology." Ph.D. diss., University of Aberdeen, 1990.

Pruyser, Paul. *The Minister as Diagnostician.* Philadelphia: Westminster Press, 1976.

Ramsay, Nancy J. *Pastoral Diagnosis: A Resource for Ministry of Care and Counseling.* Minneapolis: Augsburg Fortress Press, 1998.

Rizzuto, Ana-Maria. *The Birth of the Living God: A Psychoanalytic Study.* Chicago: University of Chicago Press, 1979.

Samuels, Andrew. *Jung and the Post-Jungians.* London: Routledge, 1997.

Sanneh, Lamin. *West African Christianity: The Religious Impact.* Maryknoll, N.Y.: Orbis Books, 1983.

Shuster, Marguerite. *Power, Pathology, Paradox.* Grand Rapids: Zondervan, 1987.

Smith-Christopher, Daniel L. "Daniel." In *New Interpreter's Bible,* Vol. 7, 97-152. Nashville: Abingdon, 1995.

Ulanov, Ann Belford. *The Functioning Transcendent.* Wilmette, Ill.: Chiron Press, 1996.

————. "The Psychological Reality of the Demonic." In *Picturing God.* Cambridge, Mass.: Cowley Publications, 1986.

Unger, Merrill F. *Biblical Demonology: A Study of the Spiritual Forces behind the Present World Unrest.* Wheaton, Ill.: Van Kampen Press Inc., 1952.

Van Deusen Hunsinger, Deborah. *Theology and Pastoral Counseling: A New Interdisciplinary Approach.* Grand Rapids: Wm. B. Eerdmans Publishing Co., 1995.

Weathers, Robert. "Dream Theory and Research." In *Dictionary of Pastoral Care and Counseling,* ed. Rodney Hunter. Nashville: Abingdon Press, 1990.

Wedel, Theodore O. "Ephesians." In *Interpreter's Bible.* Nashville: Abingdon, 1953.

Welker, Michael. *God the Spirit.* Translated by John F. Hoffmeyr. Minneapolis: Fortress Press, 1995.

Wink, Walter. *Naming the Powers: The Language of Power in the New Testament.* Philadelphia: Fortress Press, 1984.

————. *Unmasking the Powers: Invisible Forces That Determine Human Existence.* Philadelphia: Fortress Press, 1986.

Appendix

Living Fountain International Ministries Incorporated

Questionnaire for Persons Who Need Deliverance
(Strictly Confidential)

A. PERSONAL PARTICULARS

1. Name: _____

2. Meaning of Name: _____

3. Age: _____   Sex: _____

4. Address: _____

5. Occupation: _____

Home Town: _____

6. Marital Status: _____

7. Religion or Church Affiliation: _____

8. Are You Born Again (If Yes, When?): _____

_____

B. PRESENT COMPLAINTS AND DURATION

Present Problems: _____

_____

_____

C. PAST MEDICAL HISTORY (INVESTIGATIONS AND RESULTS)

_____

_____

_____

D. FAMILY BACKGROUND

1. Parents' religion or church: _____

2. Are parents alive? _____

3. Is there any history of idol worship in the family? _____

4. Any existing idols or shrines? _____

5. Name of family god: _____
   i. Father: _____
   ii. Mother: _____

6. Any ancestral and chieftaincy stools? _____
   (father or mother)

7. Do your parents belong to any of the following: Lodge, Amorc, or secret society? _____

8. Husband: Any ancestral god or stool? _____

9. Wife: Any ancestral god or stool? _____

10. Any contributory stories told by parents or relations concerning your birth and/or childhood? _____

_____

_____

_____

E. PERSONAL STRANGE PHENOMENA

1. What do you often see? _____

2. What do you often hear? _____

3. What do you often smell? _____

4. Do you miss your items often? _____

5. Do you know or see things before they happen? _____

Appendix

F. PERSONAL STRANGE CHARACTERISTICS

  1. Are you easily overtaken by:

    Anger _____

    Bitterness _____

    Unforgiveness _____

    Hatred _____

    Quarreling_____

    Jealousy _____

    Lying _____

  2. Do you have excessive fear of:

    Water (river) _____

    Snake _____

    Darkness _____

    Height _____

  3. Do you have constant urge for:

    Sex _____

    Alcohol _____

    Tobacco _____

    Eating of food _____

  4. Sexual perversion (masturbation, homosexuality, lesbianism):

    _____

  5. Do you have an undesirable attitude towards sex (married couples)?

    _____

  6. Do you have constant thought of death or suicide tendencies?

    _____

  7. Lack of seriousness over situations (laughing unnecessarily)?

    _____

  8. Worry unnecessarily over situations? _____

  9. Do you find it difficult taking people's advice and always want to have your own way (stubbornness)? _____

  10. Do you enjoy seeing other people's suffering? _____

11. Do you often feel restless? _____

12. Do you often talk to yourself when alone? _____

13. Do you often weep? (State known reason for the depression.)

    _____

14. Do you have any history of abortion? _____

    How many times? _____

15. Has someone placed any curse on you? _____

16. Any incision by spiritualist or native doctor? _____

17. Any known covenant? _____

18. Have you visited or consulted any native doctor, spiritualist, candle,

    praying churches? _____

    If yes, state all that transpired during your visit: _____

    _____

    _____

19. Do you have any occult books, rings, prayer gowns, crosses, talismans, etc.

    from a native doctor or spiritual churches? _____

    List all the things you have: _____

    _____

20. Are you a member of any of the following societies: Lodge, Amorc,

    Hinduism, Buddhism, Hare Krishna, etc.: _____

G. PECULIAR DREAMS

1. Being pressed down and unable to move and talk? _____

2. Do you attend strange meetings in your dream? _____

3. Do you go to a specific market in your dream? _____

4. Do you have sexual intercourse in your dream? _____

5. Do you swim or play in a river constantly? _____

6. Do you see and play with snakes? _____

7. Do you constantly do cooking and eating in your dream? _____

8. Have you ever dreamt of being pregnant, giving birth or carrying a baby?

   (Explain) _____

9. Have you ever received gift(s) in a dream or trance? _____

10. Have you ever dreamt of being married or wedded?[1] _____

11. Have you ever found yourself being seated on a stool or chair in a dream or trance? _____

12. Have you dreamt about receiving or wearing a ring(s) or beads? _____

13. Have you ever dreamt about wearing a crown or anything on your head?
_____

14. Do you sometimes feel some movements in or on your head?
_____

15. Do you fly constantly in your dreams? _____

16. Do you see and talk with dead relations in your dreams? _____

17. Do you always find it difficult to render services to others? _____

18. Do you always desire services of others? _____

Signature: _____

Date: _____

H. FOR OFFICIAL USE ONLY

1. Observation before ministration: _____
_____
_____
_____
_____

2. Observation during ministration: _____
_____
_____
_____
_____

3. Outcome: _____
_____

1. A distinction is being made here between the ceremony and the state of marriage.

_____

_____

_____

4. Follow-up advice: _____

_____

_____

_____

_____

Index of Names and Subjects

Abosom (intermediaries/pantheon of gods), 60, 61

Abraham, 26, 85, 176

Abronsamgyam (place of wickedness/hell), 65

Abstraction, error of, 26

Addiction, 111, 116

Adema magic, 43

Adoglo asikevee (two-tailed lizard), 59

Adzedede (witch spirit), 55

Adzemi (magic oil), 48

Adzexe (witch bird), 48

Afa diviners, 57

African Independent Churches (AIC), 15, 17, 18, 22, 40, 48, 118, 169

African Traditional Religions, 1, 6, 10, 15, 22, 28, 36, 37, 38n.16, 102, 104

Ahuntor (peace), 42

Akan: cosmologies, 36, 60-67; language, 130, 131; peoples, 17, 35, 66, 103; purification rituals, 103; religious thought, 103; symbolism, 147

Akropong-Akwapim, 14

Amea nnuto (real person), 58, 154n.42

Amedzofe (origin of human beings), 59

Amulets, 27, 42, 66

Ancestor(s), 36, 39, 40, 55-69, 103-105, 127, 128, 176n.1, 189, 192, 201; idolatry of, 105, 125, 127; Jesus as, 103. *See also Nsamanfo; Ntoro*

Ancestral cult, 103; curses, 41, 52, 66-69, 130, 174, 176; gods, 39, 40, 55-57, 68, 100; sin, 127, 177; stools, 20, 20n.11, 39

Anglican Church, 13, 14, 169

Anima, 7, 139, 145, 146, 151-53, 159, 163, 172

Animal familiars, 49-54, 123, 124; sacrifice, 57; side of man, 162; souls, 48, 61

Animism, 42

Animus, 7, 139, 145, 146, 151-53, 159, 163, 172

Anlo cosmologies, 36-60, 65-67; diviners, 69; language, 130, 131; peoples, 17, 20n.11, 35-60

Anointing, 53, 53n.39, 54, 70, 120, 128, 130

Anti-witchcraft shrines, 50, 53, 55

Anxiety, 13, 21, 46, 56, 158, 206

Apocalyptic literature, 106-109, 124

Apostles Revelation Society (ARS), 53

Archetype, 125, 139, 143-46, 152-61, 172

Ashanti, 61

Asuman (impersonal forces/minor deities), 61

Atadikpu (hot pepper), 53

Atonement, 46, 69

Augsburger, David, 9

Authority: dynamics of, 30; over evil, 4, 21,

219

70, 117, 130; figures, 30; Jesus, of, 4, 132, 192; scriptural, 72, 101; spiritual, 30, 190
Autosuggestion, 4n.3
Awasu, Wilson, 15, 16, 34, 38n.16, 39, 42, 43, 57
Aza (form of potent magic), 43

Babylon: conquest, 105n.5; destruction of, 111
Bangles. *See* Amulets
Baptism, 15, 128, 129
Baptist Church of Ghana, 15
Baptists, 14
Barth, Karl, 2-11, 30, 72-98, 99-133, 136, 158, 173-80, 201-204
Basel Mission, 14
Bediako, Kwame, 17, 101-104
Benin, 36, 49
Berkhof, Hendrick, 109
Besouled body, 88, 91, 94, 97, 98, 131, 174. *See also* Soul
Beyie bone (evil witchcraft), 61
Beyie pa (good witchcraft), 61
Blumhardt, Johann, 131, 132
Bondage, 3, 10-12, 23, 29, 67, 101, 111, 123, 128, 130, 140, 173-75, 186, 208
Born again, 19, 20, 72, 181
Brome, Violet, 146
Busia, K. A., 61

Carlson, Dwight L., 69
Center for Mission Research and Applied Theology in Akropong, Ghana, 102
Chalcedon: Council of, 179; formulations, 7n.6, 94n.66, 179, 180
Chodorow, Joan, 148
Christological anthropology, 86, 179, 181
Christology, 5, 10, 27, 75, 81, 98, 102, 174; African, 28; of Karl Barth, 5, 30, 81, 86, 87, 174
Church at Pig Farm, Accra, 135
Clebsch, William, 164
Communion: with God, 34, 39, 55, 82; rite, 55, 117

Compensation, 158
Complexes, psychological, 109, 140, 144, 154, 164
Confession, 3 44, 50-55, 68, 74, 84, 108, 110, 140, 174, 177
Cosmological warfare. *See* Warfare
Cosmologies: African, 5, 6, 15, 17, 25-27, 32-71, 100-110, 112, 130, 173, 174, 208; Barthian, 82-86, 176; Biblical, 5, 10, 26, 27, 72-74, 101-110, 112
Counseling. *See* Pastoral counseling
Covenant, with God, 78-85, 128, 208
Creation: African concepts of, 27-29, 37, 38, 58, 59; Biblical concepts of, 23, 34, 80-85, 88, 91, 102, 104, 119

Daimon, 166
Daniel, 107, 108, 137
Danquah, J. B., 62
Decalogue, 96
Deities of planets, 63
de Laszlo, Violet Staub, 138, 139
Deliverance: from demon possession, 3, 20, 21, 51, 70, 125, 130, 134, 135, 169, 175; by God, 76, 86, 91, 97, 107-110, 121, 128, 130, 201; prayers of, *see* Prayer; rituals, 51; sessions and services, 18, 21, 50, 55, 109, 123, 135, 168-70, 189, 193, 201; from spiritual oppression, 3, 12, 16, 20, 67, 68
Demon(s): activity by, 7, 11, 12, 20, 21, 41, 52, 68, 99, 100, 105, 109-112, 116, 129, 162, 186; casting out of, 4, 55, 69-71, 106, 117, 121, 128, 130; and dreams, 7, 10, 134, 163, 175, 200; and Jesus, 4, 4n.4, 106, 107, 117, 120-125, 128-33, 208; and New Testament, 114-17, 131; and Old Testament, 111-14; possession by, 3, 21, 68, 106, 111, 116, 125, 127, 131, 132, 163-71, 191; as source of sickness, 18, 51, 99, 100, 111, 116, 123, 127, 135, 140, 162, 192, 200, 203; and spirit powers, 110-111. *See also* Deliverance; Exorcism
Depersonalization of evil, 109-110
Destiny, 36, 38, 59, 63-66, 188

Dickson, Kwesi, 32
Divination, 19, 44, 55-58, 67, 111
Divine economy, 125
Diviner(s), 19, 45, 46, 56, 57, 66, 68, 69
Dreams, 7, 8, 10, 47, 49, 50, 54, 56, 59, 63,
    68, 100, 108, 134-38, 141, 143, 148-56,
    159, 163-67, 175, 183, 191-200, 203, 204,
    206
Dualism (of body and soul), 92-98
Dynamistic forces, 39, 42-44, 55
Dzo (magic), 42
Dzogbe se (destiny), 59
Dzoka (incantation), 42, 43
Dzoto/Dzotowo (magician/s), 42, 43

Ego, 139, 146-50, 153-60, 163
Emancipation Act of 1833, 13
Embodied soul, 88, 94, 96, 98, 122, 131,
    174, 177. *See also* Soul
Epileptic fits, 21
Eros, 152, 164
E-su (physical life without conscious self-
    direction), 62
Evangelical churches. *See* Independent
    Evangelical/ Charismatic Churches
    (IECC)
Evangelism, 3, 14, 17, 22, 70, 181
Ewe, the, 15, 16, 36-42
Exact sciences, 74-78, 98
Exorcism, 29, 55, 70, 99, 100, 110, 120, 129-
    31, 163, 165, 170, 208

Faith Foundation International, 68
Falleness, 75, 79-81, 87, 161
Familiars, 49, 49n.35, 51, 54, 123, 124. *See
    also* Animal familiars
Fasting, 4, 53, 100, 130, 169, 193, 201
Fatalism, 36, 38, 188
Fetish shrine, 19, 169
Foerster, Werner, 111
Food, 39, 43, 46, 50, 57, 70, 99, 100, 104,
    113, 123, 169
Forde, Cyril Daryll, 45, 46
Frank, Jerome and Julia, 22

Freud, Sigmund, 125, 151, 182, 183

Gaba, C. R., 37, 38, 43, 47, 49, 53-58
Gbogbo (divine or life soul), 58-60, 131
Gbogbo Kokoe (Holy Spirit), 131
Gerasene demoniac, 4n.4, 125
Ghanaian Independent Charismatic
    Church, 1, 135, 169
Ghanaian Mami Water Spirit, 175
Gold Coast, 14
Grace, 4n.5, 17, 26, 79, 80, 115, 117, 130, 133,
    138, 139, 161, 178, 186, 189, 199, 201, 202,
    207, 208
Gratitude, 13, 56, 188

Hanson, Paul, 107, 108
Healing, 1, 3, 5, 21, 27-30, 42, 52, 54, 55, 58,
    61, 69, 93, 99, 100, 106-110, 116, 117, 120,
    121, 127, 128, 133, 138-43, 149, 162, 165,
    170-81, 185, 186, 200, 201, 206, 208. *See
    also* Prayer: for healing
Hegel, Georg, 142n.9
Hierarchy of beings, 36, 71
Holy Spirit. *See* Spirit
Honhom (spirit-breath), 64, 65
Human autonomy, 78
Hunam (body), 65
Hunsinger, Deborah van Deusen, 6, 7,
    7n.6, 132, 179, 183-86, 205
Hunsinger, George, 90, 180
Hyatt, James, 105n.5

Imago Dei, 79, 162
Immortality, 60, 66, 91, 92
Incarnation, 5, 11, 23, 26, 27, 87, 106, 186
Incubus, 163, 164
Independent Evangelical/Charismatic
    Churches (IECC), 1, 9, 16-18, 21, 25,
    67-70, 99, 135, 169
Indissoluble differentiation, 7n.6, 94, 180
Individuation, 8, 139, 147-51, 157, 161, 162,
    190, 208
Infallibility, 101
Inner drive, 142

Interpersonal relations, 6, 51, 121, 206, 207
Israel, God of, 112; messiah of, 26, 27; people of, 23, 26, 27, 33, 40, 57, 85, 108, 120, 120n.42, 121, 121n.43

Jaekle, Charles, 164
Jeremiah, 105.n5
Job, 126, 140
Johnson, P. J., 44
Judaism, 37n.13; pseudepigraphical, 113; Rabbinical, 112-14, 124; Tannaitic, 112, 113
Jung, Karl, 2-11, 134-72, 175, 179, 203, 204

Kant, Immanuel, 142n.9
Kearney, Michael, 34
Kelsey, Morton T., 126
King Agokoli, 36
Kingdom of God, 23, 24, 24nn. 16 and 18, 106, 107, 117, 120, 121, 127
Kra (soul), 62-65

Ladd, G. E., 24, 24n.17, 107
Language of power, 118, 126, 127
Lartey, Emmanuel Y., 28
Legba (family gods), 39, 52
Libation(s), 40, 61, 67
Linnaeus, 142n.9
Literal interpretation of Scripture, 23, 35, 107
Loder, James E., 6, 7n.6
Logos, 139, 151, 152, 171
Lower Niger, 13
Luwo (personality soul), 59

MacNutt, Francis, 70, 71, 130
Malevolent spirits/forces, 12, 66, 72, 100, 113, 134, 136, 146, 175, 205
Mali, 60
Malum substantiale, 80
Mandala, 147
Mater Dolorosa, 155-57
Mawu-Lisa (Supreme Being), 37-39, 58
Messengers (Angelos), 112

Methodist(s), 14
Methodist Church of Ghana, 15
Meyerowitz, Eva, 60, 62, 64
Midwives, 47, 186, 200
Miracles, 106, 107, 114n.28, 181; gift of, 71
Missionizing, 13-16, 35, 117
Mogya (blood), 62, 65
Moreau, A. Scott, 114, 114n.28
Musama Disco Christo Church, 15, 53
Mysterium tremendum et fascinans, 56

Name, significance of, 19, 37, 38, 100, 104, 176
Nephresh, 60, 91. See also Luwo
Newbigin, Lesslie, 33
Nhebea (command), 64
Nipa (human entity), 62, 65
Nkrabea (message of destiny), 63, 64
Nkwansuo (water of life), 63
Nnipadua (body), 62
Nnutifafa (peace), 41
Nsamanfo (ancestors), 60
Ntoro (spirit of patrilineal ancestors), 63
Nutila (body), 58
Nuxe (type of sacrifice), 56, 57
Nyame Amowia (name of the deity of the cosmos), 62-65
Nyankopong, 62
Nyankopong mba (sons of the Supreme Being), 61

Obaatan (the good mother), 104
Odwira (yearly festival), 103
Okara (soul), 62
Onyame (Supreme Being), 61, 62
Origen, 70
Otto, Rudolf, 56

Pantheon of gods. See Abosom
Parachurch organizations, 18, 109
Paranormal behaviors, 140, 165-71
Parrinder, Geoffrey, 37
Passive resignation, 36
Pastoral counseling, 1-31, 35, 36, 41, 50,

67-73, 98-101, 110, 111, 118, 131, 135-40, 151, 162-65, 172, 173-208; and theology, 35, 36, 71, 72, 98, 106, 131, 136, 138, 173. *See also* Therapy
Pentecostalism, 15, 40
Pentecostalism, American, 170
Perry, Michael, 126
Persona, 7, 139, 145, 146, 149-51, 159, 204
Personalization of evil, 109, 110
Personal unconscious, 144
Personhood, 32, 58-60
Pobee, J., 15
Possession, demonic, 3, 47, 68, 88, 106, 111, 116, 125, 127, 131, 132, 163-72, 175, 191
Prayer, 4, 12, 18, 21, 21n.12, 29, 38-44, 51-54, 67, 70, 99, 100, 107, 108, 116, 117, 128-36, 140, 162, 165, 166, 181, 184, 192-201, 205-208; camps, 16; of deliverance, 3, 16, 21, 67, 116, 128, 182, 186, 192; groups, 29; for healing, 3, 20, 133, 201; meetings, 68, 106
Price, Daniel J., 132
Primal religions, 2, 102, 104
"Primitive," 141, 141n.8, 142
Principalities and powers, 105, 109, 110, 117-27, 178, 205
Projections, 150-53
Pruyser, Paul, 187-90
Psyche, 7, 34, 91, 108, 108n.12, 124, 137-63, 172-75, 204
Psychic healing, 52; homeostasis, 149; phenomena, 7, 10, 11, 134, 138, 139, 143, 146, 148; suggestion, 4; wounds, 29, 144
Purification rituals, 103

Quaque, Philip, 13
Queen of the Coast sardines, 175

Ramsay, Nancy, 30, 186
Real man. *See Wirkliche mensch*
Reductionism, 122, 126, 208
Reformed Protestantism, 6
Reformed theology, 9
Reformed tradition, 2

Reincarnation, 64, 65
Relational matrix, 5, 30
Repentance, 34, 65, 69, 178, 189
Restitution, 44
Resurrection, 24, 27, 28, 33, 71, 91, 93, 115, 121, 121n.43, 174, 208
Riis, Andreas, 14
Rites of passage, 39; "out-dooring," 68
Rizzuto, Ana-Maria, 182, 183
Roman Empire, 125

Sacrifice, 40, 44, 47, 65, 67, 102; and divination, 55-58; of Jesus, 23, 128; and medicine, 164
Salvation, 13, 28, 41, 42, 83, 106, 107, 121, 122, 127, 162, 176, 181, 206, 208
Saman (ghosts), 65
Samandow (land of ghosts or place of the dead), 62, 64
Saman pa (good spiritual being), 63
Satan, 19, 25, 28, 51, 80, 100, 107, 112, 113, 117, 122-27
Satanic: forces, 174; power, 41
Scapegoat, 102, 125
Scripture : approach to/interpretation of, 6, 23, 35, 71, 91, 92, 99, 108, 118, 128, 166, 174, 185, 201; authority of, 72; content of, 3, 23, 75, 78, 81-85, 88, 91, 92, 96, 98, 101, 111, 117, 120, 122, 129, 185, 205; use of, 9, 15, 70, 101, 161, 175, 190
Septuagint, 112
Sermon on the Mount, 96
Shadow, 7, 59, 139, 151, 159, 160, 172, 204, 206
Shuster, Marguerite, 168-71
Sierra Leone, 14
Sin, 5, 13, 29, 41, 56, 65-69, 75, 78-81, 86, 87, 96, 98, 102-106, 108, 113, 115, 122, 127-29, 140, 174-77, 185, 188, 189, 201, 202
Slain in the spirit, 170
Society of Odd Fellows/Freemasons, 20
Socrates, 166
Somatic factors, 21, 22, 51, 93, 122, 133, 134, 138, 153, 154, 168, 171, 174, 175, 177, 181, 188

Soteriology, 5, 30, 81n.21, 121, 173
Soul: Akan concept of, 61-64; Anlo
    concept of, 58-60, 154n.42; and body,
    73, 88-93, 99, 119, 131, 158, 177, 178;
    ordering of with body, 96-98; partic-
    ularity of, 93-96, 174; personality of,
    43, 47, 48, 58-60, 63; and psyche, 138,
    139, 143, 145, 172; tripartite connection
    with body and spirit, 5, 6, 10, 11, 27,
    28, 42, 58, 66, 72, 99, 100, 130-34, 174;
    union and interconnection with body,
    89, 90-93, 122, 131, 158, 174, 177, 178. See
    also Besouled body; Embodied soul
Speculative philosophies, 74-78, 98, 173
Spells, 12, 174
Spirit: ancestral, 68; of God, 18, 37n.13, 88,
    89, 98, 115, 131, 174, 177, 208; guardian,
    63; the Holy, 4, 4nn. 3 and 4, 5, 6, 16, 17,
    31, 41n.19, 88n.49, 92, 121n.43, 128-31,
    170; malevolent, 12, 19, 20, 29, 43, 52, 53,
    57, 65, 70-72, 99, 100, 109-27, 130, 135,
    136, 146, 166, 175; money-looting, 53;
    spousal, 165; tree, 61; as part of tripar-
    tite personhood, 5, 6, 10, 11, 27, 28, 42,
    58-60, 66, 72, 99, 100, 130, 131; water, 61,
    175; witchcraft, 46-55, 66, 99, 100, 105,
    135, 193, 196
Spiritual: causes of illness, 6-12, 18, 22,
    26-29, 100, 177, 186; cures, 12, 22, 140,
    176n.1; powers, 3-5, 12, 13, 19, 25, 43, 67-
    69, 99, 104, 106, 109, 127-30, 134, 169, 177,
    178, 197-205
Spouses of the god, 39, 39n.17
Succubus, 164
Suman (charm), 61
Sunsum (spirit/personal soul), 62-66
Supreme Ancestor, 103
Supreme Being, 27, 37-40, 54, 57-66, 103,
    104
Syncretism, 15, 33, 35, 104

Tanakh, 113
Televangelism, 16
Tertullian, 70

Theissen, Gerd, 125
Theophoric names, 104
Theotokos Virgin, 156
Therapy, 6-8, 11, 19, 28, 94, 138, 169, 174;
    Christian, 5, 30; family, 28; Gestalt, 28;
    Jungian, 8, 140, 142, 146-50, 155, 162,
    172; psycho-, 7, 8, 28. See also Pastoral
    counseling
Togbuizikpui. See Ancestral cult: stools
Togoland, 14
Torgovnick, Marianna, 141
Transcendent function, 154-57
Transference, 46, 47
Transpersonal power, 7
Tribal support system, 134
Tripartite constitution. See Soul: tripartite
    connection with body and spirit
Tro, 39
Trosi, 39
Tsi, 44
Tsinyefe (land of the dead), 59
Twi language, 102, 103

Ulanov, Ann Belford, 155, 159, 166, 167
Unconscious, 7, 8, 124, 125, 138-62, 172,
    204; collective, 7, 144
Unger, Merrill, 112

Vodu, 39
Voduda (snake cult), 49
Vodusi, 39, 39n.17; dynamistic forces, 39,
    42-44, 55
Vosa, 56
Vovoli (shadow), 59

Warfare: cosmological, 105; praying, 21;
    spiritual, 12, 13, 52, 72, 106-108, 123
Welker, Michael, 116
Westminster Shorter Catechism, 13
Wink, Walter, 118-26, 212
Wirkliche mensch (real man), 73-82, 86;
    Jesus as, 86-90
Witch(es), 20, 29, 59, 65, 99, 123, 124, 174;
    doctor, 3, 44

Witchcraft, 12, 15, 20, 42-52, 57, 61, 66, 99, 100, 105, 111-14, 123, 124, 143, 135, 193, 195, 196; antidotes to, 52-55, 66

Works righteousness, 201

Worldview(s) (*Weltanschauung*): African, 7, 11, 26, 27, 32-66, 69, 72, 100, 104, 130, 173, 201; Biblical, 11, 26, 83, 100, 101, 104, 173; and exact sciences, 77, 98; relationship between African and Biblical, 101, 104, 105-127; and speculative philosophies, 74-76, 98. *See also* Cosmologies

Worship: of ancestors, 39, 40, 192; African forms of, 14n.4, 15, 16, 20n.11, 25, 37-41, 105, 168; of idols, 129; of Satan, 124; of snakes, 49; westernized forms of, 14, 14n.4

Ya (wind), 58

Yahweh, 37n.13, 120, 120n.42, 124, 126, 137

Yamenusewo (archetypal spirits), 43

Index of Scripture References

OLD TESTAMENT

Genesis

1:1-2	23
2:7	88
3:8	92n.61
6:6	92n.61
8:22	23
37	137

Exodus

15:6	92n.61
15:8	92n.61

Numbers

5:14	115

1 Chronicles

21:1	126

2 Chronicles

11:15	112

Nehemiah

1:4-11	41

Job

1:6-12	126
2:1-10	126
2:11	140
19:2	140
19:4	140

Psalms

91:6	112
147:17	112

Proverbs

18:20-22	171

Isaiah

13:21	111
40:12	92n.61

Jeremiah

31:29-30	105, 128

Ezekiel

18:1-4	105, 128

Daniel

9:3-19	41
10:13	107

Zechariah

3:1	126
12:10	115

NEW TESTAMENT

Matthew

4:1	126
4:1-11	114n.28
5:21	96
5:45	178, 202
9:32-33	114n.28
10:28	91n.58
12:22-23	114n.28
12:28	23
15:19	115
16:18	4
17:14-20	132n.65

Mark

1:34	117n.36
3:27	107
5:15	4
9:29	128
9:42	93
16:17	70
17:20	128

Luke

4:18	120
4:36	118
7	115
10	117
10:11-20	117
10:17-20	117
11:14	114n.28
22:25	118

John

3:34	88
8	115
8:1-11	116
8:11	185
9	201
9:2-3	189, 201
10:10	25
11:25	91
14:17	115
16:33	25

Acts

1:6	121n.43
4:7	118
4:26	118
8:7	70

Romans

1:28	115
5:8	178
8:1	81
8:31-39	174

8:38-39	118
12:2	161
13:1	120

1 Corinthians

1:5	115
5	115
6:19	92
12	71
12-14	130

Galatians

3:29	176
5:16	122
5:20	114
5:23	122n.46
5:24	93, 114

Ephesians

1:20	108
2:1	108
2:6-8	176
3:10	108
6:10-18	12
6:12	105, 109

Philippians

4:8	171
4:11	188

Colossians

2:8	83n.27
2:15	108

2:20	83n.27
2:20-21	175

2 Thessalonians

4:13	92

2 Timothy

1:7	115

Hebrews

4:14	133
7:25	133
13:17	120

James

1:13-15	115
5:14-16	53
5:16	108

1 Peter

4:14	115

1 John

3:8	120

Revelation

9:21	114
18:23	114
20:2	126
21:8	114
22:15	114